REAGAN'S
WAR

REAGAN'S
WAR

THE EPIC STORY OF HIS
FORTY-YEAR STRUGGLE AND FINAL
TRIUMPH OVER COMMUNISM

PETER SCHWEIZER

DOUBLEDAY

New York ★ London ★ Toronto ★ Sydney ★ Auckland

PUBLISHED BY DOUBLEDAY
A division of Random House, Inc.
1540 Broadway, New York, New York 10036

DOUBLEDAY and the portrayal of an anchor
with a dolphin are trademarks of Doubleday,
a division of Random House, Inc.

Book design by Laurie Jewell

Library of Congress Cataloging-in-Publication Data is on file
with the Library of Congress

ISBN 0-385-50471-3

PRINTED IN THE UNITED STATES OF AMERICA

November 2002
First Edition

1   3   5   7   9   10   8   6   4   2

Dedicated to the memory of my father

*   *   *

ERWIN V. SCHWEIZER

WHAT IS THE USE OF LIVING IF IT BE
NOT TO STRIVE FOR NOBLE CAUSES AND
TO MAKE THIS MUDDLED WORLD A BETTER
PLACE FOR THOSE WHO WILL LIVE IN
IT AFTER WE ARE GONE?

Winston Churchill

★   ★   ★

CONTENTS

ACKNOWLEDGMENTS

MANY PEOPLE MADE THIS BOOK POSSIBLE IN A VARIETY OF WAYS. William M. Arkin, John Koehler, Lloyd Billingsley, Professor Paul Kengor, Roger Robinson, Bill Lee, Chris Lay, Mark Kramer, and Marc Thiessen all passed along information and suggestions that proved enormously helpful. I am also deeply grateful to those individuals on both sides of the Cold War divide who agreed to interviews over the past eight years.

This book includes material from numerous archives around the world in Russia, Germany, the Czech Republic, Poland, and Hungary. In the United States, I particularly wish to thank the Hoover Institution Archives, Stanford University; the International Cold War History Project; Naval Historical Center; Young America's Foundation; and the National Security Archives. I am also thankful for the assistance provided by the Ronald Reagan Presidential Library.

Thanks also to Nancy Reagan, who allowed me to use photos from the family's private photo collection.

At the Hoover Institution Archives, I received tremendous research assistance and translation help, and I wish to thank Elena Danielson, Maciej Siekierski, Zbigniew Stanczyk, and Irene Czernichowska for their help in these areas.

Considerable resources went into researching this book, and I am indebted to Owen and Bernadette Smith, who supported this project from the beginning, Richard Parillo, who provided critical funds for the collecting of the documents and research material, and the Richard M. Scaife End of Communism Initiative at the Hoover Institution, which offered support that made the completion of this project possible.

As a research fellow, I am enormously thankful for the many colleagues and friends who have provided help and encouragement over the past few years. In particular, I would like to thank John Raisian, Charles Palm, Richard Sousa, and Tom Henriksen, who never seem to tire of my phone calls and questions.

At Doubleday, I was fortunate to have the support of Bill Thomas and especially my editor, Adam Bellow, who encouraged me to draw out Reagan from the myriad of documents that I had collected over the years.

Joe Valley, my agent, provided valuable advice, as always.

Most of all, I want to thank my family for their love and encouragement. Kerstin Schweizer, Evelyn Rueb, Joe and Maria Duffus, and Richard Rueb have always been supportive of these endeavors. I thank you all for supporting me yet again. Most of all, I am indebted to my wife, Rochelle, who inspires me, helps me, and loves me unconditionally. And to little Jack and Hannah Grace, thanks for being you.

Finally, thanks to the Thursday morning guys—Dayton Jones, John Rickenbacker, and Jeff Brewer—who know what it's all about.

The author alone is responsible for the content of this book.

INTRODUCTION

RONALD REAGAN IS PERHAPS THE LEAST UNDERSTOOD PRES-
ident of the twentieth century. His life seems a conun-
drum, his ways a mystery. Even his closest friends and
advisers have been perplexed by him and what transpired
while he was president. As National Security Adviser Robert Mc-
Farlane once told George Shultz, "He knows so little but accom-
plishes so much."

In her recent book about Reagan, Frances Fitzgerald paints a
picture of a man who spouts patriotic pieties and is ignorant of the
world around him. Historian Edmund Morris, in his 874-page authorized biography, concludes that Reagan is simply incomprehensi-
ble, an airhead who has lived a charmed life. Diplomat Clark Clifford
has called him an "amiable dunce," and Nicholas von Hoffman said
it was "humiliating to think of this unlettered, self-assured bumpkin
being our president." Tip O'Neill flat out said in public, "He knows
less than any president I've ever known." Anthony Lewis of the *New
York Times* claimed he had only a "seven-minute attention span."
Author Gail Sheehy declared he was "half asleep" while he was president.[1]

Images of Reagan as the amiable dunce are particularly prevalent when it comes to his role as commander in chief. Henry Kissinger was thoroughly unimpressed, telling scholars in 1986, "How did it ever occur to anyone that he should be governor, much less president?" Historian Robert Dallek declared that Reagan's anticommunism raised questions about his "capacity to effectively govern the United States" and that his obsession with communism was an exercise in bolstering his own self-esteem. Stanley Hoffman of Harvard found him in the grips of an unthinking "ritualistic anti-Sovietism," and another observer explained that he was "provincial in background . . . content to receive a series of one-page 'minimemos' summarizing foreign and defense problems."[2]

The Cold War might have ended on his watch and the Soviet Union collapsed shortly after he left office, but he deserves none of the credit, it is claimed. Even if he had a clue about what was going on, the most important decisions of his presidency were made around him, not by him. His was, as one scholar put it, "the no-hands presidency."[3] When he did have an idea, the origins were dubious. Frances Fitzgerald claims, for example, that his interest in strategic defense stems from two movies he saw, *Murder in the Air* and *Torn Curtain,* which describe futuristic weapons that save America.[4]

★   ★   ★

FIFTY YEARS AGO, PHILOSOPHER ISAIAH BERLIN WROTE AN ESSAY titled "The Hedgehog and the Fox." Quoting from the Greek poet Archilochus, who said, "The fox knows many things, but the hedgehog knows one big thing," Berlin divided the world into two types of people. Foxes pursue many ends, often unrelated and even contradictory. Their actions are connected by no aesthetic or moral principle. Hedgehogs, on the other hand, relate everything to a single central vision, a single universal organizing principle that defines what they think and believe. Most people are foxes; Ronald Reagan was a hedgehog.[5]

The "one big thing" Reagan knew was the power and value of human freedom, which proved to be the defining principle of his worldview. It guided what he thought about domestic politics and was central to his vision for the world. For more than thirty years,

Reagan embraced a vision for dealing with the Soviet Union and ending the Cold War that was remarkably consistent and proved to be decisive. People who note his apparent lack of interest in the details of diplomacy, missile throw weights, and international law fail to see his larger strategic vision. Details that animate so many in the world of politics, academe, and journalism did not interest him so much as the "metaphysics" of the Cold War. He was, in short, a hedgehog living in a world populated with foxes.

Ronald Reagan is impossible to understand outside of his forty-year battle against communism. It was a struggle that consumed more of his attention than any other endeavor and touched the very center of his life. It cost him his first marriage and brought him his second wife; it damaged his relationship with his children; death threats while waging it left him sitting up at night, guarding his kids with a .32-caliber pistol; and it brought him three assassination attempts. When a fourth deranged assassin named John Hinckley took him an inch from death, Reagan came to believe that his life had been spared by God for a divine purpose: defeating communism.

But if it is impossible to understand Reagan separate from his war, it is likewise not possible to understand the collapse of the Soviet Union separate from Ronald Reagan; the two are intertwined.

Today it is fashionable to explain that victory in the Cold War was a group effort, including every American president from Truman to Reagan. Former president Gerald Ford says the credit doesn't belong to any one leader but to the American people, as if who happened to be in charge really didn't matter. Others, such as former secretary of state Madeleine Albright, contend that it was the ultimate team effort. "There were the Communists and there were us; the good guys and the bad guys . . . it was fairly easy to understand." If Reagan did anything, says Dallek, it was simply to stand on the shoulders of every other cold war president before him. "By the time of Reagan's presidency," he writes, "the wisdom of the containment policy was largely transparent."[6]

Another common explanation for the demise of communism is that the system was doomed to failure. This sort of historical determinism, that certain events are inevitable regardless of what actions people take, raises serious questions to begin with. But even granting for a minute that history actually can be seen this way, this explanation runs into serious problems. The fact is that the Soviet system was flawed from the beginning; it never really worked. Economic trauma was a problem dating back to the 1920s. For seventy years the Soviet economy was in a state of crisis. So why did it collapse when it did?[7]

If credit is to go to anyone, it is often given to Mikhail Gorbachev, the last general secretary of the Soviet Union. Gorbachev is credited with taking the country down the path of radical reform, which invariably caused chaos and then collapse. It was Gorbachev who was the brilliant one, says one scholar, and "Reagan's carelessness or shallowness as a foreign policy maker" was on display when he was around him. After all, it was Gorbachev who was *Time* magazine's man of the decade; Reagan just happened to be there when it all happened.[8]

Of course, Gorbachev does deserve enormous credit for choosing to allow the peaceful demise of the Soviet empire rather than trying to hold it together with force. But giving Gorbachev most of the credit raises several important questions: Why did the Kremlin feel the need to radically reform when it did? How did Gorbachev come to power? What are we to make of Gorbachev's continued insistence that his goal was to reform communism and not end it? Why did the cold war end on Reagan's terms and not Gorbachev's?

This book is not intended as a complete history of the Cold War; instead it is the story of one of the epic battles of the twentieth century. Drawing on Reagan's private correspondence over the course of forty years, classified documents from six different countries, formative life events largely hidden from the public, his own ideas and words uttered over the course of half a century, the book paints a picture of a man at war with a global empire. Passionate and courageous in battle, Reagan did have a well-developed plan seeking the demise of the Soviet Union. Developed over the course of thirty years and spelled out in detail through several top-secret national security directives when he was president, the ideas and concepts behind it were largely his own. This "self-assured bumpkin" won the Cold War.

ONE-MAN BATTALION

TALL, TANNED, AND DARK-HAIRED, RONALD REAGAN WAS often seen driving his Cadillac convertible on the open boulevards of Hollywood in late September 1946. He had been in pictures for almost ten years now. Superstardom had eluded him, but he was a star nonetheless. Only a few years earlier, a Gallup poll had ranked him with Laurence Olivier in terms of popularity among filmgoers.

Reagan knew that superstardom would probably never come, openly admitting to friends, "I'm no [Errol] Flynn or [Charles] Boyer." But life was comfortable. In August of 1945 he had signed a long-term, million-dollar contract with Warner Brothers. He was making more than $52,000 a picture and would take home the princely sum of $169,000 in 1946—and there were inviting projects on the horizon. Jack Warner, the pugnacious studio head, had offered him the lead in a film adaptation of John Van Druten's successful play *The Voice of the Turtle*. It was Reagan's first chance to play the romantic lead in a major A picture, and Warner was paying the playwright the unheard-of sum of $500,000 plus 15 percent of the gross for the story, so he clearly cared about the project. Reagan was also about to begin production on *Night Unto Night*, a dramatization of a successful Philip Wylie book.

In addition, Reagan had a wife and two little kids to go home to. Jane Wyman was a beautiful blonde from the Midwest whose own acting career was beginning to take off. Along with their children Michael and Maureen, Ron and Jane lived in a beautiful home with a pool on Cordell Drive. He owned a splendid ranch near Riverside, and when he and Jane weren't at the studio lot, they could be found playing golf at the prestigious Hillcrest Country Club with Jack Benny and George Burns. At night they often dined at the trendy Beverly Club.[1]

It was without a doubt far more than the son of a salesman from Dixon, Illinois, had ever expected out of life. But on September 27, 1946, Reagan's celluloid dreamland would be disrupted forever.

In the early-morning hours, even before the sun peeked over the east hills, thousands of picketers showed up at Warner Brothers. They were vocal and angry. Hollywood had seen strikes before, but nothing quite like this.

The strike had been called by a ruddy-faced ex-boxer named Herb Sorrell, head of the Conference of Studio Unions (CSU), who was prepared to get rough. "There may be men hurt, there may be men killed before this is over, but we are in no mood to be pushed around anymore," he warned. For good measure, he had brought dozens of tough guys ("sluggers," he called them) in from San Francisco, just in case.

Herb Sorrell had come up the hard way, beginning work at the age of twelve, laboring in an Oakland sewer pipe factory for eleven hours a day. He had cut his teeth in the Bay Area labor movement under the leadership of Harry Bridges, the wiry leader of the International Longshoremen's and Warehousemen's Union. Bridges, according to Soviet archives, was also a secret member of the Communist Party and a regular contact for Soviet intelligence.

Sorrell had joined the party in the 1930s, and under Bridges's guidance he had led two violent strikes in the Bay Area. Both strikes, he later admitted, were secretly funded by the Communists, and this time he was secretly receiving money from the National Executive Council of the Communist Party. Sorrell was a member of more than twenty Communist Party front organizations and had pushed hard for the American Federation of Labor to affiliate with the Soviet-run World Federation of Trade Unions. (AFL leaders refused on the grounds that it was simply a front group.[2])

The studio strike Sorrell organized in 1946 was no ordinary labor action. It was ostensibly called because of worker concerns, but Sorrell saw it as an opportunity to gain control over all the major unions in Hollywood. As he bragged in the early days of the action, "When it ends up, there'll be only one man running labor in Hollywood, and that man will be me!"

The stakes were high. If Sorrell succeeded, the Communists believed, they could run Hollywood. As the party newspaper the *People's Daily World* put it candidly, "Hollywood is often called the land of Make-Believe, but there is nothing make believe about the Battle of Hollywood being waged today. In the front lines of this battle, at the studio gates, stand the thousands of locked out film workers; behind the studio gates sit the overlords of Hollywood, who refuse even to negotiate with the workers. . . . The prize will be the complete control of the greatest medium of communication in history." To underscore the value of this victory, the paper quoted Lenin: "Of all the arts, the cinema is the most important."

The Communist Party had been active in Hollywood since 1935, when a secret directive was issued by CPUSA (Communist Party of the U.S.A.) headquarters in New York calling for the capture of Hollywood's labor unions. The party believed that by doing so they could influence the type of pictures being produced. The directive also instructed party members to take leadership positions in the so-called intellectual groups in Hollywood, which were composed of directors, writers, and performers.

To carry out the plan, CPUSA sent party activist Stanley Lawrence, a tall, bespectacled ex-cabdriver. Quietly and methodically he began developing secret cells that included Hollywood performers, writers, and technicians. His actions were handled with great sensitivity. Lawrence reported directly to party headquarters in New York, which in turn reported its activities to officials in Moscow. There, Comintern boss Willie Muenzenberg declared, "One of the most pressing tasks confronting the Communist Party in the field of propaganda is the conquest of this supremely important propaganda unit, until now the monopoly of the ruling class. We must wrest it from them and turn it against them."

By the end of the Second World War, party membership in Hollywood was close to six hundred and boasted several industry heavyweights. Actors Lloyd Bridges, Edward G. Robinson, and Fredric March were members, as were half a dozen producers and about as many directors. Some had joined the party because they thought it might be fun. Actor Lionel Stander encouraged his friends to become members because "you will make out more with the dames." Others who were perhaps interested in the ideas of Marx and Lenin were nonetheless gentle in their advocacy.

"Please explain Marxism to me," Sam Goldwyn once asked Communist Ella Winter at a dinner party.

"Oh, not over this lovely steak."

But many of the party members were militants, and through hard work they had managed to take over leadership positions in the Screenwriters Guild, the Screen Actors Guild (SAG), and various intellectual and cultural groups. Their level of control and influence far outweighed their numbers. It was a classic case of hard work and determined organizing.[3]

"All over town the industrious Communist tail wagged the lazy liberal dog," declared director Philip Dunne, whose credits included *Count of Monte Cristo, Last of the Mohicans*, and *Three Brave Men*.[4]

That industriousness came out of a militancy that stunned many in Hollywood. Screenwriter John Howard Lawson had a booming voice and could often be seen berating those who might oppose the party by smashing his fist into his open palm. The natural reaction of many was to simply be quiet and avoid being throttled.

"The important thing is that you should not argue with them," said writer F. Scott Fitzgerald, who spent time in Hollywood writing for movies such as *Winter Carnival*. "Whatever you say they have ways of twisting it into shapes which put you in some lower category of mankind, 'Fascist,' 'Liberal,' 'Trotskyist,' and disparage you both intellectually and personally in the process."[5]

Reagan had his first taste of this a few months before the strike, when he was serving on the executive committee of the Hollywood Independent Citizens Committee of Arts, Sciences, and Professions (HICCASP), which he had joined in 1944. The group boasted a membership roll including Frank Sinatra, Orson Welles, and Katharine Hepburn. It was what they called a "brainy group," too, with Albert Einstein and Max Weber lending their name to the organization. It was the usual liberal/left Hollywood cultural group, concerned about atomic weapons, the resurgence of fascism, and the burgeoning Cold War. But some were concerned by what they saw as its regular and consistent support for the Soviet position on international issues. Historian Arthur Schlesinger Jr. declared in *Life* magazine that he believed it was a communist front, an organization in which "its celebrities maintained their membership but not their vigilance."

Stung by this criticism, a small group within HICCASP, including RKO executive Dore Schary, actress Olivia de Havilland, and FDR's son James Roosevelt, decided to put their fellow members to the test. At the July 2, 1946, meeting, Roosevelt noted that HICCASP had many times issued statements denouncing fascism. Why not issue a statement repudiating communism? Surely that would demonstrate that the organization was wholly liberal and not at all communist.

Reagan rose quickly and offered his support for the resolution, and a furious verbal battle quickly erupted. Musician Artie Shaw stood up and declared that the Soviet Union was more democratic than the United States and offered to recite the Soviet constitution to prove it. Writer Dalton Trumbo stood up and denounced the resolution as wicked. When Reagan tried to respond, John Howard Lawson waved a menacing finger in his face and told him to watch it. Reagan and the others in his group resigned from the organization.[6]

Sorrell gathered his resources for the fight. Along with financial support from the Communist Party, he also could count on help from Vincente Lombardo Toledano, head of Mexico's largest union and described in Soviet intelligence files as an agent. The slender, well-dressed, and poised young lawyer was one of Moscow's most trusted agents in Mexico, regularly given assignments by Lt. General Pavel Fitin of Soviet intelligence.[7] Toledano immediately put his resources behind Sorrell, providing money while pressuring Mexican film industry executives not to process any film from Hollywood as a show of solidarity. He also appeared at a rally in Hollywood to encourage the strikers.[8]

Herb Sorrell had promised violence if he didn't get his way in the studio strike, and it didn't take him long to deliver. Led by his "sluggers," strikers smashed windshields on passing trains and threw rocks at the police. One studio employee went to the hospital after acid was thrown in his face. When the police tried to break up the melee, things got even worse. As actor Kirk Douglas remembered it, "Thousands of people fought in the middle of the street with knives, clubs, battery cables, brass knuckles, and chains."[9]

Sorrell and his allies wanted to shut down the studios entirely, so anyone who crossed the picket line became a target of violence. Jack Warner insisted on keeping up production and the studio remained open. To avoid injury, workers, including stars who were shooting movies, were forced to sneak into the studio lot through a storm drain that led from the Los Angeles River.

Reagan, getting ready to start production on *Night Unto Night,* was furious about the violence. And unlike his approach to the little battle with the Communists in HICCASP, he was not in a mood to retreat.

Blaney Matthews, the giant-sized head of security at Warner Brothers, had seen this sort of violent strike before. He advised Reagan and other stars to use the storm drain to get onto the lot safely. Reagan flat out refused. If he was going to cross the picket line, he was going to cross the picket line, he told Matthews.

Matthews then arranged for buses to shuttle Reagan and a few others through the human gauntlet outside the studio gate. But he offered a bit of advice: Lie down on the floor, or you might get hit by a flying Coke bottle or rock. Again Reagan refused. Over the next several days, as he went to the studio lot to attend preproduction meetings, a bus would pass through the human throng of violent picketers, with a solitary figure seated upright inside.[10]

Reagan was no doubt acting on his convictions and his determination not to be intimidated by the strikers. But he may also have seen it as an opportunity to demonstrate his courage. He had missed the action in the Second World War only a few years earlier. When he had reported for duty at Fort Mason in 1942, his medical exam had revealed poor eyesight.

"If we sent you overseas, you'd shoot a general," one doctor had told him.

"Yes," said the other. "And you'd miss him."

So instead of going off to war and serving bravely in the Army Air Corps like his friend Jimmy Stewart, Reagan was consigned to service in the First Motion Picture Unit, based just outside of Los Angeles.[11]

Not bowing to violence was Reagan's first act of defiance. Another came when Sorrell tried to get the Screen Actors Guild to fall into line and support the strike. Reagan was a SAG board member, having joined with his wife's help in 1937. (Jane Wyman was already on the board.)

SAG had a quick vote after the strike began and elected to cross the picket line. But there were Sorrell supporters and Communist Party members among the SAG leadership, and they suggested that the guild try to arbitrate some kind of solution. A small group was asked to handle the matter. Reagan was among them.

By taking the assignment, Reagan was stepping foursquare into the middle of a testy labor dispute. It was the sort of thing he had been warned against before. Spencer Tracy had always advised his fellow actors to steer clear of politics. It was bad for your career and could get you into trouble, Tracy said. "Remember who shot Lincoln," he told them.[12]

But Reagan, along with Gene Kelly and Katharine Hepburn, stepped into the breach. They met with labor officials and even with Sorrell himself. Matters were at an impasse.

Filming began on *Night Unto Night* at a dreary beach house just up the coast from Hollywood. Reagan was the lead in a story about a widow who believed her dead husband was communicating with her. The picture costarred Viveca Lindfors, an accomplished stage actress from Sweden.

After one take of a beach scene, Reagan was summoned to the telephone. When he picked up the receiver, a voice he didn't recognize threatened to see to it that he never made films again. If he continued to oppose the CSU strike, the caller said, "a squad" would disfigure his face with acid.[13]

It was the first of many threats as the CSU and their Communist Party allies grew desperate to force SAG into line. Reagan hired guards to watch his kids. "I have been looking over my shoulder when I go down the street," he told a SAG meeting.

Blaney Matthews was so concerned that he took the unusual step of making sure that Reagan got a permit to pack a .32 Smith & Wesson. From the time he got up in the morning to the time he went to bed, Reagan kept the pistol close and snug, holstered under his jacket. When he went to sleep, he kept it at his bedside. But his nights were fitful. Jane Wyman would awaken and find him sitting up in bed at two in the morning, holding the gun because he had heard an unusual sound. The dreamland he had been living in only a few months earlier was turning into a nightmare.[14]

Along with the threats of physical violence, Communist Party members in the industry began verbally attacking Reagan and others for their stand. Actor Alexander Knox, best known for his portrayal of Woodrow Wilson in Darryl Zanuck's film biography, called Reagan a "fraud" and said he was talking "out of both sides of his mouth." Actress Karen Morley called him an opportunist. The CSU called for a boycott of his movies and started handing out flyers denouncing him and other anti-Communists as "stooges." Colleagues who had previously been friendly suddenly turned on him. As he later recalled one encounter with some friends: "My smile was already forming and I had just started to greet them when one of the two thrust his face close to mine, his eyes burning with hatred. 'Fascist!' he hissed, literally spitting the words at me."[15]

Despite the attacks, Reagan stood firm. When the smoke cleared the strike had fizzled, Reagan having won people over with his courage. Jack Warner, a man who was sparing with his praise, declared, "Ronnie Reagan . . . has turned out to be a tower of strength, not only for the actors but for the whole industry, and he is to be highly complimented for his efforts on behalf of everyone working in our business." Columnist Hedda Hopper declared that Reagan, through his calmness and confidence, had "commanded the respect of his most bitter opponents." He had been a "fearless foe" of the Communists, said labor leader Roy Brewer.[16]

Reagan's opponents saw him as a key figure who had brought about their defeat. Actor Sterling Hayden, a member of the Communist Party at the time, saw firsthand the trouble Reagan had caused the party. Years later he testified before Congress about the strike and how the Communists had tried to paralyze the entertainment industry and take over the unions. When he was asked why the plot failed, Hayden explained that they had run into Reagan, "who was a one-man battalion."[17]

With the failure of the strike, Herb Sorrell was quickly eliminated as a force in Hollywood. The CSU ceased to exist, and by 1949, Sorrell had only twenty-five people in his union.

But Sorrell was not the only casualty in the battle. On March 10, 1947, Ronald Reagan and Jane Wyman attended a SAG board meeting and heard unusual news. Robert Montgomery, the recently re-elected SAG president with playboy good looks, wanted to resign. He was tired of all the extra hours that the job demanded, and the resulting wear and tear on his mind and body. But he was also weary of the political battles that were erupting. As he said to a friend, he "was very much concerned" about retribution against anti-Communists in Hollywood. He feared that "all actors and actresses who have taken such a stand will not be on the screen in ten years."[18]

Graceful Gene Kelly had been active in SAG for years, a liberal who did not take the Communist Party seriously. But the strike had hardened his attitude, and he now considered the party a real threat. After Montgomery's resignation was announced, Kelly rose and nominated Reagan to serve as the new SAG president. George Chandler, the avuncular and kindly character actor, seconded the motion. Someone also nominated Gene Kelly, and another, George Murphy. But when the secret ballots were returned, Reagan was the clear choice.

SAG was a divided organization when Reagan took over. The aims of the strike might have been defeated, but the political battles were just beginning. Reagan quickly discovered that two small cliques made up of Communist Party members were active in the SAG leadership. The strike had radicalized them and they were now posing a serious challenge.

Still shaken by the strike and concerned about party activities, Reagan and his wife sat down with FBI agents on April 10 and explained what they were facing. Thus began Reagan's secret role as an informant for the Bureau. They gave him a code name, T-10, and met with him regularly.

According to the secret FBI report about the April 10 meeting,

"Reagan and his wife advised that for the past several months they had observed during the Guild meetings there were two 'cliques' of members, one headed by Anne Revere and the other by Karen Morley which on all questions of policy confronting the Guild, followed the Communist Party line." Indeed, both women, unknown to Reagan at the time, were party members.[19]

Reagan wasn't as concerned about their ideas as he was about their tactics. SAG board members needed to be thinking solely in terms of serving SAG members. They shouldn't have a secret agenda. So, on September 16, Reagan pushed a resolution that declared that no Communist Party member could be an officer of the Guild. As the resolution put it, "A member of the Communist Party has an obligation to the Communist Party which transcends his other obligations and which would transcend his obligations to the Screen Actors Guild as a member of the Board of Directors or as an officer or executive officer of the Guild."

The resolution received stiff resistance from both Morley and Revere. But it passed in a vote among SAG members, 1,307 to 157.

In a matter of less than a year, Reagan had become immersed in the biggest political battle ever waged in Hollywood. He was passionate about it, attending meetings, reading up on the subject of communism, talking endlessly about it with friends. To his wife, it was a troubling obsession. She had been frightened during the strike when he carried a gun. After the strike ended, she had expected life to return to normal, but it hadn't. She had signed on to be the wife of an actor, not a politician.[20]

Shortly after Reagan had been elected SAG president, Wyman had headed off to Mendocino to begin production on the film *Johnny Belinda*. The story had been a smash on Broadway and had been of interest to Wyman ever since she had seen it with her husband in September 1940. Now, after considerable negotiation with Jack Warner, she had her chance to play the lead.

Her costar was Lew Ayres, best known for his role as the lead in *All Quiet on the Western Front*. Like his character in that film, Ayres was a pacifist. In March 1942, only four months after the attack on Pearl Harbor, Ayres had declared that he would not bear arms in the war. It was a stunning pronouncement, even in Hollywood, and provoked outrage across the country. Ayres spent most of the war working at a conscientious objectors' camp in Oregon.

Ayres had been married twice, first to Lola Lane and then for seven years to Ginger Rogers. When the vivacious Jane Wyman walked onto the set of *Johnny Belinda*, it didn't take long for them to fall for each other. Later, when Wyman filed for divorce, Reagan told his friend Hedda Hopper, "I think I'll name *Johnny Belinda* as the co-respondent."

In divorce papers filed in court on June 29 of the following year, Wyman claimed mental cruelty. "In recent months," she declared, "my husband and I engaged in continual arguments on his political views . . . finally, there was nothing in common between us . . . nothing to sustain our marriage. . . . Despite my lack of interest in his political activities, he insisted I attend meetings with him and be present during discussions among our friends. But my own ideas were never considered important."[21]

Reagan was shattered. His personal war on communism was costing him his wife and family. He clung to hope, telling one reporter, "It's a very strange girl I'm married to, but I love her. . . . I know we will end our lives together." But ultimately he didn't contest the suit, recognizing that a chasm existed between them that could not be closed. He blamed himself in part for the divorce. "Perhaps I should have let someone else save the whole world and saved my own home."

Only several years later, when he met a petite young actress named Nancy Davis, who shared his convictions, would he be whole again.

Even as his marriage crumbled, the political battles raged. On September 25, 1947, Reagan received a subpoena to appear before the Un-American Activities Committee of the U.S. Congress, which was conducting hearings on communism in Hollywood. Dozens of actors, directors, and writers were being ordered to appear. Reagan, along with Gary Cooper, George Murphy, and others, agreed. Others, however, including writers Dalton Trumbo and John Howard Lawson and director Edward Dmytryk, refused.

When the committee convened in Washington, the scene was a media dream: tanned, slender, handsome actors arriving in the nation's capital to discuss the political battle that had been raging in Hollywood. Amid dozens of flashing bulbs and hundreds of autograph seekers, the witnesses appeared one by one in front of the committee.

Reagan, dressed in a tan gabardine suit, blue knitted tie, and white shirt, presented his views on what had happened in Hollywood. It was a call to arms in the battle against communism. But it was also a call to fight communism by sticking to American principles. "We have spent 170 years in this country on the basis that democracy is strong enough to stand up and fight against the inroads of any ideology," he said. "I believe that, as Thomas Jefferson put it, if all the American people know all of the facts they will never make a mistake."

Under questioning from the committee (the young California congressman Richard Nixon failed to ask any questions), Reagan explained how the battle was being won in Hollywood. "I detest, I abhor their philosophy, but I detest more than that their tactics, which are those of the fifth column, and are dishonest, but at the same time I never as a citizen want to see our country become urged, by either fear or resentment of this group, that we ever compromise with any of our democratic principles through that fear or resentment. I still think democracy can do it. . . . I think that within the bounds of our democratic rights, and never once stepping over the rights given us by democracy, we have done a pretty good job in our business of keeping those people's activities curtailed."[22]

When he was finished, Reagan smiled, stood up, and quietly left the room. It was a performance that impressed even some of the skeptics in Hollywood. "Intelligent Ronald Reagan stole the show from his better known colleagues," wrote reporter Quentin Reynolds of *Collier's*. "Reagan, it was obvious, had done a great deal of thinking on the subject in question."[23]

CHAPTER II

"YOU TOO CAN BE FREE AGAIN"

IF RONALD REAGAN'S WORLD HAD RADICALLY CHANGED IN THE two years since the war, so too had the world around him. Soviet leader Josef Stalin was consolidating his hold on the nations of Central Europe. He was also looking to expand his influence by supporting communist insurgents in Greece and hoping to occupy part of Iran. At the U.S. embassy in Moscow, a State Department diplomat named George Kennan had declared that America needed to "contain" the Soviet Union. Harry Truman was moving quickly to support nations facing communist aggression and laying the grounds for the North Atlantic Treaty Organization.

Reagan liked Truman because he saw some of himself in the haberdasher from Missouri. Truman was plainspoken but could be tough when he needed to be. Reagan had been a Democrat his whole life, and he believed in the policy of containment that Truman was articulating.

But not all Democrats agreed; there was dissension in the party. Henry Wallace, vice president to Franklin Roosevelt and commerce secretary under Truman, came from the party's left and believed that the administration was being too hard on Stalin. On September 12, 1946, he spoke before a large crowd at Madison Square Garden and

enunciated his views about the world situation. Whereas he had a
few critical words to say about the Soviet Union, most of his criticism was leveled at the United States. After declaring that Russian
dominance in Central Europe was a positive development that the
United States should not interfere with, he advised Truman to go
easy on Stalin because "the tougher we get with Russia, the tougher
they will get with us."

In April 1948, a group of Hollywood stars that included Henry
Fonda, James Cagney, and Joan Fontaine hosted a dinner for writer
Arthur Koestler. The Hungarian-born British novelist had written
the novel *Darkness at Noon*, which had become an international sen-
sation. It was the story of an idealistic Communist who ended up in
Stalin's prisons. It was in some respects autobiographical, reflecting
Koestler's disillusionment with communism.

Reagan attended the event and was fascinated by what he heard.
Koestler not only attacked the Soviets, he mocked Henry Wallace,
who was running for president against Truman on the Progressive
Party ticket. Wallace was too soft on the Soviet Union. Some in the
audience were uncomfortable with the presentation because all he
was doing was attacking the left.

"They're not left," Koestler replied. "They're *East*."

All of this had a profound effect on Reagan. He was concerned
not only about the communist threat, but also the unwillingness of
some of his fellow liberals to resist it.

Reagan joined with labor leader Roy Brewer to form an organization to fight the anti-anti-Communists within the Democratic
Party. The two men formed the League of Hollywood Voters, with
Reagan as chairman, and offered support to Democrats who had denounced the Communist Party. In the presidential race, they came
out strongly for Truman and against Wallace. Truman wasn't particularly popular in Hollywood, because he had imposed loyalty oaths
for government workers. But the League brought him to town,
broadcast a radio special on his behalf, and managed to bring a few
skeptics like Lauren Bacall, Humphrey Bogart, Gregory Peck, and
Lucille Ball into the fold.[1]

In Washington, President Truman was pushing loyalty oaths. In
Hollywood, the studios and the unions were struggling with the
question of blacklists. Some of the studio heads wanted to ban any

Communist Party members from working in the industry. In their minds, blacklists were a nice, neat, simple solution to the problem.

As SAG president, Reagan opposed the idea because he believed it was grossly unfair. The threat posed by communism, as he had said in his congressional testimony, was not so much its ideas but its tactics. In a straight ideological battle between freedom and communism, he was confident freedom would always come out on top. The problem was that Communists masked their agenda and "had fooled some otherwise loyal Americans into believing that the Communist Party sought to make a better world."

In a 2,000-word article titled "How Do You Fight Communism?" Reagan wrote: "The real fight with this new totalitarianism belongs properly to the forces of liberal democracy, just as did the battle with Hitler's totalitarianism. There really is no difference except the cast of characters. On the one hand is our belief that the people can and will decide what is best for themselves, and on the other (communist, Nazi, or fascist) side is the belief that a 'few' can best decide what is good for all the rest." The secret to fighting them and winning, said Reagan, was to take the offensive and expose them for who they are. But it was critical to fight the battle within the parameters of democratic principles.

In the nation's capital, a young senator from Wisconsin named Joe McCarthy was beginning his campaign to purge the government of what he believed were hundreds of Communists. McCarthy professed to have lists of known Communists working inside several government agencies.

While not specifically naming McCarthy, Reagan explained that he was uncomfortable with McCarthy's approach. Communists were taking "advantage of our constitutional freedom to plot the death of that constitution. They are trying to operate on a 'can't lose' basis. For example, if we get so frightened that we suspend our traditional democratic freedoms in order to fight them—they still have won. They have shown that the democracy won't work when the going gets tough."

He also expressed his distaste for red-baiting. "We play right into their hands when we go around calling everybody a Communist," he wrote.[2]

As Reagan later explained about McCarthy, he "was using a

shotgun when he should have been using a rifle. . . . He went with a scatter gun and he lumped together fellow travelers, innocent dupes, and hard-core Communists."[3]

One person almost caught up by this scattergun approach in Hollywood was a young actress named Nancy Davis. In 1950, Reagan received a phone call from director Mervyn LeRoy. A young actress who was working on one of his pictures had been falsely linked to several communist front groups. It seemed that Nancy Davis, the actress, was being confused with another Nancy Davis who was involved with these groups. LeRoy thought that Reagan, as head of the SAG, might be able to help.

Reagan was glad to be of assistance. And after making a few phone calls to straighten the matter out, he met the young actress and took her to dinner at a restaurant on the Sunset Strip. Soon they fell in love and were married. The war had taken away; and now in a strange way it was giving back.

What separated Reagan from McCarthy and some of the other anti-Communists at the time was his belief in the profound weakness of communism. For McCarthy, the ideology was a thing to be feared, an ironclad doctrine with strong adherents. For Reagan, on the other hand, communism appealed to the weak. Far from being a sign of intellectual strength or political courage, its wellspring was personal weakness.

"Scratch a Hollywood Communist—especially the 'intellectual'—and you'll find a person afflicted with a kind of neurosis," he explained in a 1951 interview. "These people might otherwise have gone in for some kind of phony religion to ease their personal pressures. For them, communism filled a need. It let them blame their failures on something besides their own inabilities."[4]

It wasn't that Reagan was minimizing the threat; he believed that communism was a profound challenge. But he believed it thrived only by secrecy, threats, and deceit.

Reagan had read Koestler's *Darkness at Noon* and a 1949 book called *The God That Failed*, which included chapters by former high-profile Communists who had renounced their past. Along with a chapter by Koestler, this book contained essays by French novelist André Gide, novelist Richard Wright, Italian writer Ignazio Silone, and Louis Fischer. Some in Reagan's Hollywood set had also defected from the party. Tough-guy actor Edward G. Robinson declared, "I was duped and used. I was lied to." And he promptly left the party.[5]

Reagan had great respect for those who were baring their souls and switching sides. But he was also aware of the torment and fear that often accompanied such a move. Many stayed in the party out of fear, not because of their commitment to the ideology.

One man trying to make the break was Edward Dmytryk. The young, pipe-smoking director had been born in Canada to Ukrainian parents and moved to Hollywood to work as a projectionist. He had worked his way up and become a successful director of such films as *Crossfire* and *Murder My Sweet*. Dmytryk had joined the Communist Party in 1944 and had been called to testify before the House Un-American Affairs Committee at the same time Reagan made his appearance. Unlike Reagan, however, Dmytryk was a hostile witness, refusing to answer any questions. He became one of the so-called Hollywood Ten, spending time in jail for contempt of Congress.

If outwardly Dmytryk was a solid party man, inwardly he was troubled. He had read *Darkness at Noon* in 1945 with great interest. But when he mentioned the book to fellow party members, they pulled him aside and declared that members were not allowed to read *anything* by Koestler. He was stunned that for all their professed interest in free ideas, they had blacklisted the writer.

Finally, in 1949, Dmytryk wanted to break from the party. But his former comrades were denouncing him. They called him a "scoundrel" and a "perjurer," threatening retribution if he defected. Some anti-Communists in Hollywood thought the ex-Communist was getting what he deserved.

But Reagan and several others were sympathetic to his plight, offering to rally to his defense in the hopes of encouraging others to join him. Reagan, his friend labor leader Roy Brewer, and four others drafted a letter that they released under the auspices of the Motion Picture Industry Council (MPIC). It was published in several Hollywood trade papers and the *Saturday Evening Post*. Titled "You Too Can Be Free Men Again," it was an offer of help to those who wanted to switch sides in the cold war divide.

The letter described the attacks on Dmytryk. "These same accusations have been leveled by the Communist Party against such militant ex-Communists as Arthur Koestler, Louis Bundez, Elizabeth Bentley, and Whittaker Chambers. In each case, the records of these persons show that their disillusionment with Communism came slowly, but with it came determination to help destroy the menace which once had trapped them."

The letter explained that Reagan and the others had met with Dmytryk several times to discuss his change of heart and to offer help. "In meeting after meeting with Dmytryk, we watched the man change and gradually lose his fear that for the ex-Communist there is no road back to decent society."

The group then offered support to those who wanted to leave the party. "We will be surprised if there are not other attacks by the Communist Party on other former Communists who have the guts to stand up and be counted and to tell the truth to the proper government agencies. It takes courage and desire and time for an American to work free of the tentacles of the Communist Party. And it takes help. But there is a way out. To any Communist Party member who may be seeking that way, we say: 'You too can be free men again!' " The letter was signed by Reagan and five others.[6]

Reagan had been asked to join the MPIC planning committee shortly after the 1947 strike. It was a group made up of guild leaders and studio men that served as a cheerleader for the industry, not only in the United States but around the world.

MPIC was being run by Eric Johnston, who had recently taken over as head of the Motion Picture Association of America (MPAA). A youthful forty-nine when Reagan met him, Johnston had steely eyes but a generous smile.

Johnston was former president of the U.S. Chamber of Commerce, an unabashed believer in free-market capitalism and a virulent opponent of communism. His views had been heavily influenced by two visits to Russia. The first had come during the First World War just after the 1917 Bolshevik Revolution. As a young U.S. Marine, he had seen the chaos and carnage that had followed Lenin's seizure of power. The second visit had come in 1944, at the invitation of Stalin himself. As head of the U.S. Chamber of Commerce, Johnston spent six weeks there discussing trade issues and visiting factories around the country. He was shocked at what he saw and blunt to his hosts. "You are the most state-minded and the most collective-minded people in existence," he told them. "We are the most private-minded and the most individual-minded; and gentlemen, make no mistake: we are determined to remain so—and even to become more so."

After the war, Johnston believed that there was a great ideological struggle going on in the world, and as head of MPIC and MPAA, he believed the movie business had a critical role to play in winning it. He told studio heads that Soviet influence in the world could be countered by films depicting American prosperity. On the other hand, movies with excess—gluttony, conspicuous consumption, too much drinking—could provoke resentment in the developing world.

It was Johnston who offered Reagan his first window into the Soviet world. Johnston was spending time in places throughout the Soviet bloc, trying to convince leaders to import more Hollywood films. He told Reagan stories over dinner.

Johnston described one attempt to get the newly installed communist government in Poland to accept more American films to show in their theaters. He sat with the education minister in a tiny Warsaw theater reviewing one film in which the characters walked through the parking lot at the Lockheed plant in southern California. The minister stopped the movie.

"There, Mr. Johnston, there's what we don't like, that propaganda."

"What do you mean propaganda?" Johnston asked.

"All those cars in the parking lot. Are you trying to make us poor Poles believe that the workers in a factory in America drive those automobiles to work?"

Johnston spent considerable time trying to explain to the minister that in fact the average American did drive a car, but to no avail. The story struck a nerve with Reagan. He was still telling it to guests forty years later in the Oval Office.[7]

Reagan was intrigued by what Johnston was telling him. It provided an opportunity to combine his love of movies with his new-found mission to combat communism. Why not use Hollywood films to undermine the Soviets?

It was important for Reagan to not only be anti-Communist, but also to stand *for* something. You needed to articulate freedom and not just resist totalitarianism. Movies, he believed, could do that in a positive way. He went to Washington and met with people in Truman's State Department to discuss ways in which this "vital weapon" could be used in the battle of ideas. As he told an audience in 1951, "We are pretty proud of the fact that our government says in the ideological struggle that is going on in the world, it is the American motion picture, not with its message picture, just showing our store windows in the street scenes with things that Americans can buy, our parking lots, our streets with automobiles, our shots of American working men driving these automobiles, that is holding back the flood of propaganda from the other side of the Iron Curtain."[8]

MPIC was a conglomeration of people from throughout the motion picture industry. As a board member, Reagan got to know several people who influenced him. One was director and producer Walter Wanger. Courteous and urbane, Wanger was a Hollywood liberal who had been comfortably part of the left for years. He had won the National Peace Conference citation for his picture *Blockade* about the Spanish Civil War. He had known party members and worked with them and also been an active member of Americans United for World Government.

But the chill of the cold war had led Wanger to become a vocal anti-Communist. Without abandoning what he saw as true liberal principles, he wanted to make good movies and fight the Soviets. As he told James Reston of the *New York Times*, "I feel that if we will only organize our communications properly it will do a great deal toward winning the cold war and not leave us vulnerable to psychological warfare."[9]

Wanger was involved in another venture that he wanted to get Reagan plugged into. In 1949, the Truman administration had established a secretive body called the National Committee for a Free Europe, later called the Free Europe Committee. The committee was the brainchild of Allen Dulles, a New York lawyer who had served in the Office of Strategic Services (OSS) during the Second

World War and would later serve as CIA director under Eisenhower and Kennedy. Looking for a way to fight the Soviets with radio broadcasts and propaganda, Dulles and other veterans of the OSS had drawn up the idea while meeting in the Century Club in Manhattan.

Dulles's idea found plenty of support in the newly minted CIA, which began funding what would become known as Radio Free Europe. But to maximize these propaganda efforts, a private organization called the Crusade for Freedom was formed in 1950 to raise money.

General Lucius Clay, the man who had organized the 1948–1949 Berlin Airlift, became chairman of the Crusade for Freedom, and the organization took the American Liberty Bell as its symbol. The crusade began holding parades, rallies, and fund-raising dinners around the country, using slogans such as "Fight the Big Lie with the Big Truth" and "Help Truth Fight Communism."

Wanger had been recruited to head the Los Angeles County campaign, and he told Reagan about the organization. The Crusade was calling for a rollback of the Soviet empire under the slogan "That this world under God shall have a new birth of freedom."

The idea appealed to Reagan not only because of his fervent anti-communism but also because he understood the value and power of radio. He had spent his youth broadcasting for WHO in Iowa and well knew what you could convey to an audience through the microphone.

Reagan began appearing at Crusade rallies, encouraging people to raise money and spread the word about the Crusade. More than any other performer, Reagan embraced the cause and spread the word. He had a resolution passed by the Screen Actors Guild to encourage other performers to get involved, and he even taped a short film in support of the Crusade that was circulated to schools, civic groups, and churches around the country.

"The battleground of peace today is that strip of strategically located countries stretching from the Baltic to the Black Sea. They are not big countries geographically, but they contain several million freedom-loving people, our kind of people, who share our culture and who have sent millions of their sons and daughters to become part of these United States. Some call these countries the satellite nations. More accurately, they're the captive nations of Europe.

"My name is Ronald Reagan. Last year the contributions of 16 million Americans to the Crusade for Freedom made possible the World Freedom Bell—symbol of hope and freedom to the communist-dominated peoples of Eastern Europe."

When North Korean forces crossed the 49th parallel and invaded the south in 1950, President Truman pushed hard for a strong American response. The Cold War was becoming a war by proxy, just as many had feared might happen.

The invasion caught the Truman administration by surprise. Just months earlier, the president had announced his plans to cut defense spending. Now, with naked aggression on the Korean peninsula, Truman was promising to wage a successful war to push back communist forces.

Reagan defended Truman's decision and found himself frustrated by the fact that many of his colleagues in Hollywood were less than enthusiastic about the war. He lamented what he saw as a melting of resolve in Hollywood. Opponents of the war were not necessarily communist, according to Reagan. But they reflected a new phenomenon in Hollywood. "There seems to be a new breed in town, the anti-anti-Communist," the newspaper *Daily Worker* quoted Reagan as saying. "These are the non-communists who denounce anyone out to get the communists."[10]

The war also hardened his position on the question of blacklisting. Whereas he was still opposed to it in principle, he was growing impatient with those who were not cooperating with the government. Americans were dying at the hands of the enemy. There was now a "clear and present danger." "This country is engaged in a war with Communism," wrote the Motion Picture Industry Council in a letter signed by Reagan. "87,000 American casualties leave little room for witnesses to stand on the first and fifth amendments; and for those who do, we have no sympathy."

When the 1952 presidential election rolled around, Reagan found himself increasingly concerned about the drift of his party. He had been a Democrat all his life, growing up in the shadow of FDR and a father who worshiped the man. Reagan had liked Truman, but the Democratic nominee was cut from a different cloth. Adlai Stevenson, the lanky and thoughtful ex-governor of Illinois, was less than inspiring to Reagan.

On the other hand, Reagan found himself attracted to General Dwight David Eisenhower, who was heading up the GOP ticket. Ike was popular, pro-business, and generally conservative. Even more interestingly to Reagan, he was calling for a bolder policy for challenging the Soviet Union. John Foster Dulles, who was advising Eisenhower and would go on to serve as secretary of state, was calling the policy Liberation. It was time to move beyond the static lines of containment to an offensive strategy designed to liberate the "captive nations" of Central Europe. More than anything, it was a carbon copy of the sort of policies the Crusade for Freedom was calling for.

Reagan signed up for the Eisenhower campaign, the first time that he would campaign and vote for a Republican. He didn't change his voter registration, remaining a Democrat while heading up Democrats for Eisenhower. He made appearances for Ike and raised some money for the campaign.

On a breezy day in June 1952, Reagan went to William Woods College in Fulton, Missouri, to deliver a commencement address to the students. The speech, which Reagan wrote himself, talked about America and what Reagan saw as its unique duty to face and defeat the Soviet threat. The Cold War, he declared, was "the same old battle. We met it under the name of Hitlerism; we met it under the name of Kaiserism; and we have met it back through the ages in the name of every conqueror that has ever set upon a course of establishing his rule over mankind. It is simply the idea, the basis of this country and of our religion, the idea of the dignity of man, the idea that deep within the heart of each one of us is something so godlike and precious that no individual or group has a right to impose his or its will upon the people, that no group can decide for the people what is good for the people so well as they can decide for themselves." America was a "place in the divine scheme of things" that needed to "strive for freedom" for the sake of all mankind.

Reagan believed that America needed to face the threat of Soviet communism head-on. But as the 1952 presidential campaign moved along, he became disillusioned with the Republican ticket.

Ike lacked the spark that was needed. "I must confess my enthusiasm cooled a little as the campaign progressed," he wrote to an old friend shortly after the election. "[Eisenhower] did not grow in stature, and frankly I thought Stevenson did." But if Reagan was somewhat disappointed with Eisenhower's performance, he was disdainful of Richard Nixon, the new vice president, and questioned his commitment to the cause.

"Pray as I am praying for the health and long life of Eisenhower because the thought of Nixon in the White House is almost as bad as that of 'Uncle Joe' [Stalin]. Let me as a Californian tell you that Nixon is a hand picked errand boy with a pleasing façade and naught but emptiness behind."[11]

CHAPTER III

PILES OF CARDS
IN RUBBER BANDS

IKE CAME INTO THE WHITE HOUSE TEMPERED BY WAR. HE HAD served as Supreme Allied Commander in Europe (SACEUR) during World War II and as the first SACEUR for NATO. During the war, he had made common cause with the Soviet military in the war against Nazi Germany.

Now, as the Cold War simmered, he was deeply suspicious of Soviet intentions. He felt that the Soviets were intent on expanding their influence and dominating as much of the globe as possible. At the same time, the ideological war was heating up. The only law the Soviets seemed to understand, he told his aides, was force.

Still, Eisenhower was a reluctant strategist when it came to the Cold War. Deep inside the recesses of his mind was the belief that the Cold War was destined to end in disaster. And as a man with a supreme sense of duty, he was determined to do something about it.

"As of now," Ike wrote in his private diary, "the world is racing toward catastrophe. Something must be done to put the brake on." For the sake of peace, he was willing to "wipe the slate clean" with Moscow and forget about what had happened in Central Europe. Harry Truman had not been big on talking with Moscow, believing that there was little to say. But Ike was very interested, particularly after Nikita Khrushchev became Soviet premier following the death of Stalin. In all, there were three summits and five foreign minister meetings during the Eisenhower years. They yielded little in terms of Soviet concessions, but the usually glum Secretary of State John Foster Dulles became downright giddy about the prospects of negotiating a peace.

"Up until the time of Geneva," he told British Foreign Secretary Harold Macmillan, "Soviet policy was based on intolerance, which was the keynote of Soviet doctrine. Soviet policy is now based on tolerance, which includes good relations with everyone."[1]

If there was going to be containment of the Soviets, Ike wanted to do it on the cheap. He devoted considerable diplomatic effort to signing treaties: the Rio Pact, the Manila Pact, the Baghdad Pact, treaties with South Korea and Taiwan. But he was loath to spend money on the military. The arms race was sapping the life out of both capitalism and communism. It was "a wasting of strength that defies the American system or the Soviet system or any system to achieve true abundance and happiness for the people of this earth."[2]

In an attempt to limit the arms competition, Ike swore off any efforts to achieve American superiority. It would not be a goal of his administration, and he instructed his cabinet not to make "invidious comparisons" with the Soviet military. Instead, he wanted to "stand on the concept of having sufficient military power to deter aggression."[3]

During the 1952 campaign, Ike had been enthusiastic about rolling back the Soviet empire. But when it came to fulfilling these promises as president, he quickly backed down. Early on in his administration, a secret directive had determined that the possibility of peeling off a Soviet client state was not feasible and could be downright dangerous. So Ike was reluctant to press the matter publicly. Even when a "captive nations" resolution was introduced in early 1953 by Congress (with support from actor Ronald Reagan), the administration made it clear privately that they saw it simply as a psychological weapon and that they were not prepared to go any further.[4]

The Kremlin spent the Eisenhower years consolidating its position. With heavy investments in military programs, the Soviet Union beat the United States in the race to be the first nation to explode a hydrogen bomb and surpassed the United States in ballistic missile technology. Central Europe was also being eaten up, but not without some indigestion.

In 1953, there was an uprising in East Germany that had to be ruthlessly put down. In 1956, there was an even larger revolt in Hungary. Tens of thousands took to the streets and demanded the end of communist rule in their country. Within a matter of weeks, Soviet troops stormed into the country and took control after vicious street battles that left an estimated ten thousand dead. Many Hungarians believed that when they revolted American assistance would arrive. It never did. Privately Ike and Dulles saw the uprising as a major inconvenience, a threat to stability and American interests.

If Ike was restrained, the Kremlin was emboldened, looking confidently to the future. As one Politburo member put it in a 1957 secret session: "How is it possible not to note—even our enemies recognize this—that since 1953, the Soviet Union has enjoyed huge successes in the area of foreign policy. . . . The international authority of the Soviet Union as the leading state in the struggle for peace and security, as the friend of all peoples who are fighting against the imperialists for peace and security, as the friend of all people who are fighting against the imperialists for their national independence and freedom, has grown immeasurably. . . ."[5]

It was Nikita Khrushchev, the pugnacious and boisterous son of peasants who had risen through the Communist Party apparatus, who had taken over leadership of the Soviet Union, and he was a true believer in the cause. He also understood the psychology of the West and how to use fear to advance his interests.

He was open and frank in discussing the possibility of nuclear war.

"If a conflict results," he told Polish officials in a secret 1958 meeting, "they know full well that we are in a position to raze West Germany to the ground. The first minutes of war will decide. There the losses will naturally be the greatest. After that, the war might drag on for years. Their territory is small—West Germany, England, France—literally several bombs will suffice, they will decide in the first minutes of the war."[6]

Khrushchev was a master of theatrics, regularly telling Western leaders that he was prepared to bomb away if need be. Warsaw Pact leaders marveled at the success he enjoyed, seeing his threats for what they were—namely, a grand bluff. "For them [the West] the threat of a nuclear strike was a real threat," General Otakar Rytir, Chief of the Czech General Staff, told his colleagues in a secret meeting. "They were really scared. There was panic. Not only among the public. There was panic in the [military] staffs. And they realized what it meant, they took Khrushchev at his word; maybe what Khrushchev was saying was ninety-eight percent propaganda, but they took him at his word."[7]

★ ★ ★

FEAR. REAGAN CAME ACROSS THAT WORD NUMEROUS TIMES AS HE read through Whittaker Chambers's autobiography about his bout with communism, *Witness*. Reagan had picked up the book on a recommendation from a friend, and decades later he would be able to quote passages from memory. Chambers wrote about the use of fear to maintain party discipline and how he had broken free from that fear while watching his daughter sleep at night. He looked at the delicate features of her ear and concluded that it was something that could only be created by God. His fear was suddenly gone. The only anxiety left in him, he wrote, was the belief that by leaving the Communist Party he was joining the losing side.

As Ike had entered the White House, Ronald Reagan's life was changing. Reagan had reached middle age, when even the best Hollywood careers went into decline; his had suffered from poor roles and downright neglect. He had spent more time in the last five years on his SAG activities and political work than he had on making movies. All of Hollywood, for that matter, was changing. Television was quickly becoming king of the entertainment world.

In 1952, General Electric came calling with an offer to host and occasionally appear in a weekly Sunday-night television drama series called *General Electric Theater*. Each week the program would offer a different story.

Reagan jumped at the chance and sometimes took the opportunity to inject important themes into the program. In one episode

Reagan plays a Soviet major during the occupation of Budapest. As a military man with orders, he struggles to balance the demands of duty with the lure of freedom. After arresting two Hungarians, he lets them go. "I never knew what freedom was until I saw you lose yours," he says.

In another episode, titled "The House of Truth," Reagan stars as a member of the United States Information Service in a strife-torn Asian village when communist agitators burn down an American library. He works tirelessly to reopen the library and help the oppressed villagers resist the Communists.

But there were continual struggles with the production staff about the content of these shows. During one episode about Soviet espionage, a battle erupted. As Reagan later wrote to a friend, "At our own studio I had to fight right down to the wire to make the Communists villains. When I say 'fight,' I mean really that. On our producing staff the liberal view that Communism is only something the 'right wingers' dreamed up prevails and they literally resorted to sabotage to pull the punch out of the show. Two individuals including the director wanted to cut the whole scene about the little girl saying her prayers. Finally in a near knock down drag out—they admitted their objection was because they were atheists. T'was a merry time we had but I'd gladly do it all over again."[8]

GE Theater allowed Reagan to continue acting. But the contract he signed contained a clause that made him the company's roving ambassador. For weeks on end he would travel the country by train, visiting GE plants, talking with workers, and giving speeches. If his schedule permitted, he would drop by the local chamber of commerce or Lions Club to address the crowd. Reagan was free to say whatever he wanted.

"I am not ever going to have G.E. censor anything you say," company head Ralph Cordiner promised. "You're not our spokesman, even though you're going out under our aegis. You're speaking for yourself. You say what you believe."[9]

So, in the bedroom of his house, Reagan would sit at a large desk with his reading glasses on, writing speeches on three-by-five cards. He would labor away for hours on end, writing each word in his own version of shorthand to make them fit on the tiny cards.

"If you opened up the second drawer of that desk," recalls his son, Michael Reagan, "there were piles and piles of these cards, wrapped in rubber bands."[10]

Fear. Reagan had seen the Communists use it as a powerful tool. They had used it against defectors from their ranks in Hollywood and against Arthur Koestler and other defectors. Now he believed that Ike was succumbing to the same sense of fear. It was, he said, "painfully clear that our foreign policy today is motivated by fear of the bomb." He was troubled that when Soviet tanks rumbled into Budapest to put down the 1956 Hungarian revolution, nothing had been done by the United States. During the uprising, the Hungarian revolutionaries had pleaded over the radio: "People of the world, help us . . . listen now to the alarm bells ring. People of the civilized world, in the name of liberty and solidarity, we are asking you to help. . . . Listen to our cry." The words deeply resonated with Reagan. After all, he had raised money for the very purpose of liberating Eastern Europe. The plea had a profound effect on him, and he was still talking about the betrayal of Hungary decades later, "wondering if the conscience of man will be hearing that cry a thousand years from now."[11]

On other occasions he lamented Ike's lack of commitment to national defense. "Since 1954," he glumly told an audience in 1959, "defense spending has decreased more than a billion dollars, while non-defense government expenditures have increased more than $10 billion."[12]

One event that did excite Reagan was the so-called Kitchen Debate between Richard Nixon and Nikita Khrushchev in 1959. Nixon was in Moscow, visiting a trade show, and he began bantering with Khrushchev about the relative merits of capitalism and communism. The international media were present and picked up the conversation, which was pointed but considerate. For Reagan, who had always questioned Nixon's fortitude for the cause, the debate was a welcome revelation. He fired off a letter to the vice president congratulating him for his performance. "As the cold war continues I'm sure many people lose sight of the basic conflict and begin to accept that two nations are foolishly bickering with sane justice and right as well as wrong on each side. This 'tolerant' view ignores of course the fact that only Communism is dedicated to imposing its 'way and belief' on all the world." He applauded Nixon for challenging Khrushchev and telling him "truths seldom if ever uttered in diplomatic exchanges." He hoped that the event was "starting us back to the uncompromising position of leadership which is our heritage and responsibility."

But if Reagan was encouraged by the exchange, Nixon was not. He noted sorely that the media "suggested that if I became president I might not be able to get along with Khrushchev." Thus, he saw the need to tone down his position if he was ever to be elected president.[13]

In the shadow of Eisenhower and JFK, Reagan began to develop his idea for dealing with the Soviet empire. Continuing the policy of peaceful coexistence was for him a disaster. "There can be only one end of the war we are in," he told an audience at the Press Club of Orange County, California. "It won't go away . . . wars end in victory or defeat." If the United States stuck with its policy, he warned, it might mean the demise of the nation within a decade.

What America needed to do was to show courage and move boldly forward without fear. "Communists gauge their aggression by slicing each new gain just thin enough so that we'll say, 'that isn't worth fighting for.' They have harnessed the fear of war instead of war itself."[14]

Instead of fearing the Communists, the solution was "an all-out fight against the growing encroachment of communism in this nation and throughout the world," he declared boldly.

On note cards and in his speeches, Reagan cobbled together the seeds of a profound strategy. Rather than negotiate treaties with Moscow, America needed to ramp up the pressure and force the Soviets to compete. As Reagan saw it, the United States enjoyed the most efficient and powerful economic machine in the world. Russia and China, in contrast, were "in the grip of modern-day feudalism."[15] The United States had an undisputed advantage in the superpower competition. If those other nations tried to keep up, their system would become "unhinged," he declared in 1963.

"If we relieve the strain on the shaken Russian economy by aiding their enslaved satellites, thus reducing the danger of uprising and revolution, and if we continue granting concessions which reduce our military strength giving Russia time to improve hers as well as shore up her limping industrial complex—aren't we perhaps adding to the communist belief that their system will through evolution catch up and pass ours?

"If we truly believe that our way of life is best aren't the Russians more likely to recognize that fact and modify their stand if we let their economy come unhinged so the contrast is apparent? Inhuman though it may sound, shouldn't we throw the whole burden of feeding the satellites on their slave masters who are having trouble feeding themselves?" This was a bold view, even in 1963 when he fully laid it out. Rather than coexist with the Soviet Union, the Cold War could be won, Reagan declared. He based his view "on the belief (supported by all the evidence) that in an all out race our system is stronger, and eventually the enemy gives up the race as a hopeless cause."[16]

★ ★ ★

IN EARLY JANUARY 1961, THE ROTUND AND LIVELY NIKITA Khrushchev delivered a secret speech before Communist Party workers in Moscow. He strode confidently to the podium, convinced that the tide of history was moving in the Soviet direction. As he looked out at his audience, he declared that "a mighty upsurge of anti-imperialist, national-liberation revolutions" was taking place around the globe. Capitalism was on the retreat and Soviet gains were apparent everywhere. In Cuba, Fidel Castro had swept into power with his band of guerrillas from the Sierra Maestra. In Southeast Asia, insurgents were gaining a foothold in Laos and advancing in South Vietnam. In Africa, there were revolutionary groups, backed by Moscow, that were pushing out colonial powers. In short, there was "a growing change in the correlation of forces in favor of socialism." These revolutions could not be defeated, Khrushchev declared with smug historical confidence. "Communists fully and unreservedly support such just wars and march in the vanguard of the peoples fighting wars of liberation."

A few months later, Khrushchev received the outline of a secret plan from the KGB, a grand strategy designed to advance the Soviet cause worldwide. It called for supporting revolutionary movements with arms, intelligence, and money. The Central Committee quickly endorsed it.

★ ★ ★

TWO DAYS AFTER HE WAS INAUGURATED AS PRESIDENT, JOHN F. Kennedy was in the Oval Office reading Khrushchev's secret speech. He read the entire twenty-thousand-word text in one sitting, shocked by the contents. He gave copies to all his top advisers and read portions aloud at the first session of the National Security Council.

John Kennedy had been narrowly elected president, defeating Richard Nixon in a hard-fought contest. Kennedy considered himself an ardent anti-Communist and had campaigned against Nixon on the grounds that the Republicans had allowed a "missile gap" to develop in favor of the Soviet Union.

Moscow had taken a keen interest in the election, and the Kremlin had a clear preference. Khrushchev considered Nixon an "aggressive anti-Communist" who "owed his career to that devil of darkness McCarthy."

Not that they didn't have their doubts about Kennedy. The young man from Massachusetts could be "outright bellicose," warned a secret intelligence assessment. But they believed he was a "typical pragmatist" who would change his position and accommodate adversaries if it served his interests. The report said that Kennedy could flip-flop easily, noting that as a senator he had been supportive of Joe McCarthy. But during the Senate hearings held a few years later to censure him, Kennedy had refused to take a position, failing to even vote on the matter.

For the 1960 election the KGB resident in Washington was ordered to "propose diplomatic or propaganda initiatives, or any other measures, to facilitate Kennedy's victory." Khrushchev went so far as to delay the release of American U-2 pilot Gary Francis Powers, who was being held in prison after being shot down on a spy mission over the Soviet Union. Khrushchev waited to release him until after the presidential election. It was his way, he declared, of "voting" for Kennedy and against Nixon.[17]

For Kennedy the test came early in his short presidency. Two months after his inauguration, communist guerrillas armed with new shipments of Soviet weapons advanced deep into the eastern reaches of Laos, which bordered Vietnam. The peaceful country's loyalty was supposedly guaranteed by the 1954 Geneva Accords, but the Viet Cong and North Vietnamese wanted to use the country as a supply line for their forces fighting in the south. Having occupied eastern Laos, the Viet Cong began using what came to be called the Ho Chi Minh Trail to arm their forces fighting in South Vietnam. Kennedy was apprised of the situation and elected to do nothing.

In April 1961, a large force of Cuban exiles began landing on the beaches of Cuba, near the so-called Bay of Pigs. They had been trained and equipped by the CIA with the intent of liberating their country from Fidel Castro. The plot was something that Kennedy had inherited from Eisenhower, and he had reluctantly signed off on it. But he had nixed a critical ingredient: When the force hit the beaches, it did so without American air strikes or naval bombardment. The exile army was driven back in a matter of days. The operation was an unmitigated disaster.

★   ★   ★

AT ABOUT THE SAME TIME THAT RONALD REAGAN WAS BEGIN-ning to deliver speeches about the inability of communism to compete with the West, Soviet-bloc leaders were privately fretting about the same thing. Nowhere was the efficiency of capitalism and the failure of communism more apparent than in Germany. West Berlin, a tiny free enclave in the heart of East Germany, was attracting thousands of refugees. Communist Party officials were worried, and the pugnacious party boss Walter Ulbricht was reaching the same conclusion that Reagan had reached about the difficulty communism faced in competing with the West.

Ulbricht secretly wrote to Nikita Khrushchev and explained his dilemma. "The experiences of the last years have proven that it is not possible for a socialist country such as the GDR to carry out peaceful competition with an imperialist country such as West Germany with open borders," he admitted bluntly.[18]

In the early hours of August 13, 1961, West Berlin residents awoke to see that a massive wall had been erected through their city. Within a matter of hours, they had been encircled by concrete and barbed wired. Suddenly, friends and family were divided.

Kennedy was furious at the action, but he was not prepared to go very far in countering it. He called up the reserves, sent troops to Europe, and proposed a substantial increase in the military budget. But again, he was concerned about the prospect of war. "It seems particularly stupid," he told aides, "to risk killing a million Americans over an argument about access rights on the Autobahn."[19]

For Nikita Khrushchev, the failure at the Bay of Pigs and successes in Laos and Berlin were proof that he could have things his way. He told a visiting American, Robert Frost, that Kennedy was "too liberal to fight." Far from preventing a confrontation that could "risk killing a million Americans," Khrushchev was now encouraged to pursue his most dangerous gambit.[20]

In May 1962, Khrushchev announced to the Politburo his secret plans to put Soviet nuclear missiles in Cuba. In Havana, Fidel Castro was eager for the missiles because he felt they would deter another Bay of Pigs–type invasion. Khrushchev thought that if he could pull off the plan it would shift the balance in the arms competition, because his shorter-range ballistic missiles would now be capable of reaching the United States.

The Soviet premier, seemingly always the gambler, was hoping to build the missile sites before the United States even detected them. On the chance that they were discovered, he believed, Kennedy would fear a confrontation and not take any substantial action.

Throughout late 1962 and most of 1963, Soviet transport ships brought material and specialists to Cuba, where construction crews busily worked on the missile batteries. The plan seemed to be going as Khrushchev hoped until an American U-2 spy plane flying over the island uncovered the scheme. When President Kennedy learned about it, he was furious and immediately confronted the Kremlin.

Kennedy ordered an immediate naval blockade of the island nation and regular U-2 flights to monitor the situation. He explained his position to Khrushchev in unambiguous terms: remove the missiles and the personnel to man them or military action would be imminent.

Khrushchev, mulling over the situation in his Kremlin office, knew the strategic situation favored the United States. Not only did America have nuclear superiority, it had the overall strategic advantage. Cuba was just off the American coastline, whereas the Soviet Union was halfway around the world. Kennedy had called his bluff. A bargain needed to be struck.

Khrushchev agreed to withdraw the missiles, but he wanted something in return. For his ally Fidel Castro, who was furious about any suggestion that the missiles be pulled out, he wanted a pledge that the United States would never attempt to invade Cuba again. And for good measure, he wanted U.S. nuclear missiles in Turkey, which were pointed at Soviet forces, removed as well.

On Saturday, October 27, 1962, as the crisis reached a crescendo, Soviet Ambassador Anatoly Dobrynin went to the U.S. Justice Department for a private meeting with Attorney General Robert Kennedy, who was serving as an adviser for his brother.

Dobrynin, the shrewd silver-haired diplomat who would serve almost three decades in Washington, walked into Kennedy's office and noted almost immediately, according to a secret memo he sent back to Moscow, that Kennedy "was very upset . . . I've never seen him like this before." Dobrynin sensed that Kennedy seemed to be losing his nerve.

Bobby Kennedy explained that war might be imminent and expressed a desire to seek some sort of solution. Dobrynin told him that Moscow wanted an agreement also, but that the Soviets' conditions had to be met.

Moscow might have been negotiating from a weak position, but President Kennedy didn't press the matter. His brother was prepared to take a no-invasion pledge to the Soviets, and he would pull the Jupiter missiles out of Turkey.

But Bobby Kennedy cautioned that the deal needed to be done quietly. "The president can't say anything public in this regard about Turkey," he told Dobrynin pointedly. It would be too much of a political embarrassment. The missiles would be withdrawn under some pretext and without consulting NATO allies. Dobrynin agreed to the secret bargain and it was never mentioned in public.[21]

Indeed, Bobby Kennedy was so secretive about the deal involving missiles in Turkey that when his diary account of the crisis was later published as *Thirteen Days: A Memoir of the Cuban Missile Crisis*, the book contained nary a word about the missiles. The editor of the book, Ted Sorensen, had purposely deleted any mention of them.[22]

★ ★ ★

LIKE THE REST OF AMERICA, RONALD REAGAN SPENT MUCH OF October 1962 watching closely the duel between Kennedy and Khrushchev. When the crisis ended, he was of course pleased. But he fretted that Kennedy had given up too much, faulting him for agreeing to a no-invasion pledge. "Are missile bases enough," he said, "or will we insist on freedom for all Cubans?"

Reagan had always had his doubts about Kennedy. In January 1962, during a speech at Huntington Memorial Hospital in California, he expressed his concerns about whether Kennedy could handle "the roughnecks of the Kremlin." He was surrounded by "well-meaning and misguided people" who failed to understand the Soviets, Reagan believed. Kennedy's failure to challenge the communist move into Laos meant that they were ready "to drink the bitter cup of capitulation" in Southeast Asia.

These were blustering attacks, and they began to cause discomfort at General Electric. *GE Theater* no longer seemed to be faring well against the competition, so it was canceled in 1962. Reagan's speeches were also creating problems.

GE had been supportive of Reagan's sharp-edged message for close to eight years, never asking him to edit anything. But now the company was facing difficulty in Washington. Several company executives were under federal indictment for price fixing, and Bobby Kennedy was deciding their fate. Reagan was now the most popular man on the lecture circuit after the President himself, and he was spending his time criticizing the Kennedy administration. Getting rid of him was better than risking the wrath of Washington. The company informed him of its plans in 1962, and offered him a job as a pitchman for GE products. But Reagan wasn't interested in pushing toasters. He was more interested in the larger ideas he had been developing over the course of the last decade.[23]

These ideas were attracting attention around the country. In early 1962, Reagan made an appearance before the Phoenix, Arizona, Chamber of Commerce. His father-in-law, Loyal Davis, was in the audience, along with a slender and stern-looking senator named Barry Goldwater. Reagan had first met Goldwater in 1952, shortly after Goldwater won his first election to the U.S. Senate. Loyal Davis had been a strong supporter, and the Phoenix doctor had introduced the two men, knowing they would have a lot in common.

There was a mutual attraction. Reagan and Goldwater shared a love of the American West and the outdoors. Both men loved horses and the independent cowboy spirit of the West. They also had similar opinions about economics, the size of government, and the threat of communism. They would chat about horses, taxes, the Soviets, atomic weapons. Goldwater would joke, "Let's lob one in the men's room of the Kremlin."[24]

When Reagan gave his Phoenix speech in 1962, Goldwater had already decided to run for president in 1964. That afternoon, as Reagan smoothly explained his vision for America, Goldwater saw that Reagan's straightforward message, uncompromising tone, and the reassuring manner in which he delivered it would be a great asset. Goldwater believed in those very same ideas, but he could never present them with Reagan's soothing confidence.

After the speech, Goldwater asked Reagan to join his campaign and serve as cochairman in California. His GE days were behind him, but Reagan was still busy, giving speeches, working on *The Killers* (his last movie) for NBC, and hosting a new television series, *Death Valley Days*. But he promised to stump for Goldwater around the state.

One evening in 1964, Reagan was standing before eight hundred Republicans at the Coconut Grove in Los Angeles. As the guests dined amid the forest of palm trees, Reagan gave them his message on reducing the size of government and how to defeat communism. The Goldwater campaign was struggling, having failed to get any traction against Lyndon Johnson. But the crowd was enthused by Reagan's message, and after the speech a delegation of high-powered Republicans approached Reagan with an idea. If his speech was delivered before a nationwide audience, it just might provide the energy that the campaign needed. If the party bought time on nationwide television, would he be willing to address the nation?

Reagan agreed and drafted a speech that incorporated the themes he had developed over the past ten years on the lecture circuit. Sitting down in front of a live audience in Los Angeles, he taped a speech that was released on the night of October 27. Millions of Americans saw it. Few had ever heard his prescriptions for fighting the Cold War.

Dressed in a conservative suit and dark tie, he declared that American policy had been guided by "a utopian solution of peace without victory. They call their policy 'accommodation.' And they say if we only avoid any direct confrontation with the enemy, he will forget his evil ways and learn to love us."

But these assumptions were flawed, he told the American people. The threat to peace came from the nature of the communist system itself. There could be no peace without freedom in the Soviet bloc.

"We cannot buy our security, our freedom from the threat of the bomb by committing an immorality so great as saying to a billion human beings now in slavery behind the Iron Curtain, 'Give up your dreams of freedom because to save our own skin, we are willing to make a deal with your slave-masters.' Alexander Hamilton said, 'A nation which can prefer disgrace to danger is prepared for a master, and deserves one!' Let's set the record straight. There is no argument over the choice between peace and war, but there is only one guaranteed way you can have peace . . . and you can have it in the next second . . . surrender!"

Containment and peaceful coexistence with the Soviet Union was nothing more than "appeasement . . . it gives no choice between peace and war, only between fight and surrender. If we continue to accommodate, continue to back and retreat, eventually we have to face the final demand—the ultimatum."

The stakes were enormously high. "You and I have a rendezvous with destiny. We will preserve for our children this, the last best hope of man on earth, or we will sentence them to take the last step into a thousand years of darkness."

It was the sort of uncompromising speech that you rarely saw on the eve of an election. The response from the public was stunning. Eight million dollars poured into the beleaguered Goldwater campaign.

Barry Goldwater lost to Lyndon Johnson in a landslide. Johnson, after a long career in the Senate and close to three years as vice president, had taken the mantle from JFK after his death. Tough but pragmatic, he was promising a "Great Society" at home and a firm and steady course on the world stage.

But Reagan had clearly captured the national imagination. *Time* magazine hailed Reagan's speech as "the one bright spot in a dismal campaign." David Broder of the *Washington Post* declared it "the most successful national political debut since William Jennings Bryan electrified the 1896 Democratic Convention with his 'Cross of Gold' speech." The GOP, which had for so long been a liberal party, was now being reborn as a conservative force, thanks in part to Reagan's contributions. And in Michigan, a group of people formed "Friends of Reagan" in the hopes of convincing him to run for political office.

CHAPTER IV

A BULLET WITH HIS NAME ON IT

L YNDON JOHNSON BROUGHT MANY AMBITIONS WITH HIM TO the White House. But before too long he found that everything would become clouded by the war raging in Vietnam. LBJ had inherited the commitment of fifteen thousand U.S. advisers in that country from JFK. Even if Johnson had wanted to pull out of Vietnam (and he did not), it would have been impossible, because he would have been abandoning the policy of a revered, fallen predecessor.

Johnson's goal in Vietnam was not to seek outright military victory, which he considered nearly impossible, but to negotiate a settlement with the North Vietnamese. "We are not trying to wipe out North Vietnam," he declared. "We are not trying to change their government. We are not trying to establish permanent bases in South Vietnam . . . we are there because we are trying to make the Communists of North Vietnam stop shooting at their neighbors . . . to demonstrate that guerrilla warfare, inspired by one nation against another nation, can never succeed. . . . [W]e must keep on until the Communists in North Vietnam realize the price of aggression is too high—and either agree to a peaceful settlement or to stop the fighting. . . ."[1]

Johnson adopted what he called a "slow squeeze" strategy.

American military might was unmatched in the world, but the key was to apply it selectively. Using too much power, Johnson believed, was as bad as using too little. You needed to fight the war in a calibrated way. Borders were not to be crossed, and bombing would be intensified and reduced depending on whether he wanted to provide inducements or punishments to Hanoi. McGeorge Bundy, the national security adviser, put a fine point on it: "We should strike to hurt but not to destroy. For the purpose of changing the North Vietnamese decision on intervention in the South."[2]

To make sure the job was done right, bombing targets were selected in the White House, with the President monitoring the outcome of individual missions. Far from unleashing the dogs of war, Johnson was determined to keep them on a tight rein. In a 1966 memo regarding bombing missions, for example, it was declared that the piers in North Vietnam's Haiphong Harbor could be hit only if no tankers were there, vessels firing at American planes could be bombed only if they were "clearly North Vietnamese," and no air strikes would be allowed on Sundays (which Johnson apparently considered a day of rest).

As Johnson held back, Moscow pressed onward, dramatically increasing its support for the North Vietnamese and the Viet Cong. Up until 1965 the Kremlin had provided small German arms to the Viet Cong. But seeing that the insurgency had a real opportunity to succeed, the Kremlin suddenly began providing the latest in surface-to-air missiles, jet aircraft, rockets, and field artillery. In exchange, the North Vietnamese agreed to transfer models of captured U.S. military hardware for inspection.[3]

As the war raged on, Johnson clung to hopes that the Kremlin would help him get out of the Vietnam mess. When he met with a group of Soviet citizens at his Texas ranch, he explained to them his belief that the war would eventually end with a settlement negotiated in part by Moscow. "After all," he was quoted as saying in a KGB report on the meeting, "it is the United States, not Vietnam which is the main partner of the Soviet Union."

★ ★ ★

I N JANUARY 1967, RONALD REAGAN WAS SWORN IN AS GOVERNOR of California. During his inauguration ceremony, he had a special flag placed on the state capitol building. It was a small, slightly torn flag that had been carried into battle in a rice paddy in Vietnam by a Sergeant Robert Howell. The young Californian had been severely wounded in battle, and Reagan wanted the flag fluttering in the Sacramento breeze as a symbol of freedom and a testimony to Howell's courage.

Following the Goldwater speech in 1964, a group of California Republicans had convinced Reagan to run for office. Facing off against California governor Pat Brown, Reagan had trounced him by more than a million votes. The election had been about state issues: taxes, welfare, and regulation. But the Vietnam War was not far from Reagan's mind. Reagan was watching closely the situation in Vietnam. After the election, he spoke by phone with military officers like General Daniel "Chappie" James, a black four-star general. He read eagerly the ideas for winning the war of World War II generals like Arthur Trudeau and Omar Bradley. At one point he was briefed by the SAC commander, General Thomas S. Power, who was outspoken in how he thought the war should be fought. (The famously blunt General Power told LBJ in a 1964 briefing that he was going about the war the wrong way entirely. "[The] task of the military in war is to kill human beings and destroy man-made objects" and to do it "in the quickest way possible." Johnson's advisers, Power told him, "didn't know their ass from a hole in the ground."[4])

America needed to be in Vietnam, Reagan believed, because it was in our national interest. But the war "must be fought through to victory," he declared. Johnson was "naive" to think that slow escalation was the way to succeed. Instead you wanted to strike fast and hard "to win as quickly as possible."

Barely nine months on the job as governor, Reagan led the charge within the Governors' Association to withdraw support for Johnson's prosecution of the war. He was reluctant to abandon Johnson at a time of conflict, but he was upset with the "conduct of the war during the last year."[5]

The United States needed to get out of Vietnam or get serious. While Johnson was sending memos about precisely how to bomb

Haiphong Harbor, Reagan suggested that the United States needed to close it completely, an option that was being proposed by retired Generals Bradley and Trudeau. He also pushed for an amphibious invasion of North Vietnam, a replay of what MacArthur had done in Korea at Inchon. "Or at least post constantly the threat of invasion to pin down an enemy force that has got to stay home and guard the store," he said.[6]

As for nuclear weapons, Reagan did not expressly recommend their use, but he clearly believed that ambiguity on the matter would help. "The North Vietnamese should go to bed each night being afraid we're going to use such weapons."

Reagan had strong views on Vietnam that distinguished him even from Richard Nixon. Reagan's opinion of Nixon seemed to vary depending on the circumstance. He had supported Nixon in Nixon's 1960 presidential run and again in his ill-fated 1962 governor's race in California. But as Nixon geared up to run against Johnson in 1968, Reagan was clearly doubtful about his fellow Republican's ability. They disagreed about Vietnam, where Nixon believed that "economic détente" would lead Moscow to broker a deal to end the war. Reagan clung stubbornly to the notion that a military victory was still possible. The divide was so great that it led Reagan to a brief fling as a presidential candidate in 1968.[7]

As governor of California, of course, Reagan wasn't fighting the war in Vietnam. But he was fighting a war of sorts in his own state—namely, on the college campuses. And as far as his personal safety was concerned, the stakes could almost be as high.

Reagan had campaigned for governor against "the mess in Berkeley" and was always taking shots at the radical left, which was determined to disrupt campus life there as much as possible.

"I had a nightmare about going broke," he would say on the stump. "I dreamed I owned a Laundromat in Berkeley."

He called the radical students "brats," "freaks," and "cowardly fascists," and his willingness to do battle with the campus left won him plenty of fans in California. "Give 'em hell," people would tell him as he traveled the state. During the 1966 election he captured a third of the labor vote, largely because of his stance on Berkeley.

On the campus an assortment of self-described anarchists,

Maoists, Trotskyites, followers of the revolutionary Che Guevara, and would-be future Fidel Castros were holding protests, organizing sit-ins, and sometimes doing even worse. During one eleven-month period on the Berkeley campus, there were eight bombings or attempted bombings; police confiscated more than two hundred rifles, pistols, and shotguns, nearly a thousand sticks of dynamite, and dozens of Molotov cocktails.

Weeks after Reagan was inaugurated as governor, the Berkeley chapter of the radical group Students for a Democratic Society (SDS) organized a violent protest to stop Navy recruiters from meeting with students. Rocks were thrown, would-be recruits were assaulted, and windows were broken. University president Clark Kerr called the police but spoke of the need for moderation. Reagan was furious.

"In all the sound and fury at Berkeley," he declared after the melee, "one voice is missing. And since it is the voice of those who built the university and pay the entire cost of its operation, I think it's time that voice was heard."

A board of regents meeting was planned at University Hall on the Berkeley campus. When campus activists found out Reagan was going to attend, they gathered on a grassy slope near the front entrance of the building to protest. The numbers swelled to several thousand and security officials began to worry about violence, given what Reagan had been saying. They quietly suggested to Reagan that he slip into the meeting through the back of the building to avoid the protesters. It must have seemed strangely reminiscent of the 1946 strike in Hollywood when security had advised him and other movie stars to slip onto the studio lot through a storm drain.

As he had in 1946, Reagan refused to arrive for the meeting through a circular route. Instead he entered through the front of the building, with thousands of students watching and many of them jeering.

Ever since the so-called Free Speech Movement in 1964, the university's administration had been trying to gently tolerate campus sit-ins, protests, and harassment of students. Reagan believed that the process had gone too far and that other students were having their right to an education infringed by the activists. If a student wanted to meet with a Navy recruiter, by what right did another student deny him that chance?

Reagan arranged for Clark Kerr to be promptly fired. And he promised to get tough with violent protesters. He was drawing the line, declaring that it had to be done for the sake of the country's future. If he failed to draw the line, he said, America would continue to lose its will.

"We have been picked at, sworn at, rioted against, and downgraded until we have a built-in guilt complex, and this has been compounded by the accusations of our sons and daughters who pride themselves on 'telling it like it is.' Well, I have bad news for them— in a thousand social-science courses they have been informed 'the way it is *not*.' . . . [A]s for our generation, I will make no apology. No people in all history paid a higher price for freedom. And no people have done so much to advance the dignity of man. We are called materialistic. Maybe so . . . but our materialism has made our children the biggest, tallest, most handsome, and intelligent generation of Americans yet. They will live longer with fewer illnesses, learn more, see more of the world, and have more successes in realizing their personal dreams and ambitions than any other people in any other period of our history—because of our materialism. . . . I think on our side is civilization and on the other side is the law of the jungle. . . . We all have to recognize that this country has been handed the responsibility, greater than any nation in history, to preserve some 6,000 years of civilization against the barbarians."[8]

If Reagan was already held in low regard by the radical left, throwing down the gauntlet helped to make him their biggest enemy. Mere months later, Black Panther Party leader Eldridge Cleaver, who had been released from prison on a rape conviction less than two years earlier, led five thousand students in cheers of "F—— Ronnie Reagan" from the university's Sproul Plaza.

Reagan said he was glad to have a dialogue with his critics, but not the four-letter-word kind. Instead, he met with student leaders in Sacramento. And he traveled to Yale University to spend four days on the campus as a Chubb Fellow. With a jagged smile and deep lines fanned out from his eyes, he glowed warmly as he walked around the campus. Secretaries were leaning out of office windows to wave at the aging movie star, and some students rushed to shake his hand. But the reception from the campus left was decidedly cool. He took questions in a history class with a young history professor seated behind him, sneering and rolling his eyes as he spoke. One student rose and asked: "Weren't people who held your views convicted at Nuremberg of crimes against humanity?"[9]

But Reagan remained the happy warrior, willing to exchange views and mix it up with his critics. In May 1967, he appeared with Bobby Kennedy on an international forum with youth from around the world and broadcast by CBS. They discussed the arms race and Vietnam, among other issues, taking questions from students. When one student pressed him on Goldwater's declaration in 1964 that "extremism in the defense of liberty is no vice," Reagan said he agreed with the statement. "The idea is as old as Cicero," he explained. When the subject turned to the Cold War, Reagan suggested that Moscow could demonstrate its peaceful intentions by tearing down the Berlin Wall, an idea that he would express more famously as president two decades later.[10]

But lurking behind the debate was the seemingly ever-present threat of violence.

One night back in Sacramento, Reagan, his wife Nancy, and his children Patti and Ron Jr. were startled out of bed by the sound of gunfire. Reagan, dressed in his pajamas, jumped up and ran down the hallway, where he was met by a Secret Service agent running in the other direction. "Stay away from the windows!" the agent shouted. Outside Reagan's bedroom window, the Secret Service had spotted two men lighting gasoline bombs. An agent had fired at them—it was no warning shot—but the two had managed to get away. The FBI determined weeks later that there was a plot afoot to try to kill Reagan, and security was dramatically increased.[11]

Violence erupted on the Berkeley campus in the spring of 1969 over a vacant plot of land. The university had been planning to build more dormitories on the campus but lacked the money to proceed. In the interim, an assortment of drifters, hippies, antiwar protesters, and street people had made the plot their refuge, planting trees, sleeping on the ground, smoking pot, making love, and playing rock 'n' roll music throughout the night. It didn't take long before nearby residents began complaining. There were nudists wandering around on Telegraph Avenue high on drugs, and dealers selling the stuff to anyone interested in buying. Residents expressed fear about going out at night, and they couldn't abide the loud music.

University chancellor Roger Heyns, a natty pipe-smoking academic, recognized the problem and tried to build a fence around the property to settle the matter. But as word of his plan spread, three thousand students gathered at Sproul Plaza. One speaker stood up and declared that the mob should "go down and take the park." In a matter of minutes, the crowd surged down Telegraph Avenue and proclaimed the land "People's Park."

The crowd was met by police who had encircled the fence. Before long students were throwing rocks and slabs of concrete off the roofs of nearby buildings at the police. The crowd moved forward, and forty-two police officers were trampled so badly that they had to be treated at a hospital.

Art Goldberg, a veteran Berkeley radical and self-described Marxist, saw the violence as "the beginning of resistance." Berkeley mayor Wallace Johnson called it "a diabolically clever idea by that motley bunch of Bohemians and hippies." Governor Reagan, at the suggestion of the mayor, called in the National Guard.

The Guard moved in quickly and quelled the violence. Berkeley remained deeply divided over the fate of the park. Reagan remained an enemy of the militant left and the threats continued.[12]

Every time he spoke out, there seemed to be a nasty threat.

"Death threats were a daily occurrence," recalls William Clark, who served as chief of staff while Reagan was governor. Clark recalls one incident in particular: A few days after Reagan made some remarks about communism in Cuba, he received a package in the mail with an undertaker's needle and thread inside. "You're going to need this," the letter warned, and it was signed by "friends of Cuba."[13]

The Berkeley SDS started to splinter in 1968, and quickly fell into factions. One group formed the Weathermen and convened a war council in Flint, Michigan, declaring their commitment to go underground and initiate an armed struggle against the United States government. They met in a house that featured a large room where a cardboard cutout of a machine gun hung from the ceiling, pointing at the wall. On the wall there was a banner with drawings of several large bullets. One of them had Reagan's name written on it.[14]

"The goal is the destruction of US imperialism and the achievement of a classless world: world communism," they claimed in their manifesto.

The Weathermen were not students philosophizing about a revolution after reading Karl Marx in Poli Sci 101. They began an armed struggle and maintained extensive contact with foreign intelligence agents in countries such as Cuba, Hungary, Czechoslovakia, and North Vietnam.

Miniskirted Bernadine Dorhn and the group's other leader, Mark Rudd, would travel to New York and meet with spies from the Cuban Mission to the United Nations. There they arranged for Weathermen to be trained in the use of weapons by Cuban military officers during visits to Cuba. They received money and advice on organizing their movement. North Vietnamese intelligence officers gave them advice on how to find recruits who were physically capable of doing battle with the police. And when the Weathermen had to flee the FBI, Cuban spies developed a system of codes that permitted secret communication with the radical group.

"SDS was the group we concentrated on in those days," an ex–Cuban intelligence agent told the FBI. "Oh, we didn't start it. But we radicalized it, we gave it form. Every leader came and left [Cuba] with new ideas."[15]

One of those who traveled to Cuba was Gregg Daniel Adornetto. After his visit he joined an underground terrorist group in the San Francisco area known as the Emiliano Zapata Unit. The group bombed literally dozens of targets in the Bay Area, and maintained contact with a Cuban intelligence officer named Andres Gomez. The FBI broke up the group with a series of raids, arresting seven of its members. Adornetto was among them, and he began talking to agents. Gomez, he said, had been working with the group on a special project. The plan was to kill Ronald Reagan. "If Gomez dies, his body must be burned and his fingers cut off so he cannot be identified," Adornetto said he was instructed.[16]

CHAPTER V

THE DEAL

I T WAS EARLY 1969, AND HENRY KISSINGER WAS WAITING IN THE
White House Map Room for a secret visitor.

Only a few months earlier, Richard Nixon had been
elected president by the slimmest of margins and had appointed
Kissinger as his national security adviser. The two had first met in
1967 at a swank Manhattan party hosted by Claire Booth Luce.
Nixon had come away from the party impressed by the Harvard
professor's grasp of history. Kissinger had found that Nixon was a
rather impressive student of international affairs himself.

Nixon was the son of a California grocer, a lawyer who had run
for Congress and emerged on the national stage as the anti-
Communist who stared down Alger Hiss. Kissinger had grown up
amid the chaos of pre–World War II Germany, served in the U.S
Army, and gone on to study for a Ph.D. in history at Harvard. The
two men were very different. Yet for all their differences, they had
a common vision for how to shape America's role in the world.

Nixon had won the 1968 presidential election over Hubert
Humphrey and George Wallace by the slimmest of margins, largely
with his promises to end the war in Vietnam honorably and fast.
There were 540,000 troops in Vietnam when Nixon was sworn in,

and thousands of protesters had lined the parade route to chant "Ho, ho, Ho Chi Minh, the Viet Cong are going to win."

Kissinger was in the White House Map Room waiting for Anatoly Dobrynin, the Soviet ambassador to the United States. Dobrynin had been on Embassy Row since the Kennedy administration and was familiar with Nixon's public reputation as an anti-Communist. During the 1968 election, the Kremlin had approached Hubert Humphrey with offers of financial help to keep Nixon out of the White House, according to Dobrynin. Nixon was the dark prince with whom the Kremlin did not want to deal.

But shortly after Dobrynin arrived and began chatting with Kissinger, he found himself pleasantly surprised by what his host, in his signature German accent, was telling him.

There were no American note takers at the secret meeting. But according to memoranda that Dobrynin sent back to Moscow, Kissinger was interested in a deal with Moscow. He hoped "relations would enter a constructive phase, different from those relations which existed during the 'cold war' and unfortunately continue to make themselves apparent even now." Then he got down to business and proposed that both sides work together to help each other out of particularly thorny problems.

Nixon wanted out of Vietnam. There was a need, Kissinger told the Soviet visitor, "to solve the Vietnam question." By doing so, he said, they could together "guarantee [Nixon] reelection as President of the USA."

In exchange, Kissinger offered Moscow a reprieve from tensions over Eastern Europe. Less than a year earlier, there had been another in a series of anti-Soviet uprisings in the region, this time in Czechoslovakia. Soviet and Warsaw Pact tanks had rolled into Prague and brutally crushed the reform movement. In the months that followed, Moscow had been roundly condemned by world opinion.

Kissinger coolly told Dobrynin that in exchange for help on Vietnam, the Kremlin could ignore any protestations from Washington on events in Eastern Europe, because these events would be of little concern to the administration. "It is not necessary to pay attention," he told Dobrynin, "to isolated critical public comments about some East European country because that is only a tribute to the mood of certain sub-strata of the American population which play a role in American elections."[1]

Dobrynin listened intently, and when the meeting ended, both men left apparently encouraged with the results. More secret meetings between the two would follow, creating what would become known as the "back channel."

It was a back channel that could be used to great effect by Moscow. Dobrynin and other Soviet leaders came to view Kissinger as someone motivated less by strategic interests than by his own political ambitions. "Kissinger himself," Dobrynin wrote to the Politburo in 1969, "though he is a smart and erudite person, is at the same time extremely vain."[2]

Political calculation would figure prominently in any negotiations Kissinger had with Moscow. According to a 1971 KGB report on the anti–ballistic missile (ABM) treaty negotiations, Kissinger at one point expressed concerns about the timetable for negotiations. "Kissinger in a private talk," reported KGB chief Yuri Andropov, "said that from the political point of view it may be more beneficial for Nixon if the agreement with the USSR were to be achieved closer to the presidential election." He hoped that Moscow might speed up the negotiating timeline to boost the administration's political fortunes.[3]

Five years later, when Kissinger had been elevated to secretary of state in the Ford administration, he was again asking Moscow for help, this time to maintain his own political viability. As the Soviet Union was aggressively supporting Marxist forces fighting in Angola, Kissinger "pleaded" with Soviet diplomats to curtail their activity, according to Soviet diplomatic cables. Continued support would do "irreparable damage," Kissinger bluntly told senior officials. But the damage he spoke of was not to superpower relations but to his own credibility. "Five years from now it will make no difference" who is running Angola, he told the Soviets.[4]

★   ★   ★

RICHARD NIXON OWED HIS EARLY POLITICAL CAREER TO HIS image as an ardent anti-Communist. He had gone after Alger Hiss, worked aggressively as a member of HUAC, and represented the United States abroad as vice president. While traveling overseas he had spoken frequently on the evils of communism. But what helped his career early on he later came to see as a hindrance. The so-called Kitchen Debate in 1959, in which he had a detailed exchange with Nikita Khrushchev over the merits of communism versus capitalism as all the world watched via television, Nixon believed had hurt him in the 1960 presidential election. He didn't look *presidential*.

So in the run-up to the 1968 election, Nixon ran with promises of being the tough negotiator who could seal a deal with Moscow, whether over Vietnam or in arms control. It was a campaign approach that worked, and once he was elected, Nixon made it clear that the transformation was real.

In the early weeks of his administration, Nixon signed a secret directive that ordered a review of American foreign policy by his National Security Council (NSC). Over the next several months, Robert E. Osgood, an NSC senior staff member who had been a graduate school friend of Kissinger's, worked in his small office on the third floor of the Old Executive Office Building cobbling together a review of what Nixon administration policy would be. When he was finished with the 109-page document, Nixon reviewed it and signed off on it.

Beginning with a "reappraisal of containment," the secret document made it clear that the Cold War standoff of the 1950s was part of a bygone era. "Containment no longer adequately describes the organizing concept of American foreign policy," it read flatly. Instead, the Nixon administration believed that it was facing a new world where the traditional Cold War concern about Soviet communism no longer applied.[5]

Nixon envisioned a world made up of five great economic powers—the United States, the Soviet Union, China, Japan, and Europe. The President could be found frequently in the Oval Office with a legal pad propped up on his lap as he scribbled comments to Kissinger about where he wanted his policy to go or making notes about his speeches. In his mind there was no longer a tight Cold War divide, a world neatly divided between East and West, but instead each of these five powers could negotiate and benefit from economic cooperation and competition. Containing the Soviet Union was not the overarching goal; instead the United States would follow a "pentagonal strategy" that would promote peace and economic development in all five powers.[6]

Keeping the peace was a balancing act, so none of the five great economic powers could be too strong or two weak. "The only time in the history of the world that we have had any extended period of peace is when there has been balance of power," President Nixon told *Time* magazine. "It is when one nation becomes infinitely more powerful in relation to its potential competitors that the danger of war arises." For this reason the United States had a stake in seeing that the Soviet Union not fail. "I think it will be a safer world and better world if we have a *stronger, healthy*, United States, Europe, *Soviet Union*, China, Japan, each balancing the other, not playing one against the other, an even balance."[7]

It was because of this perceived need for balance that Nixon and Kissinger plotted their dramatic opening to China. The need for a balance of power was also a reason to curtail American military spending. President Nixon asked his staff in June 1969 to provide him with "their best judgment as to what our force level should be." Forget about superiority or parity, he advised them. Instead, tell me what a "sufficient force" would be. His aides mulled over the issue, and a few months later, Nixon proposed a defense budget that would leave the American nuclear arsenal at a stable level and continue to accelerate the demobilization of American forces from Vietnam.[8]

Henry Kissinger defended the notion of sufficiency on the basis that "strategic superiority" was outdated. As he once famously would ask, "What in the name of God is strategic superiority? What is the significance of it, politically, militarily, operationally, at these levels of numbers? What do you do with it?" This was not simply his view, Kissinger explained in testimony before the Senate. Even Moscow shared this view, he claimed.[9]

But lurking in the back of Nixon's mind was the reality of the political situation. There was little interest on Capitol Hill in large defense budgets. If anything, there was a race to see who could cut the most. The Brookings Institution suggested a $12.5 billion cutback in defense out of a budget of just over $76 billion, a plan that would eliminate half the strategic bomb and land-based ICBM forces and most air defenses. The Navy would lose four of its sixteen carrier task forces and most of its ship-building program. The Air Force would lose the F-15 development program and the Army six active brigades. On Capitol Hill, senators like Hubert Humphrey endorsed the proposal, while others, like Senator George McGovern, in agreement with the *New York Times* editorial page, proposed even deeper cuts. Even if Nixon had wanted more for defense, it is doubtful he would have gotten it.[10]

★ ★ ★

O N A HOT DAY IN LATE JULY 1969, AT ABOUT THE SAME TIME THE Nixon administration was rewriting American Cold War and military policy, Soviet premier Leonid Brezhnev convened a special meeting of Soviet senior military officials at a resort in the gentle hills above the town of Yalta. With a majestic view overlooking the Black Sea, these senior officials, representing the military and the KGB, sat around a table adorned with bottles of Georgian wine and Ukrainian pepper vodka.

For Brezhnev, the meeting represented a watershed in Soviet history. The son of a steelworker, Brezhnev had known deprivation throughout his early life. Born in 1906, he had grown up against the backdrop of the First World War, the Bolshevik Revolution, and the protracted civil war that followed. His young eyes had seen bloody combat in the Ukraine during the Second World War, and he had participated in the occupation of Czechoslovakia after the Nazis retreated. He had become General Secretary in 1964 after the fall of Khrushchev, who had been humiliated in his attempt to place nuclear missiles in Cuba.

In the months after he became General Secretary, Brezhnev and the Soviet Politburo had issued a series of sweeping directives to begin the massive shift of resources necessary to forge a world-class military arsenal. They were determined to never again face the need to back down as they had been forced to do in October 1962.

In a matter of a few years, the balance of world military might had begun to shift. By 1965, Moscow was building between 200 and 250 new silo launchers and seven or eight nuclear-powered ballistic missile submarines each year. By the summer of 1969, the Soviets believed that parity existed between the two superpowers.

Now Brezhnev was ready to move on to a new task.

Seated next to him was Dmitri Ustinov, a stocky, sandy-haired man who was the head of military industry. Wearing gold-rimmed spectacles and speaking in short, clipped bursts, Ustinov possessed little charm or charisma. But when it came to building a military arsenal fast and under difficult conditions, no one was better than this genius of logistics and industrial planning.

Perhaps more than anyone, Ustinov had been responsible for the Soviet victory in World War II. In the bleak late fall of 1941, when the Red Army was reeling and the Nazi blitzkrieg threatened to overwhelm the Soviet Union, it was Ustinov who had been put in charge of the Herculean task of moving Soviet war industries from the front lines of western Russia two thousand miles away to the Ural Mountains. In a matter of months he saw to it that Soviet tanks, trucks, and weapons were being mass-produced where only weeks earlier there had been no factories. By 1943, his armament plants were outproducing those of Nazi Germany.

Brezhnev had called the meeting in Yalta to establish an unprecedented fifteen-year plan to build up the Soviet military machine. Only this time the goal was not to catch up with the Americans, as it had been after the Cuban missile crisis. Instead, "the desire was to get ahead of the U.S. competition," recalls Soviet general Andrianna Danilevich, a general staff officer who participated in the meeting. Military superiority was now within their grasp, the assembled leadership believed. And if they could achieve it, enormous political returns would result.[11]

These plans for military superiority were not drawn up under clouds of fear that the United States might attack. "We inside the General Staff did not really believe that [the United States] would attack," recalls General Danilevich. Instead, the motivation was strategic. The Nixon administration might be questioning the value of strategic superiority as they talked about "sufficiency." But the Kremlin viewed matters differently.[12]

"The Soviet civilian and military leadership did not concern itself with foreign concepts and ruminations about stability and other abstract subjects," recalls General Nikolay Detinov. "Superiority over the United States was seen by Moscow as something highly valuable in political and ideological, not to mention strategic terms."[13]

Over the course of several days, the Soviet leadership laid out their plans for the construction of the largest military force the world had ever seen. The Nixon administration might have capped the American arsenal at 1,000 Minuteman ICBM launchers and 41 Polaris/Poseidon missile-capable submarines. But with the stroke of a pen, Leonid Brezhnev committed the Soviet Union to a course that would dedicate almost one-third of its gross national product to military needs.

The strategic nuclear force continued to grow. More than 242,000 men were added to the Soviet armed forces. And massive sums of money were spent on exotic schemes to fight and win a nuclear war.

Nine hundred meters below the surface of the earth in Moscow, construction began on a labyrinth of facilities more than two hundred miles long. The so-called D-6 subway included everything the Soviet leadership would need to survive the apocalypse. There were underground factories that would produce weapons, fifteen communication bases for the KGB, and a transportation system for both freight and passengers. More than eight thousand people were trained to run this underground world, and there was great attention to detail. Even the creature comforts the Soviet Politburo knew so well were accounted for. Several sleek black Zil limousines, prized by the leadership, were placed underground for safekeeping.

Hundreds of miles away, construction also began deep inside the Ural Mountains. This was to be a postnuclear city the size of Washington, D.C., that could support a hundred thousand apocalypse survivors. Construction on this subterranean behemoth, code-named Krasnoyarsk 26, would consume 2 percent of the Soviet gross national product over the next two decades.[14]

Near the remote Siberian city of Novosibirsk, tucked inside the thick birch forest, a secret research facility was built to develop exotic new weapons. It was one link in a chain of fifty-two research sites controlled by the Ministry of Defense, employing fifty thousand people who worked feverishly to transform microbes into weapons of war.

One of the best minds working at the Vector facility in western Siberia was Dr. Nikolai Ustinov, a young scientist assigned to develop the Marburg virus, a cousin to the dreaded Ebola virus. One day Ustinov was holding a guinea pig as a colleague attempted to inject the animal with the virus, missed, and accidentally plunged the needle straight into Ustinov's finger. Ustinov faced certain death, but the work went on.

Over the next two weeks, his coworkers watched from behind glass in an observation facility as his body slowly decomposed. Ustinov kept a death diary during those two weeks, describing in grisly detail the facts of his pending death. "It was blood everywhere," recalls a colleague, "from nose, from eyes, mouth, ears."

Ustinov's wife, Dr. Yevgenia Ustinov, also watched through the glass, able only to talk to him over the phone.

After he died, the urgency that the Soviet government assigned to this work was revealed when it was ordered that his liver and spleen be removed and his blood siphoned out by syringe. His bodily fluids were compressed and used for research purposes and for making weapons.[15]

★   ★   ★

IN EARLY APRIL 1970, MORE THAN TWO HUNDRED SOVIET SHIPS and submarines moved into strategic positions around the world, from the Baltic Sea to the Bering Strait, and into the heart of the western Pacific, and began conducting highly complex military maneuvers. It was dubbed Okean 70 by the Soviets; U.S. Navy Secretary John Warner would later call it the Soviet Navy's "coming out party." Eager to find out what the Soviets were up to, the United States put several Navy vessels to sea to collect intelligence. In the Sea of Japan, the USS *Waddell*, a guided-missile destroyer, began tracking the movements of the Soviet Pacific Fleet. As the exercise continued, Captain Peter Cullins brought his ship to within a hundred yards of a Soviet destroyer. Tensions were high, so as intelligence officers took photographs, Captain Cullins put the ship's rock band up on deck to entertain the Russian sailors. The band warmed up with the Beatles' "Back in the U.S.S.R.," and later on took requests.[16]

When Okean finally ended a few days later, the Pentagon gathered satellite intelligence and the information collected by ships like the *Waddell* for analysis. After a few months, Pentagon brass came to a startling conclusion. The Soviet Navy, historically thought of as a shoreline nuisance, was now a blue-water threat to the United States.

Using submarines and surface ships, Moscow could deny the United States the ability to reinforce its forces overseas in Europe and make it more difficult to supply forces fighting in the developing world. The Soviet Union was now a military power with a global reach.

Shortly before Okean, the Chief of Naval Operations had estimated that the U.S. Navy had a 55 percent chance of winning in a conventional war with the Soviets. A year later, after the data from Okean had been fully assessed, he privately briefed the Navy Secretary that the Soviets now maintained a 65-to-35-percent edge.[17]

This was a startling turnaround. The Soviet Union had been a Eurasian land power since its founding in 1917. Even after the end of the Second World War, when Josef Stalin commanded the largest army in the world, Harry Truman took comfort in the fact that Stalin's ability to venture into the seas was limited. But beginning in the 1960s, Moscow embarked on a massive buildup in naval forces. In January 1968, when the British government announced its plans to withdraw Britain's military forces from east of the Suez, the Soviets demonstrated their growing power by quickly moving in to fill the void. Two months after the British retreat, a Soviet naval squadron set sail for the Indian Ocean. Made up of a Sverdlov-class cruiser, two destroyers, a nuclear submarine, and a tanker, it made calls at various ports in South Asia and East Africa. For the first time, U.S. naval forces in the Indian Ocean found themselves shadowed by the Soviet Navy.

The United States was not alone in recognizing that the balance of power at sea was slowly beginning to shift. Moscow knew it, too, and was beginning to flex its muscles. Soviet warplanes flew out of bases in Egypt to conduct mock attacks on the American Sixth Fleet. On July 3, 1970, a Soviet Badger fighter-bomber diagonally buzzed across the bow of the USS *Wasp*, just as a U.S. fighter was about to be catapulted into the air. A few months earlier, the Soviet ship *Khariton Laptev* had threatened to ram a surfacing American submarine operating off Block Island, Rhode Island.[18] In another incident a few years later, an American frigate was rammed by a Soviet Echo II–class submarine in the Ionian Sea, broadsiding the American frigate near the stern. Water poured into the aft steering compartment and part of a propeller was sheared off. One sailor was injured when he was tossed from the 01 deck onto the main deck.[19]

As the massive Soviet buildup accelerated, the Kremlin was confronted with a troubling reality. As Brezhnev confided to his Politburo colleagues, the burden was putting a heavy strain on the economy. The ambitious plans that had been established in July 1969 were absorbing the best technical and scientific capabilities in the Soviet Union. The Central Committee determined that close to 50 percent of Soviet scientists, engineers, and technical experts were tied up in military research. If the United States decided to match this buildup and truly compete in the arms race, Brezhnev and others knew the Soviet Union could not keep up. An official assessment written by Soviet military analyst Sergei Blagovolin concluded that the United States alone, even without the help of NATO allies, could outproduce the entire Warsaw Pact. The Americans, if they really wanted to, could produce fifty nuclear submarines and fifty thousand tanks per year.[20]

This was the very problem Reagan had identified in 1963: Moscow couldn't compete in a real arms race. How would Moscow deal with this problem?

Parallel to the military buildup, Moscow also turned to arms control as a tool in the effort to achieve military superiority. President Nixon saw arms control as a way to achieve stability, but the Kremlin was thinking otherwise. In the words of General Detinov, who served as the Defense Ministry representative to the strategic arms talks, "The concept of obtaining strategic superiority through international arms agreements [became official Soviet policy]."

The approach was simple, recalls Detinov. "By the formulation of a clearly one-sided negotiating position and a tenacious adherence to it during negotiations," the Soviets could force the United States into concessions that would aid them in their efforts to achieve superiority.[21]

This was all borne out by the manner in which the Soviets approached the negotiations. Unlike in the United States, where negotiating positions were worked out among several bureaucracies, such as the Departments of State and Defense, in the Soviet Union the Ministry of Defense had sole responsibility for determining the negotiating position. Indeed, few diplomats even knew the full size, capability, or composition of the Soviet arsenal.[22]

CHAPTER VI

FIRE AND HEAT
MAKE STEEL

"F———YOU, RONALD REAGAN!" SOMEONE SHOUTED FROM THE crowd, just before an orange was hurled in the air at him.

It was January 4, 1971, and Governor Ronald Reagan was being sworn in for a second term of office at the state capitol in Sacramento. Only a few months earlier, he had soundly defeated Jesse Unruh in a bitterly fought contest in which Vietnam was an important issue. Reagan had firmly defended the bombing of Cambodia and declared that antiwar protesters were giving "aid and comfort" to the enemy. When a riot broke out in Santa Barbara at the height of the campaign, Reagan hadn't flinched. William Kunstler, attorney for the Chicago Seven, had given a rousing speech at the nearby University of California. Hours later, demonstrators set fire to a branch of the Bank of America and began pelting passing cars with rocks. Local police moved in but failed to restore order, and Reagan showed up in Santa Barbara the next day and declared a "state of extreme emergency." He also called out the National Guard.

After his swearing-in, during which Viet Cong flags carried by protesters fluttered in the overcast sky, Reagan stood on the steps of the capitol and began making brief comments about his plans for the state. He spoke loudly so as to be heard over shouts of "Bull——!" coming from the crowd, then left after fifteen minutes with more than a hint of anger on his face.

"They're like mosquitoes and flies," he said of the protesters. "They're part of the world, and you have to put up with them, I guess."[1]

Despite attending to the details of governing California, Ronald Reagan was keeping his finger firmly on the pulse of the Cold War. And as he looked at the world, he did so with great trepidation. Richard Nixon was not a close friend, and Reagan had long since begun to hold serious doubts about what sort of president he would be. Those doubts and his own ambitions had led Reagan to make a halting try for the Republican presidential nomination in 1968. Traveling the country, speaking out on the issues—Vietnam, the Cold War, taxes, the size of government—he didn't officially declare his candidacy and he never criticized Nixon by name. But you could hear it in the language he used on the stump; Nixon was not exactly his man. When the 1968 Republican Convention finally rolled around, Reagan declared himself a candidate, but his insurgent campaign failed when Nixon locked up the delegates he needed.

Nixon came to see Reagan as both an ally and a threat. At the 1969 presidential inauguration, he rudely snubbed both Ron and Nancy Reagan. And he was painfully aware that some of his own supporters might jump ship and support Reagan against him in 1972 if the California governor decided to challenge him.[2]

Senator Mark Hatfield of Oregon sounded such a warning in the summer of 1970, mentioning that he knew several Nixon supporters who wanted Reagan in the Oval Office in Nixon's place. "There's no secret that Governor Reagan and the President are not the closest of political friends," he said. Tom Wicker of the *New York Times* went so far as to declare that "the Specter of Ronald Reagan" was haunting the Nixon White House. If Nixon moved too far to the left in his foreign and defense policies, Reagan would be a very real threat in 1972.[3]

But Nixon also needed Reagan.

One of Nixon's boldest strategic plans was the opening to mainland China. It was a daring diplomatic move that exposed him to serious criticism both at home and abroad. On Capitol Hill, conservatives like Senator Barry Goldwater believed that opening relations with China was a sellout to the Communists. In Asia, traditional allies such as Japan, Taiwan, Thailand, and South Korea were nervous because the plan came in the wake of America's retreat from Vietnam. Was the United States still a reliable ally?

If some conservatives were critical of Nixon's move, Reagan instinctively understood the value of what he was trying to do. As he wrote to a friend critical of the gambit, "Russia is still enemy number one. Russia is still the country that very shortly will have the power to deliver an ultimatum [to us]. So the president, knowing the disaffection between China and Russia, visits China, butters up the warlords, and lets them be, because they have nothing to fear from us. Russia, therefore, has to keep its 140 divisions on the Chinese border; hostility between the two is increased; and we buy a little time and elbowroom in a plain, simple strategic move. . . ."[4]

In early October 1971, Reagan found himself on a White House 707 jet flying over the Pacific Ocean on a mission to Asia. America's Asian allies were worried and Nixon had appointed Reagan to soothe their nerves. Traveling with Nancy, his son Ron Jr., and several aides, Reagan flew first to Taipei for a meeting with Chiang Kai-shek.

It was Taiwan's National Day when they arrived, and the mood in the country was gloomy. Compounding the danger posed by Nixon's opening to China, there were efforts afoot to push Taiwan out of the UN and give the seat to mainland China. Chiang Kai-shek, the steely and now aged generalissimo of Nationalist China, delivered his annual message to the people, declaring that they must not lose hope. He criticized those who wanted to compromise with communism as morally weak, certainly a message that Reagan would be comfortable with: "They turn away from the call and the appeal of an outstanding but persecuted people who have chosen to resist Communism to the bitter end."[5]

After the speech, Reagan entered the generalissimo's office and the two sat down for tea. Reagan had been given a prepared text for the meeting, but he dispensed with it and instead chatted about Vietnam, the United Nations vote, and communist China. Henry Kissinger was leaving shortly for Beijing to make arrangements for

Nixon's visit the following February. Reagan told Chiang it was a done deal, but that he could trust Kissinger and Taiwan would be protected.

From Taipei, Reagan jetted off to Singapore and then to Bangkok. He tried to soothe anxieties in both countries before continuing on to Saigon. The Vietnamese capital was by now a very tense place. There were only 140,000 U.S. troops in the country, down from 540,000 only two years earlier. The last U.S. combat soldiers were expected to leave in less than a year. The Viet Cong had succeeded in infiltrating the capital and were in the midst of a bombing campaign.

Shortly after landing at the airport, Reagan was taken by helicopter to the U.S. embassy. En route, he chatted with the young pilot, who asked Reagan to contact his mother when he got back to California and tell her that he was all right. When the Reagans returned, Nancy did call the mother, and Reagan wrote the pilot telling him his mother expected to see him by Christmas.

Security for the visit was being managed by the Secret Service and was, in their words, "extraordinarily tight." The Secret Service planned to have Reagan travel everywhere by helo—even the four-block trip from the embassy to the presidential palace—fearful that if he traveled by car his motorcade would be subject to attack. But after Reagan arrived at the embassy and discussed the matter with Ambassador Ellsworth Bunker, it was decided that he would drive to the presidential palace instead. It was the same sort of symbolic act of defiance Reagan had carried out during the Hollywood strike and the protests at Berkeley.

That afternoon, Reagan lunched with President Thieu and they discussed the war and prospects for peace. Reagan's own views about the war had already begun to change. As he had written to a friend before the trip, no American president was going to be able to prosecute this war in the way that was needed to win. Nixon's effort to pull out, while giving heavy support to the South Vietnamese, was the only option. Reagan told Thieu that both he and Nixon would not abandon Saigon. "There will be no change in the course of our policies," he assured him.[6]

From Saigon, the Reagans' 707 headed north, first to Seoul,

South Korea, where he met with President Park Chung Hee. Like Thieu, Park was a military man who had taken over in a coup d'état. Tough, aggressive, and not easy to deal with, Park also had concerns about Nixon's policies toward the East bloc. Reagan discussed matters briefly with Park and explained that Nixon would not abandon him. After Seoul, Reagan was off to Tokyo for consultations with Premier Eisaku Sato and Foreign Minister Takeo Fukuda.[7]

Once he was back in Sacramento, Reagan called Nixon in the Oval Office and filled him in on the trip. According to a transcript of the conversation (Nixon secretly taped it, as he did so many), Reagan asked Nixon pointedly if he would indeed back the Asian allies if they were attacked. Nixon said he would. Reagan then told him the situation in Vietnam (things "seem to be going well" given the circumstances) and they hung up.[8]

★ ★ ★

THIS WAS A TROUBLING TIME FOR REAGAN, WHO WAS USUALLY THE eternal optimist. The collapse of American commitment in Vietnam bothered him deeply. It was not so much a failure of American muscle, he believed, but of American resolve. The country was losing its sense of purpose and duty.

It was this sense that had propelled his old Hollywood friend Audie Murphy into acts of heroism during the Second World War. Murphy had won the Medal of Honor and thirty-three other awards while fighting in nine major campaigns in which he was wounded three times. When Murphy was killed in a plane crash in 1971, Reagan wrote to his widow, drawing a sharp contrast between Murphy's spirit and the spirit of some Americans in the midst of Vietnam.

"I know this is a difficult time for young people to see heroism in any act associated with war, and that is too bad. Some men will go through life and never find themselves in a position where they are the only one who can do the dirty job that has to be done. Some will face such a moment and fail. Some, like Audie, accept and do the dirty job because there is no one else there to do it, and they know in their hearts it must be done."

Vietnam was America's current "dirty job" in Reagan's mind,

and the country's leaders had failed to see it through. It was, in short, a failure of spirit. In an exchange of letters with a young Navy ensign who was perplexed at the realities of the Vietnam War, Reagan expressed his frustration at how America's leaders had let down her soldiers. "War very often brings out the noblest in men," he wrote the young man from his office in Sacramento. "By the same token, particularly when it drags on the way this has with no apparent goal in sight, it can bring out the worst. I fear very much this has happened."

Reagan had long believed that America had a divine mission or purpose: to spread freedom around the world. He had written on the subject and spoken about it during his days with GE. Now, with its failure in Vietnam, America seemed to have lost sight of its purpose, or no longer had the courage to follow it. In either case, he wrote in a philosophical letter to a friend, this was the worst possible fate that could befall a person or a nation. "Some with little faith and even less testing seem to miss their mission, or else we perhaps fail to see their imprint in the lives of others. But bearing what we cannot change and going on with what God has given us, confident there is a destiny, somehow seems to bring a reward we wouldn't exchange for any other. It takes a lot of fire and heat to make a piece of steel."

In contrast to the failure of America's leadership to deal with the test in Vietnam, Reagan was inspired by the exploits of General George S. Patton, "Ol' Blood and Guts," who had plowed through German defenses with his Third Armored Division during World War II. The 1971 release of the film *Patton*, starring George C. Scott, brought the general to life for millions of Americans. The film's producer, Frank McCarthy, was an old Reagan friend who had been trying to get the film made for twenty years. When Reagan finally saw it, he considered it one of the best films ever produced. But he watched it with a hint of disappointment. As he wrote to McCarthy, "I told you once I would hate anyone who ever played that role other than myself."[9]

Fire and heat were a reality for everyone. How you responded was a testament to your character, and it required making tough choices. As he wrote in a letter to his son, Ron Jr.: "Everything in life has a price and our biggest mistakes are when we don't really ask the price before we make our choice."

The questions firmly in his mind were: Could America pass the test? Would it be willing to make the difficult choice?

The Vietnam War was not an abstraction for Reagan, but something profoundly real and human. As he walked about the governor's office and the state capitol in Sacramento, dangling from his wrist was a metallic POW/MIA bracelet. Engraved on it was the name of Marine captain Stephen Hanson, who was missing in action. Reagan never took the thing off, wearing it to political functions, around the ranch, even to bed. He even met Hanson's wife, Carole, in the capitol as her young boy, Todd, gently tugged at his coat.

When it was discovered in 1973 that Hanson had in fact been killed in combat, Reagan finally took off the bracelet and had it put in a display case honoring Vietnam vets set up in the corridor of the Capitol Building in Sacramento. Then he sat down and wrote a letter to Carole Hanson.

"I've worn it so long I feel as though I had a personal knowledge and friendship with Steve. For some strange reason I have a feeling without the bracelet on that I, too, shall miss him."[10]

For American soldiers returning from Vietnam, Reagan held prayer breakfasts and receptions in the state capitol, proclaiming them heroes while denouncing the fact that we had been "dragged into a winless war." Soldiers seemed to appreciate his support, and gave him items that told of their ordeal—prison spoons, North Vietnamese cigarette packs, even old bullet casings. He also exchanged letters with soldiers and was sometimes asked to carry out special missions. One young soldier wrote to him from Vietnam with a strange request: Could Reagan express to the man's wife how much he missed her and loved her? Reagan gladly took up the task and showed up on the lady's doorstep. "Hello, I'm Ronald Reagan," he told her, cradling a dozen red roses in his arms. "Your husband asked me to deliver these flowers to you and to tell you that he loves you."[11]

★   ★   ★

IF RONALD REAGAN CAME TO ACCEPT NIXON'S VIEWS ON HOW TO proceed in Vietnam, he was not supportive of everything Nixon was doing. He certainly was not privy to the secret negotiations taking place between Henry Kissinger and Anatoly Dobrynin, nor did he have access to the policy discussions that were taking place. But what he did know he was concerned about. As he wrote privately to a friend, there were many things he would "have chosen to do differently" from Nixon. But he was reluctant to say so in public. As he wrote to one supporter, "We cannot afford division. . . . I believe there is a better chance to advance my conservative principles with a Republican president, even though I disagree with some of what he does. I believe that we have a better chance to elect a conservative president in 1976 if he doesn't have to run against an incumbent Democrat."

Reagan was willing to work with Nixon, "pressuring on behalf of our own views." And he encouraged his supporters to "be critical, be vocal and forceful in urging your views on the President."

But he recognized the realities that they were facing. Nixon was hemmed in. "The President has to deal with things as they are, not as he would like them to be. Bluntly, he inherited a situation in which the Democratic leadership has allowed the strength of the nation to deteriorate until we are in a situation where the possibility exists of the Soviet Union delivering an ultimatum."

He wanted to support Nixon and believed that the President would do the right thing. "If I am wrong in this," he wrote to a friend, "I will be the first to repudiate him."

CHAPTER VII

MOVING FORWARD

O N MAY 30, 1972, SHORTLY BEFORE MIDNIGHT, PRESI-
dent Nixon and Soviet Premier Leonid Brezhnev were
standing in the green and gold hall of St. Vladimir in
the Kremlin's Grand Palace. After pulling a silver
Parker fountain pen out of his pocket, Nixon inked his name to a series of documents. Television cameras were there to capture the mo-
mentous event, and flashbulbs popped like lightning.

The two superpowers were taking "an irreversible step" toward
building a "structure of peace," Nixon declared.

The two men signed a strategic arms limitation (SALT) agreement, which would freeze offensive missile construction for five
years, and an anti–ballistic missile (ABM) treaty, which would severely limit the deployment of missile defense systems. Several trade
agreements then followed. Finally came the innocuous-sounding
"Basic Principles of Relations Between the United States and the
Union of Soviet Socialist Republics." This agreement committed
both powers to the concepts of "peaceful coexistence," "mutual ac-
comodation," and "non-interference in internal affairs."[1]

These basic principles had been hammered out between U.S.
and Soviet negotiators during the previous week. President Nixon

and Henry Kissinger, who were housed in the Czar's Apartments in the Kremlin, paid little attention to the contents of the agreement. Kissinger had barely discussed it with his Soviet counterparts, and it received only limited attention among aides before it was signed. But in Moscow the agreement was highly valued, not because of what the document said but for what it represented. The agreement marked the first time that the Soviet Union was recognized as an equal by the United States on the world stage.

It was a sign of the times. The United States had been weakened by Vietnam. Days before the signing, Kissinger had met with Leonid Brezhnev to discuss the summit meeting. In a conversation that was jovial and humorous, Kissinger confided in the Soviet leader about America's policy in Vietnam. "In the spirit of personal confidence that I believe characterizes our discussions, I must tell you the determination the President has to bring about some solution, whatever price he has to pay."[2] The administration hoped for diplomatic help from Moscow in extracting U.S. forces from Southeast Asia, which Kissinger had proposed in his first meeting with Dobrynin in 1969, but this help never materialized.

But if America seemed to be faltering, less than confident in herself, the mood in the Kremlin was buoyant.

The SALT agreement allowed the United States to retain launchers for 1,054 ICBMs and 656 submarine-launched ballistic missiles (SLBMs). Moscow, on the other hand, was permitted 1,608 ICBM launchers and 740 SLBM launchers. Nixon and Kissinger were convinced that American technological superiority would mean that the United States would retain its position of parity with Moscow. But the Kremlin saw it otherwise. General Detinov, who was a member of the Soviet negotiating team, remembered the jubilation in the Soviet General Staff. They had "managed to gain major American concessions" without giving up much at all.[3]

A. S. Kalashnikov, a chairman of the Soviet Strategic Rocket Forces, recalls the same sense of excitement moving through the military. Because of the SALT agreement and the ongoing military buildup, senior officers were confident they "had amassed a superior first-strike arsenal." They had, in short, "achieved superiority" over the Americans.[4]

In the Politburo, Leonid Brezhnev and the master military planner Ustinov were also pleased with what had been accomplished. The agreed-upon strategy of using arms control as a tool to help achieve military superiority seemed to be working. "The evaluation was as follows," recalls Ambassador Oleg Grinevsky. "[In] the SALT I talks we won a victory over the Americans and this treaty gave us an opportunity to deeply change the structure of our forces. The number of missiles in the Soviet Union in these five to seven years was increased seven-fold, while in the United States the number remained dormant. But there was [also] an increase of 22 times in [Soviet] warheads."[5]

The SALT agreements also proved valuable for another reason. During the negotiations, virtually all of the data on Soviet strategic weapons used for the talks were provided by U.S. intelligence. Scouring through the data, a stern but brilliant military officer named Marshal Nikolai Ogarkov was able to determine how the Americans were getting their satellite intelligence. With the approval of the Soviet Council of Ministers, he worked feverishly with the secretive Scientific and Technical Committee of the General Staff to develop a comprehensive strategic deception program to hide from Washington the true size of the Soviet arsenal.[6] The plan worked wonderfully. For the rest of the Cold War, the United States would never be able to fully grasp the size and scope of the Soviet nuclear arsenal. By 1990, the United States was guessing that the Soviet Union had produced 30,000 nuclear weapons and 500 to 600 tons of enriched uranium. In reality, Moscow possessed 45,000 nuclear weapons and had created 1,200 tons of enriched uranium.[7]

With Moscow's success came certain temptation. A decade after their missiles had been forced out of Cuba, the Soviet military was on the cusp of achieving its dream of military superiority. They even began to think about the unthinkable: launching and winning a nuclear war. General Danilevich, who served as a senior special assistant to the chief of Main Operations in the Armed Forces, remembers the cold calculation that was made. "We considered that we held advantages in certain areas, such as throw-weight, land-based systems, in control systems, in silo protection, in numbers of weapons, so we thought that we could win a nuclear war by striking at the Americans and then using our general superiority to bring the nuclear war to victory."

But there were reasons for the Kremlin to be optimistic other than the shifting military balance. In addition to the SALT agreement, the Moscow summit had also included a series of economic and commercial agreements. As Brezhnev had predicted in 1969, the arms buildup was a heavy burden on the economy, consuming something like 40 percent of all the machinery produced in the Soviet Union. The trade deals inked with Nixon would lighten the burden.

Six weeks after the summit, the Nixon administration approved the sale of $750 million worth of grain to Moscow at bargain prices. The prices were so low and the terms of repayment so easy that the deal quickly became known as the "Great Grain Robbery." It was the first in what would become a blizzard of deals that would give the Soviet economy a much-needed boost. Nixon supported a program to finance Soviet purchases of U.S. technology using long-term loans through the Export-Import Bank. Kissinger, in a March 14, 1974, secret decision memorandum, approved the sale of advanced computers to Moscow for the first time.[8] As a result, Soviet imports of technology increased sevenfold over the next several years.

The hope was that these trade deals would, in Kissinger's words, "foster a degree of interdependence that adds an element of stability to the political relationship."

Just how damaging these deals proved to be would not be known for another decade. A top-secret CIA analyst revealed that the trade and finance deals allowed the Kremlin to continue its ambitious military buildup without significantly reforming the economy. "Soviet hard currency imports—especially machinery, ferrous metals, and foodstuffs—have played a critical role in many high-priority industrial, agricultural, and military programs, including those for raising energy production and meat consumption," noted the report. Particularly helpful were a series of buyback deals with the West involving purchases of Western industrial plants and equipment. According to CIA estimates, oil pumps purchased from the United States in the 1970s "added as much as 2 million barrels a day of capacity to Soviet oil production." At the same time, machinery imports allowed Moscow to accomplish an ambitious fifteen-year plan for motor vehicle production, something that would not have been possible without American help. The Soviet chemical industry also received a tremendous boost. As the CIA report concluded, "By providing economic gains from trade that relieve bottlenecks and improving the efficiency of the economy they thereby reduce the burden of defense."[9]

These trade deals also led to an explosion in Soviet borrowing from the West. In 1971, the Soviets borrowed $8 billion; by the end of the decade the figure was $80 billion.[10]

★ ★ ★

TRADE EXPANDED AND TREATIES MULTIPLIED, BUT SOVIET AP-petites and ambitions did not wane. In East Germany, large underground storehouses had been built near several Warsaw Pact military installations. Hidden away in these cavernous facilities were interesting tokens. There were literally hundreds of street signs printed with names like Karl Marx Platz and Friedrich Engels Strasse. There were also enormous stacks of crisp new money, unlike any other currency in circulation. And thousands of military medals were stacked neatly in large crates.

These were the necessities of an expected conquest. The medals had been stamped and minted to honor Warsaw Pact soldiers who would serve gallantly in a future war against the West. The money was currency to pay East German, Polish, Czech, Hungarian, and Russian troops when they occupied "the adversary's territory." And the street signs were new road names for what would be occupied Western Europe.[11]

There might have been talk of arms control and warming East-West relations. But for the militaries of the Warsaw Pact, the preparation for war continued. When the armies of the Soviet bloc conducted war games, they hardly ever practiced defensive maneuvers, believing an attack from the West would not come. War games always included attacking and defeating the enemy.

Warsaw Pact military plans were detailed and direct, designed around deep thrusts into Western Europe, in the hopes of achieving early military victories in West Germany and Denmark. Then the

Soviet bloc would move to take over the Netherlands, Belgium, Luxembourg, and France. The final surge would include the occupation of the Iberian Peninsula.

There were sixty Warsaw Pact divisions waiting to be used in the first wave of attack. But the Soviets also expected to use nuclear weapons early and often, regardless of whether NATO planned to use them. They expected to destroy half of NATO forces along the front with these weapons. All in all, they believed it would take only fourteen days to reach the French coast.[12]

General Danilevich, who served on the Soviet General Staff, recalls: "We had some plans which called for an advance to the English Channel. Later we limited our appetites, our goals, but we thought it was realistic to achieve victory in Europe using our strategic advantage."

For all of this planning, however, Europe was not the prime arena of conflict. As the Kremlin leadership eyed the developing world, it was here that they saw the best opportunity to expand. American troops had been driven out of Vietnam. And with Moscow's own growing military might, the Soviets were increasingly interested in flexing their muscles.

When war erupted in the Middle East on October 6, 1973, President Nixon expressed his determination to support Israel by any means necessary. Vice Admiral Daniel Murphy, commander of the Sixth Fleet, was aboard his flagship *Little Rock* in the Mediterranean when orders came from Washington to put his fleet to sea. Two aircraft carriers, the *Independence* and the *Franklin D. Roosevelt*, supported by forty-six other vessels, began moving east toward the area of conflict.

Since the end of World War II, American naval power had been supreme. But as the Sixth Fleet moved into position, a new reality awaited them. The Soviet Mediterranean naval squadron, named the Fifth Eskadra, was assembling off the island of Crete. With fifty-seven cruisers, destroyers, frigates, and corvettes, it was a formidable force. And it would only continue to grow.

Three days after the *Little Rock* headed to sea, sonar readings from the ship indicated there was something new to worry about: Soviet subs were tagging behind the *Independence*. Over the next several days, more Soviet naval units joined the Fifth Eskadra as subs and surface ships from the Black Sea Fleet made their way through the Dardanelles. Admiral Murphy feared he might be vulnerable to a quick strike, so he split his fleet. The *Independence* would remain south of Crete while the *Roosevelt* took up position in the western Mediterranean.

By the end of October, the number of Soviet ships tracking the Sixth Fleet was eighty, and below the waterline ten American submarines were trying to keep track of an untold number of subs. Murphy was now forced to keep his fleet constantly moving. He was outnumbered and no American ships were on the way.

"By October 31," recalled Murphy, "SOVMEDLFT strength had increased to 95 units, including 34 surface combatants and 23 submarines, possessing a first launch capability of 88 surface to surface missiles." A devastating first strike, effectively destroying most of Murphy's fleet, was now a real possibility.[13]

With Israel's military victory days later, the possibility of a naval showdown diminished. Both navies gradually withdrew from the Mediterranean basin. But for Murphy and the U.S. Navy, it was a strange new world. They no longer ruled the oceans unchallenged. As Admiral Elmo Zumwalt, the Chief of Naval Operations, put it, "I doubt that major units of the U.S. Navy were ever in a tenser situation since World War II ended than the Sixth Fleet in the Mediterranean was for the week after the alert was declared."[14]

As the Soviet Navy extended the arteries of Soviet power into the world's oceans, Leonid Brezhnev was plotting the use of the Soviet Army in a way that would roll up victories in the developing world. Back in early 1961, Nikita Khrushchev had launched an ambitious plan to support National Liberation Movements around the world. Now Brezhnev wanted to up the ante by secretly using Soviet soldiers to advance the cause.

Brezhnev called them the "internationalists," young, specially trained men who would disguise themselves as teachers, doctors, and agricultural experts. They were an army in waiting, and when they were needed, they would don foreign military uniforms, use Soviet military equipment painted with insignias of another country, and join the myriad of civil wars that were ravaging the developing world. In all, one and a half million Soviet soldiers became internationalists, fighting in the rice paddies of Southeast Asia, the dry plains of Africa, the jungles of Latin America, and the hill country of Southwest Asia. They were pilots, artillery officers, and common foot soldiers. For their service, Brezhnev saw to it that they received special commendation medals cast in silver and gold. But because their missions were so secret, they were forbidden to wear their medals publicly.[15]

Yuri Andropov, the bespectacled chairman of the KGB, had prime responsibility for organizing the effort to win the cold war in the developing world. The son of a railway worker, he had joined the Young Communists at age sixteen and proved to be a loyal party member. Soon he was off to a special intelligence agency and began a public career as a diplomat. When Hungary revolted in 1956, Andropov was the Soviet ambassador in Budapest. Quietly and professionally he helped to organize the invasion and suppression of the country. In 1967, he was appointed chairman of the KGB.

Though you wouldn't know it by his dour look and rigid demeanor, Andropov was an optimist. As he scanned the globe in the early 1970s, he saw decolonization creating new opportunities. If Moscow handled matters delicately, he wrote in a secret report, it could yield big gains at the expense of the United States, in part because the Americans had erroneously concluded that "in the coming years the Soviet Union does not plan a broad offensive." It was time to move quickly.[16]

The question was: where to strike? Soviet military intelligence (the GRU) saw opportunities in Africa, where colonial powers were retreating and leaving a region abundant in natural resources up for grabs. Andropov shared that view, and his attentions were quickly drawn to Angola, a mineral- and oil-rich country that was on the verge of independence from Portugal. A guerrilla leader named Agostinho Neto and his MPLA were fighting several other insurgent groups, all seeking to seize power once the Portuguese left.[17]

Since the mid-1960s, the Kremlin and her allies Cuba and East Germany had been supplying arms and money to Neto. But Andropov was prepared to raise the stakes, offering not only to boost the level of material support but also to provide "internationalists" to serve in his guerrilla army. In exchange for the support, Moscow was expecting Neto to begin conducting military operations against other countries in the region, including mineral-rich Zambia, Zaire, and Congo. Neto, in secret meetings with Soviet officials, agreed to these terms.[18]

The Soviet push into Angola came at an opportune time. Back in Washington, the Nixon administration was under siege because of Watergate. Nixon's abuse of presidential power was moving many on Capitol Hill to consider impeaching the president; many legislators were also working to severely restrict the president's power by taking away his option to sell arms or provide military assistance, and limiting his ability to use covert operations. When Nixon finally resigned in August 1974, he was replaced by Vice President Gerald Ford. The new commander in chief was certainly aware of what Moscow was doing in Angola, thanks to a secret CIA report. But Congress was in no mood to check the Soviet advance, and Ford's hands were tied. This sense of paralysis extended even to Vietnam, where more than fifty thousand Americans had died. As North Vietnamese forces violated the terms of the peace accords and advanced on Saigon, Congress turned back Ford's request for military aid to the Thieu government.

So Moscow continued to pour it on. Neto received shipments that included six hundred trucks, sixty fighter aircraft, thirty surface-to-air missile systems, a thousand artillery pieces, and two hundred armored personnel carriers. Hundreds of Soviet internationalists arrived, flying MiG-21 fighter aircraft and HIND helicopter gunships. Famed General of the Army V. V. Varkenikov was secretly flown into the country to command Neto's forces and guide them to victory.[19]

Thousands of Cuban soldiers also flew in to join the fight. As Fidel Castro would later brag to East German leader Erich Honecker during a secret meeting, "We are giving Angola a great deal of military support. At the end of the liberation war, 36,000 Cuban troops and 300 tanks were deployed."[20]

When Agostinho Neto finally seized power in 1975, the victory gave Moscow an enormous boost of confidence. Yuri Andropov and the Soviet military brass had managed to wage a military campaign more than five thousand miles from Moscow. Victory came only months after the North Vietnamese, equipped by Moscow, had over-run Saigon. As Leonid Brezhnev sat in the Kremlin gloating, he declared that détente with the West had changed everything. Angola and Vietnam were proof that "active solidarity with peoples" around the world with the help of military assistance was perhaps the most valuable tool in his arsenal for winning the Cold War.[21]

At the Soviet Defense Ministry, Cuban defense minister Raul Castro would soon pay a visit for consultations. According to a secret transcript of the meeting, both sides were elated and confident about the future. Soviet military supplies and Cuban troops had made all the difference in Angola. Now it was time to move farther afield to seek new victories.

CHAPTER VIII

ATHENS OR SPARTA?

I N THE SPRING OF 1972, ONLY WEEKS AFTER NIXON AND BREZH-
nev met in Moscow, Governor Reagan was touring the National Weapons Laboratory at Los Alamos in New Mexico. It
was not that Reagan had an affinity for weapons. Reagan abhorred war. At age twenty, he had written a short story he titled
"Killed in Action," about two soldiers in a foxhole. They were fired
on and then gassed in the trenches. Later in life one of them died a
tramp, scarred by his experiences in the war. Reagan had been in
Hollywood when atomic bombs were dropped on the Japanese cities
of Hiroshima and Nagasaki. While he defended Truman's decision to
use the new weapons, he also joined efforts to counteract their
spread. When his friend Eddie Arnold returned from the Pacific,
Reagan sat quietly and listened as Arnold described the horrors of
Tarawa. Later, as governor, he heard similar stories from Vietnam
vets with whom he met on a regular basis.

War was a horror. But preparing for war was one of those grim
necessities you could not avoid. And Reagan considered it an absolute duty.

Reagan believed he had a small but important role to play in this.
As governor, he was head of the University of California Board of

Regents, the body that oversaw the state's entire university system. When the weapons lab had been built at Los Alamos, and another called Lawrence Livermore was later constructed outside of San Francisco, it was done under the auspices of the University of California at Berkeley's physics department. So Reagan had oversight of the two labs, and appointments to head them were subject to his approval. Over the course of his eight years as governor, Reagan would make yearly visits to both facilities.

"He didn't come with the regents," recalls Harold Agnew, who was director of Los Alamos at the time. "He came alone. He would tour the weapons lab, chat with people, and ask a few questions."[1]

Both labs were on the cusp of developing exotic new weapons systems that some believed could change the military equation. In November 1967, Reagan became the first California governor to tour Lawrence Livermore. Invited by Hungarian-born physicist Edward Teller, who had been involved in the development of the hydrogen bomb, Reagan spent the day touring the laboratory and discussing the current projects. At the time, work was being done on an anti–ballistic missile (ABM) system called Safeguard. Lab scientists had built the Spartan missile, tall and fast-burning, which could fly up to the heavens and explode a massive six-megaton warhead to destroy incoming enemy missiles. Those warheads that survived the blast would then in theory be picked off by a smaller and faster missile called Sprint.[2]

Reagan never pretended to understand the science behind Safeguard.

"He didn't really focus on the technology per se," recalls Ed Meese, who was a counselor while Reagan was governor. "He just kept saying, 'Every time an offensive system is built a defensive system rises to meet it. Swords led to shields, horse cavalry to the tank, the tank to anti-tank missiles.' "[3]

The great attraction of the ABM for Reagan was that it undermined the ability of Moscow to use fear as a tool. He had said repeatedly in the 1950s and early 1960s that Eisenhower and Kennedy had backed down in the face of a Soviet challenge because of what he called "fear of the bomb." Take away that fear, he reasoned, and the Soviets had nothing.

Reagan was an instant convert to Safeguard, and at the 1969 Republican Governors' Association meeting in Louisville, he took the unusual step of giving an impassioned presentation in favor of the system to his fellow governors. He then asked them to pass a resolution supporting its deployment. Vice President Spiro Agnew, who was also at the meeting, caught wind of Reagan's efforts and opposed them. Passing such a resolution would be too divisive and partisan, he declared.[4]

But Reagan caught the ABM bug and continued discussing the general concept with scientists in California. Sometimes old friendships yielded a strange convergence.

Maxwell Hunter was a scientist at Lockheed and one of America's greatest experts on rockets and missiles. He had been in on the design of just about every major American rocket—Honest John, Thor, Nike-Zeus, and the Saturn S-IV for the Apollo moon program. He was interested in the concept of missile defense, too.

As chance would have it, Hunter's wife was Irene Manning, an actress and singer from Hollywood's Golden Age. (She costarred with James Cagney in the 1942 hit *Yankee Doodle Dandy*.) Her career had intersected with Reagan's and she was good friends with his longtime friend Cagney. While he was governor, Reagan reestablished the friendship and the two couples would sit down for dinner in Los Angeles. They would talk about the old days in Hollywood and Reagan would ask what Max was working on. Max would start talking about his vision for a new weapon that was like no other: a space-based laser that could shoot down incoming missiles.[5]

As his term as governor wound down, Reagan spent considerable time reading books, many of them unorthodox tomes on the Cold War. An old friend from Hollywood named Laurence Beilenson had written two books on the subject that Reagan read repeatedly.

Beilenson had been general counsel of the Screen Actors Guild and had represented Reagan during his divorce proceedings with Jane Wyman. It was Reagan "who awarded me my gold life membership card," Beilenson recalled years later. "We've been fast friends for years."

Beilenson had spent the Second World War as a commanding liaison officer with the Chinese Army. Now in retirement, the lawyer was spending his time reading history books at the UCLA library. He was particularly fascinated by questions of war and peace and the nature of communism. In 1969, he wrote a book called the *Treaty Trap,* which examined the history of treaties between nations. His central point in the book was that arms control agreements were useless because nations obeyed them only when it was in their interest to do so. Two years later he wrote another book, called *Power Through Subversion,* in which he examined how Communists used subversion to advance their ends. Beilenson's solution to the challenge was simple: Do unto them as they do unto us. He proposed that the United States support insurgents and guerrilla armies in the struggle against the Soviet Union. "The United States should give to dissidents against all Communist governments protracted sustained aid—initially for propaganda, with supplies and arms added where feasible and warranted by the developing situation."[6]

Beilenson was no strategic expert, but the influence of his books on Reagan was profound. Both books "should be required reading for every employee of our State Department," he said.[7] For Reagan, a good idea was a good idea regardless of whom it came from, and he would adopt Beilenson's ideas and turn them into an approach to foreign policy that came to be called the Reagan Doctrine.

★   ★   ★

IN MOSCOW, NIXON AND BREZHNEV HAD SIGNED BOTH A STRATEgic arms treaty and the ABM treaty. Reagan was opposed to both of them. Out of deference to Nixon, however, he avoided voicing criticism in public. There were also concerns about the treaties in Europe, where leaders found that they had largely been ignored in the midst of the negotiations. To mollify their concerns, Nixon again tapped Reagan as his special envoy.

Two months after the Moscow summit, Reagan, accompanied by a dozen Secret Service agents, boarded a 707 and flew to Western Europe. Over the next several days he met with NATO General Secretary Joseph Luns, the foreign ministers of France and Spain, and the prime ministers of Denmark and Great Britain. Reagan tried to reassure the Europeans, but he grumbled privately that Nixon had been forced into giving up too much to Moscow. "He endorsed and got, by the skin of his teeth, approval for the B1 Bomber," he wrote a supporter. "He got ABM by one vote. Congress is dead set against any military spending." Likewise, he believed Vietnam was ending in disaster because Nixon had no "public support" to "escalate the war and try for victory."[8]

The collapse of Vietnam pained Reagan, who had seen a stream of wounded soldiers returning to the United States from Southeast Asia. He had visited and spent time with them. He had also spent time in Saigon with South Vietnamese president Thieu. When Thieu came to the States to meet with Nixon, he made a point of seeing Reagan in Los Angeles. But in 1975, as North Vietnamese troops advanced on Saigon, Reagan watched in desperation and sadness. He had supported Nixon's Vietnam policy "with the understanding that we would provide weapons and ammunition to enable South Vietnam and Cambodia to resist if the North Vietnamese violated the negotiated ceasefire." He blamed Congress for failing to provide the funds desperately needed for the Saigon government, and he equated it with the acts of Neville Chamberlain, the British prime minister who had appeased Hitler.

But Reagan also blamed Gerald Ford for failing to do everything possible to rescue Saigon. "Can anyone think for one moment that North Vietnam would have moved to the attack had their leaders believed we would respond with B 52s?" he asked.[9]

When Reagan's second term ended in Sacramento, he returned to private life. A debate was raging about America's fate, and it was encapsulated by speculation on whether the country would follow the course of the Roman Empire, Greece, and other great civilizations that had declined. America was on the retreat, and there was of course plenty of evidence to support the idea that her best days were in the past. The Arab oil embargo had sent the economy reeling and the failure in Vietnam had created national self-doubt.

In 1974, Admiral Elmo Zumwalt revealed in his memoirs what he claimed was Henry Kissinger's take on present-day America. In a series of private conversations, Kissinger had reportedly told Zumwalt that America was a modern-day Athens, decadent and struggling to maintain its fighting spirit. The Soviets, on the other hand, were Sparta, the disciplined power that was militantly challenging Athens.

"The day of the United States is past," Kissinger allegedly said. "And today is the day of the Soviet Union. My job as secretary of state is to negotiate the most acceptable second-best position available."

Whether Kissinger actually uttered those words is not known. But it is certain that he did have a Spenglerian view of the human condition and believed that America needed to accept decline gracefully.

Reagan had pondered this question himself, although without the depth and breadth of historical knowledge that Kissinger could muster. Still, in 1969 he had compared America to Rome. The country was becoming soft and lacking in moral courage. Speaking before the American Legion in 1972, he declared that perhaps America was like Carthage, which, having lived in luxury and abundance, was overrun by the Romans.

But Reagan's vision of an America in decline clashed with his belief, expressed as early as 1952, that America was a nation with a divine purpose. He still believed it, even in the midst of Vietnam and Watergate. "You can call it mysticism, if you want to, but I have always believed that there was some divine plan that placed this great continent between two oceans to be sought out by those who were possessed of an abiding love of freedom and a special kind of courage," he said in 1974. Even with its troubles, America was still "the last best hope of man on earth."[10]

When you looked at the decline of empires and compared it with America, Reagan declared, "the parallel is almost eerie." But America was still in a position to write its own history.[11]

The fate of America rested in the choices that were made, and that came down to leadership. What Reagan meant by leadership is perhaps best illustrated by an exchange he had with students on a television program aired by CBS in 1967. When asked about Barry Goldwater's dictum that "extremism in the defense of liberty is no vice," Reagan said he agreed with it. The statement was simply a total commitment to liberty that "was as old as Cicero."[12]

All the choices America was making with respect to the Soviet

Union were for Reagan the wrong choices. After Richard Nixon resigned, Reagan no longer felt compelled to remain quiet in deference to the White House. He openly criticized the ABM treaty and the SALT agreement, declaring that America was falling behind the Soviets in the arms race (an opinion shared in Moscow). He also rebuked the very notion of détente. Trade deals like those that had been signed during the Moscow summit were only helping a troubled Soviet economy. Aren't we "adding to our own danger by helping the troubled Soviet economy?" he asked openly. "Nothing proves the failure of Marxism more than the Soviet Union's inability to produce weapons for its military ambitions and at the same time provide for their people's everyday needs."

He also declared that America needed to have an endgame for the Cold War. "The Russians have told us over and over again their goal is to impose their incompetent and ridiculous system on the world. We invest in armaments to hold them off, but what do we envision as the eventual outcome? Either that they will see the fallacy of their way and give up their goal or their system will collapse or—(and we don't let ourselves think of this) we'll have to use our weapons one day. Maybe there is an answer," he declared. "Stop doing business with them. Let their system collapse, but in the meantime buy our farmer's wheat ourselves and have it on hand to feed the Russian people when they finally become free."[13]

Reagan had serious doubts as to whether the Ford administration would take such a course. The administration was continuing to pursue détente, and out of deference to Moscow, Ford was refusing to invite recently exiled Russian writer and Nobel Prize winner Aleksandr Solzhenitsyn to the White House. Ford had offered Reagan his choice of a job in the administration. But Reagan had politely declined.

Reagan was now sixty-four years old. In 1968, he had flirted with the idea of running for president. If he wanted to achieve his ambition, now was the time to do it. He might never have another chance.

He joined the 1976 presidential primary campaign, announcing his plans at the National Press Club on a gray fall day in Washington, D.C. While he criticized Ford for his domestic policy and his failure to deal with inflation, it didn't take long for Reagan to turn his attentions to foreign policy on the campaign trail.

Ford had only recently signed the Helsinki Accords in Europe. In exchange for recognition of Moscow's domination of Central Europe, the Kremlin was promising to improve the human rights situation behind the Iron Curtain. Reagan lambasted Ford for signing the agreement, claiming he was "putting our stamp of approval on Russia's enslavement of the captive nations. We gave away the freedom of millions of people—freedom that was not ours to give." Reagan also rejected the administration's policy of parity and sufficiency in the arms competition with Moscow, calling instead for the restoration of American "military superiority."[14]

These frontal attacks on détente gave much-needed momentum to Reagan's campaign. He won primaries in North Carolina and Texas by focusing on the issue of America's slipping position against the Soviet Union. But his outspokenness also garnered attention from the KGB, which noted with displeasure his call to arms. Yuri Andropov ordered Service A, which was responsible for "active measures," to develop a plan to undermine Reagan. It was apparently the first and only time that Moscow would try to influence the outcome of an American political primary.

KGB agents began digging for material that could be used against Reagan in the media. When nothing useful turned up, they dissected his family background, paying particular attention to his father's struggles with alcohol. Still coming up empty, they elected to launch a propaganda campaign to discredit Reagan. In the end, they successfully planted anti-Reagan articles in Denmark, France, and India.[15]

Despite grueling hours on the campaign trail and hundreds of speeches, Reagan came up short. Ford, buoyed by a string of victories in the Midwest, locked up the delegates he needed for his party's nomination at the Republican National Convention in Kansas City. Facing certain defeat and a divided Republican Party, Reagan showed up in Kansas City a wounded man. He believed that perhaps the chance to be president had passed him by.

Conservative Republicans had largely lined up behind Reagan, whereas moderates and liberals were supporting Ford. There was talk of unity in the air, an effort to unite the party to take on the

Democrats in November. "Take the VP spot," Reagan's family and aides advised him. "You may never get another chance like this." But Reagan wasn't interested in being Ford's vice president. And besides, Ford wasn't offering it.[16]

As Reagan watched the convention proceedings on television from his hotel suite, his son Michael joined him on the sofa. They watched together, and then father turned to son. "You know, Michael, what I really wanted was to get the presidential nomination and then win the presidency in November because I was looking forward to negotiating the SALT Treaty with Brezhnev. It has been a long time since an American president has stood up to the Soviet Union. It seems that every time we get into negotiations, the Soviets are telling us what we are going to have to give up in order for us to get along with them, and we forget who we are. I wanted to become president of the United States so I could sit down with Brezhnev. And I was going to let him pick out the size of the table, and I was going to listen to him tell me, the American president, what we were going to have to give up. And I was going to listen to him for maybe twenty minutes, and then I was going to get up from my side of the table, walk around to the other side, and lean over and whisper in his ear, 'Nyet.' It's been a long time since they've heard 'nyet' from an American president."[17]

CHAPTER IX

NOT ENOUGH STATURE

RESIDENT GERALD FORD LIMPED INTO THE 1976 GENERAL election after his bruising primary battle with Reagan. Burdened by the weight of Watergate, his pardon of Nixon, and a divided Republican Party, he faced former governor of Georgia Jimmy Carter. Despite Reagan's endorsement of Ford, the conservative wing of the party was less than enthusiastic about Ford's candidacy.

As he traveled the country—Los Angeles, Houston, Indianapolis, Minneapolis—Ford promised a resolute administration. Carter, with his call for a more open government, was a decent man, Ford declared, but he was not really prepared to be president. When it came to matters of war and peace in particular, better to leave it in competent hands.

As the race entered the final stretch in early fall, polls indicated that it was very tight. The candidates gathered for the presidential debate, where every word might make the difference between victory and defeat. But attention quickly turned to the Cold War when Max Frankel, the acerbic and feisty editor of the *New York Times*, asked a question about the recently concluded Helsinki Accords.

Reagan had been critical of the accords in the primary, and

Frankel was concerned, too. Weren't they a tacit acceptance of Russian dominance of Eastern Europe? he asked.

"It just isn't true," the President responded sternly. "There is no Soviet dominance of Eastern Europe, and there never will be under a Ford administration."

Frankel, like almost everyone else in the room, was visibly shocked by what Ford said. Thinking that the President had misunderstood the question, Frankel asked a follow-up so Ford could correct himself. "Did I understand you to say, sir, that the Russians are not using Eastern Europe as their own sphere of influence and occupying most of the countries there and making sure with their troops that it is a communist zone?"

Instead of modifying what he had said, however, Ford pressed on. "I don't believe that the Yugoslavians consider themselves dominated by the Soviet Union. I don't believe that the Romanians consider themselves dominated by the Soviet Union. I don't believe the Poles consider themselves dominated by the Soviet Union. . . ."

Ford's words seemed to hang in the air as everyone sat and listened in disbelief. Later Ford would explain that this was a simple slip of the tongue. But the damage was done; it may very well have cost him the election. And the statement seemed to be more than a slip of the tongue, at least according to what some in the Ford administration were saying. Kissinger, who was now Ford's secretary of state, had made clear in his meetings with Soviet ambassador Dobrynin that he was willing to accept the Soviets' dominance of Eastern Europe and even avoid criticizing them over it. And in April 1976, State Department counselor Helmut Sonnenfeldt, at a private conference of American ambassadors, declared that "an organic relationship" existed between the Soviet Union and Eastern Europe. The implication of his comments, which were quickly dubbed the "Sonnenfeldt Doctrine," was that the United States needed to accept Soviet dominance in the region and not seek to change it.[1]

After Ford's verbal slip during the debates, the Carter camp became increasingly confident about their chances of winning the election. Carter had made a point of campaigning against what he called the "Nixon-Kissinger-Ford" foreign policy, which he said was "covert, manipulative, and deceptive in style." But with the prospect of victory looming, Carter was not going to take any chances.

In September 1976, Carter sent a secret emissary to Moscow. Averell Harriman was one of the grand old wise men of American Cold War policy. He had been secretary of defense and ambassador to the Soviet Union. What he said, particularly in private, was weighed heavily by Soviet leaders.

According to Georgii Kornienko, first deputy foreign minister at the time, Harriman "gave assurances that if elected president he [Carter] would take steps toward the rapid conclusion and signing of the SALT II Treaty, and then would be ready to continue negotiations on an agreement on substantial reductions in strategic weapons." Harriman was there to tell Moscow that Carter would be easy to deal with. In short, don't do or say anything that might help Ford win.

Soviet leaders listened politely and liked what they heard from Harriman. They had been watching the election closely. And while they welcomed Ford's embrace of détente, they believed that Carter might be willing to go further. "Many of his statements influenced the mood of the Soviet leadership," Kornienko later recalled.

The Kremlin sat on its hands in the fall of 1976, waiting to see the outcome. A Ford victory meant continued détente. A Carter win offered the promise of more. As Kornienko put it, "There were no regrets in Moscow over Ford's defeat and Carter's victory."[2]

At KGB headquarters, Yuri Andropov watched the election results with particular interest. As the election campaign had heated up, the KGB had managed to recruit a Democratic Party activist with direct access to senior levels of the Carter camp. The new agent, who passed political intelligence along to the Second Chief Directorate of the KGB, had a wide circle of influential contacts, including Senators Alan Cranston, Eugene McCarthy, Edward Kennedy, Abraham Ribicoff, and J. William Fulbright.

It was the best source the KGB has ever been known to tap inside a presidential campaign. The agent provided valuable inside information on the campaign strategy and offered a detailed profile of Carter himself. On one occasion the agent apparently spent three hours with Carter, Governor Brown of California, and Senator

Cranston discussing the election in the candidate's room at the Pacific Hotel in California. According to the KGB report sent to the Politburo, the agent had "direct and prolonged conversations" with Carter. After Carter won in November, KGB chief Andropov forwarded his reports to all the members of the Politburo.

But Andropov had more in mind than simply collecting intelligence. He wanted an agent of influence who could push Moscow's agenda within the administration. To accomplish that task, he turned to a disarmingly friendly academic named Georgi Arbatov. Arbatov was head of the Moscow Institute of United States and Canada and a KGB agent code-named VASILI. With his urbane charm and ostensible academic credentials, Arbatov was able to cultivate relationships with Western academics and intellectuals interested in international politics. Former Swedish prime minister Olaf Palme had put him on his international peace commission. Now, with Carter's victory in the election, one of Arbatov's contacts seemed particularly promising.

During his many trips to the United States, Arbatov had formed a warm relationship with Cyrus Vance, former undersecretary of defense in the Johnson administration. Vance had impressed Arbatov with his intellect and his apparent interest in fostering closer relationships with the Soviet Union. The KGB gave Vance the code name VIZIR and began cultivating him as a possible agent. KGB files note that during a spring 1973 visit to Moscow, Vance had told Arbatov of the need to "increase the level of mutual trust" in U.S.-Soviet relations and strongly criticized Nixon as being too hawkish. In 1976, Vance and Arbatov had dinner in New York, where the conversation took on a similar tone. Months later, when Vance was tapped by Carter to serve as secretary of state, the KGB was enormously pleased.

Arbatov continued to develop this friendship, but the special relationship Moscow had hoped for never materialized. The Soviets did, however, try to support Vance within the administration.[3]

As Carter formed his national security team in 1977, it became apparent that two camps were emerging. Vance, as secretary of state, was strongly in favor of warmer relations with Moscow and building on détente. But for his national security adviser, Carter tapped Zbigniew Brzezinski, a hawkish academic who had concerns about the Soviet threat. In some respects, it was personal for Brzezinski: As a Pole, he had firsthand experience with the terrors of Soviet power.

The Kremlin knew about this divide within the administration. "From the military-strategic point of view, there are two policy links in the USA leadership now: the line of the National Security Council, and the line of the State Department," noted one top-secret Soviet report.[4] Although Arbatov had never been able to recruit Vance, the Soviets wanted to do what they could to support him. Brzezinski, with his suspicions about communism, was "a cunning devil," Cuban leader Fidel Castro told East German leader Erich Honecker during secret consultations. The divide within the administration was something "we have to exploit."[5]

To support Vance and a softer line in the Carter administration, Service A of the KGB set out to end Brzezinski's influence by seeking his dismissal. An active-measure operation code-named MUREN was launched, designed to discredit him. The KGB's Service A drafted bogus reports claiming that Brzezinski was an anti-Semite, and intelligence agents searched for compromising material on his relationships with his deputy, David Aron, his special assistant Karl Inderfurth, and Ambassador Richard Gardner. The agents found nothing, but they did their best to undermine Brzezinski by spreading rumors.

★   ★   ★

CARTER'S STRONGEST CRITICISM OF FORD AND KISSINGER HAD been their lack of moralism in foreign affairs. Kissinger had advanced détente because it helped maintain the global balance of power. Carter saw it instead as an opportunity to rid American foreign policy of its emphasis on power politics. For too long, America had subscribed to the idea that military might and power could solve problems.

Shortly after he became president, Carter traveled to the University of Notre Dame to deliver an address on his vision for America. The country was still suffering a hangover from losing in Vietnam. But Carter saw defeat as something therapeutic. It would show us that power and military might were not the answer to the world's problems. "Through failure we have found our way to our own values," he declared. Far from being the noble cause that Ronald Reagan thought it was, the Vietnam War was for Carter a profound mistake, the result of "our inordinate fear of communism."

The threat was not communism, said Carter. Instead, American values in the world needed to be focused on human rights. What Carter actually meant by "human rights" was spelled out by Cyrus Vance in an April 1977. There were three kinds of human rights that particularly mattered: brutality toward individuals, economic rights, and broad political liberties like freedom of speech. Of these three, broad political liberties would receive the least emphasis, said Vance. After all, he declared, "we have no wish to tell other nations what political or social system they should have."

Carter and many of his top advisers, like Cyrus Vance, seemed plagued by a profound sense of guilt over the Vietnam War. Unlike Reagan, who had been critical of Johnson's execution of the war, Carter and Vance had been strong supporters. Vance had been a deputy to Defense Secretary McNamara when the disastrous policy had first been laid out. Carter had also staunchly backed the conduct of the war. While governor he had firmly defended Lt. William Calley, the officer in command during the My Lai massacre, and asked Georgia residents to turn on their headlights as a form of protest when he was brought up on charges.

Now in the White House, Carter and Vance came to believe that often the blame for the violation of human rights around the globe lay with the United States and her allies. Countries such as Argentina, Chile, Nicaragua, and El Salvador soon found economic and military assistance cut back or eliminated altogether. These countries were run by "retrogressive Fascists," said the administration's coordinator for human rights. At the United Nations, Carter-appointed ambassador Andrew Young blasted America's Cold War policies for fostering "an apparatus of repression" and "imperialism, neocolonialism, capitalism, or what-have-you." All presidents before Carter were racist, Young allegedly said. And America's closest ally, Great Britain, "practically invented racism."

Carter was promising to check any evil that might come from

the U.S. government. In words that no doubt created anxiety and paralysis in Washington, he declared, "If the CIA ever makes a mistake, I'll be the one, as president, to call a press conference and I'll tell you and the American people, 'this is what happened, these are the people who violated the law, this is the punishment I recommend, this is the corrective action that needs to be taken,' and I promise you it won't happen again."[6]

Carter was promising to talk tough and to be tough, if necessary, with human rights violators. But while he enthusiastically pursued American allies, his passion evaporated when it came to dealing with the Soviet bloc.

In September 1977, Soviet Foreign Minister Andrei Gromyko arrived in the White House for private consultations with Carter. After exchanging pleasantries, the two sat down to talk about the superpower relationship. They discussed the ongoing SALT II treaties and events in Africa. But according to secret Soviet transcripts of the meeting, Carter never mentioned human rights abuses in the Soviet Union. He asked Gromyko to free several individual dissidents who were languishing in Soviet prisons. But as he did so, he went to great lengths to assure Gromyko that "we do not want to interfere in the domestic affairs of any state or put you in an awkward position." His crusade for human rights did not really extend to the Soviet Union, Carter candidly told his guest. Above all, he was concerned about human rights "in our hemisphere."[7]

Three months later, when Polish communist boss Edward Giereck was ushered into the Oval Office, Carter went even further. In this conversation, Carter actually "expressed appreciation for Poland's support for the Helsinki Agreement and its commitment to human rights," according to the classified White House transcript of the meeting.[8] Carter offered no criticism of the Polish government's human rights record whatsoever, despite the fact that one month earlier the Polish secret police had attacked thousands of workers protesting food price increases. Four people had been killed in the melee, and hundreds of others were arrested and savagely beaten in prison.

The situation was so bad that while the State Department was criticizing American allies, some were making creative excuses for communist regimes. Roberta Cohen, Carter's deputy assistant secretary of state for human rights, remembers that some State Department "desk officers argued that writing up the Berlin Wall as an economic development measure in the human rights reports would prove more palatable to the East German government."[9]

Carter did boldly campaign on behalf of individual dissidents, something Nixon and Ford had failed to do. Dissidents such as Vladimir Bukovsky personally benefited from the Carter administration's tireless efforts to secure their release. But even these limited efforts worried Carter, who feared that Leonid Brezhnev might take them the wrong way. As he wrote in his personal diary: "It's important that he [Brezhnev] understand the commitment I have to human rights first of all and that it is not an antagonistic attitude of mine toward the Soviet Union."

★   ★   ★

AS BRZEZINSKI TOOK UP HIS POST AS NATIONAL SECURITY ADviser, a pessimistic intelligence report crossed his desk. A National Intelligence Estimate (NIE) done by the CIA warned that "direct comparison between the USSR and its major opponents shows the USSR in increasingly favorable positions." Moscow had been heavily investing in its military for more than a decade and it was optimistic about the future. "The Soviets still see basic trends in the world as positive for themselves and negative for the United States."[10]

As if to underscore that point, the Kremlin was asserting itself around the globe, testing American ships with aggressive maneuvers. In the Mediterranean, Soviet destroyers and frigates repeatedly trained their gun turrets on passing P-3 Orion reconnaissance aircraft and helicopters. By May 1977, the U.S. Navy had accused Moscow of twenty-four provocative acts. Most of the complaints centered around the Soviets' directing weapons and fire-control radar at U.S. ships and aircraft.[11]

Brzezinski was himself concerned about Moscow's ambitions and asked for a detailed report on the Soviet military buildup. When the report came back, it confirmed his worst fears. Moscow had spent 75 percent more on its intercontinental nuclear attack programs than the United States had over the past five years. The trend was expected to continue.[12]

Carter inherited a weakened defense base that had been in a steady state of decline for nearly a decade. In the eight years prior to his becoming president, the defense budget had declined 35 percent in real dollars. But despite the gloomy intelligence assessments and Moscow's assertiveness at sea, Carter continued cutting back on defense. One of his first acts as president was to slash the budget by another six billion dollars. By the middle of Carter's term, the U.S. defense budget was 20 percent lower than it had been in 1964, prior to the heavy commitment in Vietnam. Especially hard hit was procurement. The Pentagon was compelled to limp along at about 75 percent of what it needed.[13]

The consequences of the budget shortfall were real. The U.S. Navy had less than a week's supply of most major defensive missiles and torpedoes. In spare parts for both aircraft and ships, there was only a third of the minimum requirement. In the submarine service, where President Carter had served his country, men were retiring in record numbers. The budget cuts caused strained maintenance schedules and an unprecedented spate of accidents. On September 20, 1977, the USS *Ray*, with navigation equipment in need of repair and a young crew, drifted fourteen miles off course and smashed into a coral reef off Sicily. In all there were fourteen major submarine accidents in the Atlantic submarine fleet that year—so many that the fleet's admiral had to send out a cautionary note.[14]

Shortly after Carter delivered his speech decrying America's "inordinate fear of communism," Soviet Politburo member Boris Ponomarev made a visit to Washington. Ponomarev was the chief ideologist of the Politburo, stiff, doctrinaire, but also charming in a strange sort of way. Ponomarev made the rounds with several members of the administration and members of Congress. Before he left, he was ushered into the White House for a face-to-face meeting with Carter. The two men sat down in the Oval Office and over the next hour engaged in a lively discussion about arms control, human rights, and the third world.

Ponomarev's purpose in coming to Washington had been to size up the President. He arrived back in Moscow with strong opinions about the United States and Carter. "The prestige of the USA Administration is lower than ever before due to Watergate and Vietnam," he confided to East German party officials in a secret meeting. "And Carter has not shown enough stature."[15]

Fifteen years earlier in Vienna, Nikita Khrushchev had sized up President Kennedy and calculated that he was "too liberal to fight." That assessment had led to the installation of missiles in Cuba. Now the Kremlin was coming to the conclusion that it had another green light, and it quickly moved to advance its position in the developing world.

One of the most promising opportunities for the Soviets was the strategic choke point of the Red Sea. In early February 1977, shortly after the United States announced that it was cutting off aid to Ethiopia, Ethiopian leader Mengistu Haile Mariam met with the ambassador of Cuba, Jose Peres Novoa, and declared that he intended to "follow Cuba's example." He was tired of dealing with the Americans and wanted to join the winning side. To follow Cuba, however, he needed the "necessary quantity of weapons" to hold on to power. The request was relayed to Moscow, which quickly complied by sending Soviet advisers.

These were Brezhnev's "internationalists," and they dressed in Ethiopian uniforms without rank or insignia. In all, 11,000 Soviet internationalists served in Ethiopia, and they proved decisive in maintaining Mengistu's hold on power. Tens of thousands of Cuban troops soon joined them.[16]

The Carter administration watched as the country fell into the Soviet orbit. An official from the National Security Council was dispatched to discuss the situation. But the message he delivered was tepid at best. The United States did not "oppose the socialist choice of new Ethiopia," he told officials. And when he met secretly with Soviet representatives in Addis Ababa, he wondered how the United States could keep its influence in the region in a way that would "not be counter to the interests of the Soviet Union."[17]

Ponomarev got the same impression during his meeting with Carter. As he told his colleagues, Carter "*pretended* to be concerned about Soviet arms deliveries in Ethiopia."[18]

When war broke out between Ethiopia and neighboring Somalia over a bitter land dispute, Moscow jumped in quickly. Over a three-month period in late 1977, 225 Soviet transport aircraft ferried arms, troops, and war matériel to Ethiopia, landing on average every twenty minutes. Cuban troops took up their positions and were launched into battle. To secure victory, according to a secret Soviet Foreign Ministry report, Cuban soldiers "were used in the main lines of attack."[19]

As the Soviets and Cubans moved in, Secretary of State Cyrus Vance declared that to "oppose Soviet or Cuban involvement in Africa would be futile." Instead, we needed to accept the new realities in the region, because "the fact is that we can no more stop change than Canute could still the waters."

Brzezinski, although he was more suspicious of Moscow, nevertheless held the view that revolutionary change in Africa was inevitable. "The world is changing under the influence of forces no government can control," he declared. Vietnam had been "the Waterloo of the WASP elite," he added grimly. We should never again make the mistake of intervening in a third world battle zone.[20]

★   ★   ★

THE SITUATION WAS HARDLY BETTER ELSEWHERE IN THE WORLD. While Carter insisted that America need not fear communism, the Kremlin and its allies continued to make impressive gains. A pro-Moscow faction took power in Yemen, a small nation on the tip of the Arabian peninsula. In Southeast Asia, Vietnam, Laos, and Cambodia had all fallen. In the Caribbean, the Cuban-backed New Jewel Movement had taken power in Grenada. Moscow was also pursuing ambitious plans in Latin America.

In Nicaragua, a guerrilla army known as the Sandinista National Liberation Front (FSLN) had been waging a decades-old war against the dictatorship in that country. To many in the West, these were merely frustrated democrats who were tired of trying to peaceably oust Somoza. But Moscow viewed the Sandinista movement as a powerful ally. FSLN founder Carlos Fonseca Amador was not a frustrated democrat but "a trusted agent," according to KGB files, who received considerable financial support and weapons from both Moscow and Havana. Support had begun to flow back in 1966, and the Sandinistas were considered so loyal to the cause that KGB officers had remarkable plans for the group. The KGB organized members into secret sabotage and intelligence groups that could be stationed on the U.S.-Mexican border—in towns like Ciudad Juárez, Tijuana, and Ensenda—to strike targets in the United States.

The strike team leader was a young revolutionary named Manuel Ramon de Jesus Anara y Ubeda (code-named PRIM), who spent considerable time in Moscow learning sabotage tactics and the use of explosives. When he returned to Mexico, he came equipped with a detailed target list. The team was expected to cross the border to attack U.S. military bases, missile sites, and the oil pipeline that ran from El Paso, Texas, to Costa Mesa, California.[21]

The Sandinistas took orders from Havana, and they would target American diplomats when ordered to do so. On the night of December 27, 1974, U.S. Ambassador to Nicaragua Turner Shelton was at a Managua dinner party given by the former minister of agriculture, Jose Maria Chema Castillo. It was a regal event, with plenty of music and drink. Shelton, however, ended up leaving early; he had business to attend to back at the embassy. This bit of extra work was fortuitous for Shelton: Moments after he left, a team of thirteen members of the Sandinista National Liberation Front (FSLN) stormed the mansion.

The plan was to kidnap Shelton and hold him for ransom. Frustrated that Shelton was gone, the FSLN team instead shot Castillo and held the other guests as hostages. After hours of negotiation, they struck a bargain with the Somoza government. In exchange for freeing the hostages, the Sandinistas received a million-dollar ransom and a plane ride to Cuba. According to KGB files, the attack had been supported by the Cuban intelligence service (DGI) and sanctioned personally by Fidel Castro himself.

Deprived of military aid by the Carter administration, the corrupt Somoza government struggled to deal with the mounting insurgency. At the same time, Moscow began secretly supporting leftist insurgencies in El Salvador and training guerrillas from Uruguay, Argentina, and Panama. According to secret directives, the Kremlin had big plans for the region.[22]

★ ★ ★

A S THEY WERE DOING IN AFRICA, THE CARTER ADMINISTRATION tried to accommodate their enemies in Latin America. After suspending aid to several Latin American allies for human rights violations, Carter began a secret dialogue with Fidel Castro. There were high hopes that this sort of diplomacy could solve a variety of regional problems. But where Carter saw good faith, Castro saw weakness.

In a confidential Cuban intelligence report, officials noted that "the process of relaxation in Cuban-American relations" had been initiated by Carter and pushed "by an influential group of individuals in his close circle," including Andrew Young, George McGovern, and others. (The report made a point of mentioning the claim that "the son of Senator McGovern is currently enrolled at the University of Havana.")

Cuba now had tens of thousands of troops fighting in Africa, but the intelligence reports noted that in the secret discussions the Carter administration didn't really raise the subject.[23]

Fidel Castro relished these U.S. attempts at diplomacy as evidence that America was weak. After all, he told the Soviet ambassador in Havana, the Americans were reeling from "a series of crippling defeats suffered by American imperialism in the Western hemisphere." In Castro's mind, the most important defeats for American imperialism had been in Nicaragua and Grenada.[24]

★   ★   ★

F OLLOWING THE 1976 CAMPAIGN, RONALD REAGAN'S LIFE FELL into a steady rhythm that seemed both familiar and comfortable. He and Nancy were financially secure, and despite his loss to Ford in the primary, he had not fallen into a funk. Instead his life seemed much as it was when he was working for General Electric. He had financial security and the freedom to study and speak out on the issues he cared most about.

Gone were the resources Reagan had known in Sacramento. Instead of a large staff and an expansive office, he spent much of his time working in his Pacific Palisades home or at the Rancho Del Cielo (literally, "Ranch in the Sky"). The ranch was his favorite place to spend time, and he would drive up the narrow, winding road into the Santa Ynez Mountains to work on the small nineteenth-century ranch house or to clear brush from the ranch's more than six hundred acres. Reagan found that riding his horses on the trails that lined the ranch was particularly helpful when it came to sorting out difficult issues.

For the first time in more than ten years, he was not serving in public office or running for election. But he maintained a vigorous schedule, speaking to audiences around the country, meeting with visitors, and reaching thousands with a weekly radio commentary.

The radio commentaries were a natural for Reagan, something that he had dreamed up as a way to stay in touch with his supporters and get his message out. He had been in radio back in Iowa during the 1930s, and he knew how with the right tone of voice and the right choice of words a radio personality could develop an intimacy with the audience. As a result, he himself wrote many of the scripts he read. Sitting in his study with a black pen and a yellow notepad, surrounded by stacks of fraying newspaper clippings, reports, and books sent to him by friends and supporters, he would compose a script on the most pressing issue of the day. It was by no means a sophisticated operation. He seemed guided by instinct more than anything else, but he proved to be remarkably adept at crystallizing the core issues.

When the federal government declassified NSC-68, the Truman administration's secret document concerning Cold War strategy, Reagan read it and analyzed it over the course of two radio broadcasts. "We must realize that the Cold War is a real war and the survival of the free world is at stake," he warned. He also read the impassioned speeches of Aleksandr Solzhenitsyn, the Russian Nobel Laureate who was warning about the moral disarmament of the West, and reports on the Soviet threat written by James Angleton, the former chief of counterintelligence for the CIA.

A group of concerned individuals had formed the Committee for the Present Danger (CPD) in November 1976. This was an odd assortment of New Deal Democrats, conservative Republicans, New York intellectuals, old-line labor leaders, and retired military officers who believed America was in danger of losing the Cold War. One of the cofounders of the group was Richard Allen, a former Nixon national security adviser who had left that administration disillusioned. Allen had gotten to know Reagan, and soon Reagan was receiving all of the organization's publications. Many CPD members were concerned about throw weights on ICBMs, the accuracy of SLBMs, and other minutiae of the strategic balance. Reagan took some interest in these issues, but he remained focused on larger questions. Richard Allen recalls sitting down to talk with Reagan in 1978 about the SALT treaty and arms control. "My idea of American policy toward the Soviet Union is simple, and some would say simplistic," Reagan told him, leaning back in his chair. "It is this: We win and they lose. What do you think of that?"

The story would seem unbelievable except for the fact that Reagan had been calling for victory in the Cold War ever since the 1950s.[25]

Reagan took a keen interest in the committee's work. This was his introduction to the burgeoning neoconservative movement. In 1979, Reagan would be asked to join the group's board, and dozens of CPD members would come to serve in his administration.

In his radio commentaries Reagan was remarkably adroit at discerning precisely what the Soviet Union was up to. In July 1978, he penned a commentary that completely captured Brezhnev's secret 1969 decision at Yalta to strive for strategic superiority over the United States. (He even got the date right.) In November 1978, he wryly noted that Moscow was concentrating its arms control negotiating strategy on limiting American technological advances while giving itself an advantage in the areas it favored. In doing so he was perfectly describing the secret strategy General Detinov was seeking to carry out—namely, using arms control to gain superiority.[26]

Reagan watched with grave concern as Carter unfolded his foreign policy. In Africa, said Reagan, "we blustered and made demands unbacked by action," leading to Soviet victories in Angola and Ethiopia. Carter's human rights policy was a disaster, Reagan said: You were better off violating human rights and being America's enemy than violating human rights and being her friend. "We continue to seek friendship with the rulers in the Kremlin, selling them our technology and our wheat," he said. "We even lend them the money so they can buy more."

But Reagan was more than a critic crying out against his political opponents in Washington. He clung stubbornly to the ideas he had developed in the 1950s for defeating Moscow.

The Soviet Union was no colossus, Reagan said. It was weak and vulnerable. He noted with interest the reports of discontent in the Soviet Union, seeing the Russian people as a potential ally. "The Soviet Union is building the most massive military machine the world has ever seen and is denying its people all kinds of consumer products to do it," he said into the studio microphone. "We could have an unexpected ally if citizen Ivan is becoming discontented enough to start talking back."

Reagan was also heartened by the actions of Soviet dissidents, who were showing real courage, perhaps the human quality that he admired most. Dissidents were not "skulking in alleys and basements trying to create an underground movement," Reagan wrote in one script. "They are speaking out openly, citing their rights under the Soviet Constitution. . . . Sixty years of unceasing propaganda has not made the people a docile mass of willing slaves." In their example he saw a lesson and the seeds of a strategy for the West. Instead of trying to warm relations with the Kremlin, concentrate on the Soviet people, Reagan advised. "Let our State Department take heed—a little less détente with the politburo and more encouragement to the dissenters might be worth a lot of armored divisions."[27]

Reagan watched with great interest when Pope John Paul II returned to visit his homeland of Poland in 1979. Reagan knew full well the charisma of a pontiff: He had met Pope Paul VI during a visit to Europe in 1972. But John Paul II seemed to have a particular hold on him, perhaps because this pope had grown up under communism and had retained his Catholic faith. Richard Allen was sitting with Reagan in his living room when television reports showed John Paul being greeted by hundreds of thousands of young Poles. Reagan was entranced by what he saw, and tears welled up in his eyes. Later he retreated to his study and penned another commentary. "Now with the eyes of all the world on them they have looked past those menacing weapons and listened to the voice of one man who has told them there is a God and it is their inalienable right to freely worship that God. Will the Kremlin ever be the same again? Will any of us for that matter?"

In 1978, Reagan took two trips overseas. In early April, he

traveled with Richard Allen to Japan, Taiwan, and Hong Kong. Six months later, they were off to Europe. First they went to Great Britain for meetings with Margaret Thatcher and Winston Churchill II, then on to France and Germany. The most poignant part of the trip, however, was not in his meetings with these leaders. Instead, it came as they neared the Berlin Wall. Allen could see Reagan's countenance darken with each approaching step.

They entered East Berlin through Checkpoint Charlie and proceeded to a department store to look around. "As we departed," recalls Allen, "we stood on the platz, observing the silent shuffling of the people passing by—no merriment, not much talking, very drab. At that moment a pair of Volskpolitsen ["People's Police"] sauntered past and within thirty feet of us stopped a citizen carrying shopping bags, forcing him to drop them on the spot and show his papers. One officer poked him with the muzzle of an AK-47 and the other probed through the bags with his gun."[28]

It was a vivid reminder of the brutality of communism.

As Reagan watched the episode, someone was secretly watching him. The East German secret police had been following him ever since they had crossed through Checkpoint Charlie. There were agents on the street and an unmarked car watching his every move. An eight-page dossier, including six photographs of the visit, was assembled and put in his file.[29]

CHAPTER X

EXPLOSIONS

O N A HOT JULY NIGHT IN 1979, THOUSANDS OF PEOPLE adorned in revolutionary red-and-black colors were dancing and singing in Managua, Nicaragua's central plaza. They were celebrating the demise of the country's dictator, Anastasio Somoza, and the arrival of the Sandinistas.

For close to twenty years, the FSLN had been conducting a war against Somoza, so their triumph was not a complete surprise. Less than a year earlier, the Sandinistas had demonstrated their strength and resolve when twenty-four men had stormed the national palace in Managua in a daring raid. There had been bombings, assassinations, and military strikes ever since. But it was the Carter administration that gave Somoza a shove: Aid was cut off, and with the support of other Latin American governments, Washington had formally called for his removal from power. A broad coalition government, including the Sandinistas, should take Somoza's place, Carter said.

Ronald Reagan, watching events from California, was horrified by the inclusion of the Sandinistas. They "bear a Cuban label," he warned three months before they came to power. "There is no question but that the rebels are Cuban trained, Cuban armed and dedicated to creating another communist country in this hemisphere."

But Carter and his administration saw it otherwise. The "evolutionary change" in Nicaragua was not a result of "Cuban machinations," Carter said reassuringly. Instead, this was an effort to "let the people of Nicaragua choose their own form of government."[1]

Reagan and other critics misunderstood the Sandinistas, the State Department said. The Sandinistas were committed to democracy. If they appeared pro-Soviet, it was because Somoza had "radicalized the opposition." Deputy Secretary of State Warren Christopher appeared before the Senate Foreign Relations Committee to say the Sandinistas were going to build "a new Nicaragua through popular participation that is capable of meeting basic human needs." As a vote of confidence in the new government, Carter pushed through a $75 million aid package.[2]

Back at KGB headquarters in Moscow, there was elation that nearly matched the euphoria of the celebration in Managua's central plaza. KGB general Nikolai Leonov had boldly predicted the Sandinistas' success months earlier and now reveled at the first revolutionary victory in the Americas. The KGB had been steady sponsors of the Sandinistas since 1966, offering training and financial support. Now Leonov was thinking of how to help them consolidate their hold on power and how to use the country as a springboard for further revolutionary gains.

Doing so, however, would require a deft hand. The true nature of the revolution needed to be concealed. There would be no open declaration of a communist revolution; that would set off alarm bells in Washington and the rest of Latin America. Instead the Communists would proceed quietly with their plans. As a secret communiqué from the International Department of the Communist Party put it: "The FSLN is the ruling political organization. The leadership of the FSLN considers it essential to establish a Marxist-Leninist Party on the basis of the front, with the aim of building socialism in Nicaragua. At present, for tactical reasons and in view of the existing political situation in the Central American region, the leadership of the FSLN prefers to make no public statements about this ultimate goal."[3]

Days after the celebration on Managua's central plaza, the new Sandinista Interior Minister, Tomas Borge, received a visit from a colonel in the East German secret police. "Fielder," as Stasi files identify the colonel, arrived with a folder full of secret documents, including terms for a secret intelligence-sharing agreement. Borge was a longtime rebel leader, trained behind the Iron Curtain, with responsibility for consolidating the revolution. He needed advice on how to deal with domestic enemies of the revolution, and no one was better at establishing a secret police than the East Germans.

In exchange for their help, Borge was willing to allow both the Stasi and the KGB to establish an intelligence post in his country. There were secrets to be gleaned in Central America and the region was ripe for revolutionary expansion.

Thus began a close collaboration between the Sandinistas and the Soviet bloc. Less than a year later, Borge and two of his aides, Hugo Torres and Marcos Somariba, visited the capitals of several Soviet-bloc states—Moscow, Prague, Sofia, and East Berlin—to solidify those ties.

They went first to Moscow, to pay their respects to KGB Major General Yakov Medyanik, deputy chief of the First Main Directorate. On April 1, 1980, they traveled to East Berlin and were ushered into the office of Interior Minister Erich Mielke, who had effectively built the East German police state. Stern and colorless, Mielke knew about the necessity of brutality: He had shot a policeman in his youth and engaged in street fighting against anti-Communists.

Mielke assembled a team of Stasi experts to advise his Nicaraguan guests, Major Generals Horst Janicke, deputy chief of foreign espionage, and Wili Dam, chief of the Stasi Tenth Department. They greeted their Latin comrades and briefed them on how to handle dissidents. Lt.-Col. Horst Scheel then arrived to talk about how revolution could be spread to the rest of Central America.

Mielke sat through all of these meetings and was particularly adamant on the need for the Sandinistas to lock up their domestic enemies. According to the Stasi transcript of the meeting, he said they needed to pay particular attention to "strengthening and solidifying the organs of power, particularly the state security organs."

Borge heartily agreed. "Repressive measures have already been taken," he explained.

Mielke was clearly impressed by what he heard from Borge. One month later, he convened a special meeting in Berlin with KGB chief Yuri Andropov to assess the situation. Janicke was there, along with KGB General Medyanik. The Czechs, Bulgarians, and Cubans also had representatives on hand.

"Since we know that Lenin's words about the difficulties of defending a revolution have been confirmed many times, we all have the obligation of defending a revolution, we all have the obligation to do our share for strengthening and securing the revolution in Nicaragua," said Mielke.

The Czechs and the Bulgarians pointed out that they had already sent some 1,500 submachine guns, 50 light machine guns, and 12,000 pistols to Managua, along with more than two million rounds of ammunition. Medyanik praised them for their efforts but concluded that more needed to be done. They needed training in intelligence and help with their subversive operations against other countries. This was the sort of help only the KGB and the Stasi could provide.

What did Moscow have in mind? asked one representative.

Medyanik introduced a Colonel Kolomyakov, who was chief of the KGB Latin American section, foreign espionage directorate. Kolomyakov explained that the plan was to ship arms, uniforms, and other equipment that guerrillas in the region could use. The meeting closed with Mielke urging everyone to stand vigilantly with their new Central American ally.[4]

★ ★ ★

NICARAGUA WAS NOT THE ONLY GAIN IN THE AMERICAS THAT excited Soviet-bloc leaders. In March 1979, a charismatic and dynamic young leader named Maurice Bishop seized power on the tiny Caribbean island of Grenada. Bishop was a committed Marxist who had a close personal relationship with Fidel Castro, having met him several times over the course of his political career. Bishop put General Hudson Austin, a trusted comrade from the New Jewel Movement, in charge of the armed forces, and Austin immediately went about integrating Grenada's small military and intelligence service with the Soviet bloc, just as Borge was doing. Grenada was strategically located in the Caribbean and was a good transit point between Cuba and Latin America. KGB head Yuri Andropov was all too willing to help. Thank you "once again for the tremendous assistance which our armed forces have received from your Party and Government," Austin wrote him after one shipment of arms.[5]

The CIA was well aware of the Cuban connection to Maurice Bishop. In a classified report issued a few months after the revolution, the CIA noted: "Prime Minister Maurice Bishop is now heavily indebted to Havana for the reported shipment of enough rifles, revolvers, and light machine guns to equip up to 2,000 troops; an unknown quantity of heavy machine guns; and four antiaircraft guns."[6] Senior Carter administration officials read the report but did nothing, believing that Bishop was more of a nationalist than a Marxist.

★ ★ ★

SUCCESS IN NICARAGUA AND GRENADA ADDED TO THE WAVE OF optimism that was running through the Soviet bloc from Moscow to Managua. Fidel Castro, who had played a significant role in both revolutionary successes, was particularly buoyant when he met secretly with East German leader Erich Honecker. Two men could not have been more dissimilar: Castro the fiery orator and guerrilla leader, and Honecker the typical party hack who had worked his way through the communist bureaucracy. But they shared a commitment to the communist cause, and each seemed slightly amused by the other.

"For thirty years, we have been isolated, on our own, [and] now there are already three of us in the region: Grenada, Nicaragua, and Cuba," Castro told Honecker. "Grenada has important implications in the Caribbean, where there is instability after the success of revolution in Nicaragua."

Honecker agreed that revolutionary gains in the region were a critical turning point. Cuba "provides a stimulus for the anti-imperialist revolution in Latin America," he told Castro. "They [the Americans] had to swallow the fact that Cuba is revolutionary, but Nicaragua came as a great surprise to them. As we all know, events in Cuba did not fall out of the blue, and they felt that the Nicaraguan revolutionaries had the moral and material support of Cuba. Add to this the events in El Salvador. The USA imperialists have a strong interest that all is quiet in their 'backyard.' But there is a new revolutionary wave in Latin America."[7]

Castro shrewdly pointed out that now was the time to consolidate the revolutionary gains in the Western Hemisphere. Carter had backed himself into a corner with his talk about the "inordinate fear of communism." As for the communist gains in Nicaragua and Grenada, Carter wanted to avoid mentioning them—he felt they were an embarrassment.

"It is not in Carter's interest to raise this issue, because his political opponents could exploit it," Castro aide Jose Antonio Arbesu explained to the Soviet ambassador in Havana. "If Carter claims that Cuba interferes in Nicaraguan affairs, it would give a reason for his opponents to blame him for not giving the necessary support to Somoza; and this is not in his interest." More than anything, Carter needed to downplay the communist orientation of these revolutions.[8]

Castro was clearly enjoying what he considered evidence of America's impotence. He relished telling Honecker how he was toying with Carter, negotiating with him for better relations while supporting anti-American revolutions at the same time. He told the East German leader that at one point the United States had planned a military exercise near Guantanamo Bay, where there was still an American military base. The plan was foiled, Castro said, when he organized a mass protest to stop it.

"At this point they [the United States] proclaimed the suspension of the exercise," Castro explained with obvious glee. "The very same day! This is the first time that they set up something like this on such a big scale, and they have suspended it without any conditions."[9]

These were indeed heady times for Soviet-bloc leaders. The Americans had not only been kicked out of Vietnam, Castro told Honecker, but they had also been forced out of Iran. "It has become clear that détente, which has its primary basis in Europe, does the imperialist circles no good. . . . Détente eliminates the possibility of a global conflict, but at the same time eliminates the possibility of local conflicts and also the opportunities for repression and attacks on the liberation movement."

There had been seven conflicts in the developing world in which the Soviet bloc had substantially supported one side. In five of those conflicts they had won; the other two had yet to be resolved.

★ ★ ★

O N NOVEMBER 13, 1979, RONALD REAGAN WAS STANDING IN the ballroom of the New York Hilton Hotel. He was sixty-eight years old, his face generously covered with lines and creases, the sort you might find on worn saddle leather. In a voice that was steady and calm, almost a breathy whisper, but with words that were as uncompromising as ever, he announced his plans to run for president.

"I don't agree that our nation must resign itself to inevitable decline, yielding its proud position to other hands," he said. "I am unwilling to see this country fail in its obligation to itself and to the other free peoples of the world." He shifted at the podium and tilted his head in that familiar way. "Though we should leave no initiative untried in our pursuit of peace, we must be clear-voiced in our resolve *to resist any unpeaceful act wherever it may occur.* Negotiation with the Soviet Union must never become appeasement."[10]

Reagan began traveling the country in what many dismissed as a quixotic campaign. His message was considered too conservative for the times, his ideas so simplistic that they were laughable. But in expressing his ideas he vowed to go where no one else would. He talked about not simply containing the Soviet Union but reducing the size of the Soviet empire. "We have not helped those who want to be free of Soviet and Cuban domination," he said bluntly. And although Vietnam was still a tender wound in the American psyche, he raised the topic often and defended the effort to defeat the Communists in Southeast Asia as just. Far from an ugly chapter in American history, Vietnam was "in truth a collective act of moral courage." Any ugliness came from the failure of American leaders to seek victory. For his part, Reagan was determined never to commit that grievous error as president. "There will be no more Vietnams. Regardless of price or promise—be it oil from Arabia or an ambassador sitting in Peking—there will be no more abandonment of friends by the United States of America."[11]

★ ★ ★

I T WAS NIGHTFALL ON CHRISTMAS DAY, 1979, WHEN A MASSIVE SO-viet military aircraft touched down at Afghanistan's Kabul Airport, the first of many transports carrying hundreds of commandos. Next came aircraft carrying heavy weapons, equipment, vehicles, and armor. By daybreak, the equipment and troops had been hidden away in enormous hangars at the edge of the runway. Brezhnev's internationalists were now in place.

Two days later, a Soviet armored column with Afghan military insignias moved out of the airport in the direction of the presidential palace. It was led by Soviet commandos dressed in Afghan uniforms, members of the KGB's Special Operations Group dubbed "Department 8." In command was Colonel Boyarinov, a combat veteran who had been trained at Balashika, the best commando school in the Soviet Union.

The column moved slowly, and when it reached a checkpoint near the presidential palace it came to a stop. Afghan security officers gathered around the lead vehicle to ask for papers. Suddenly the flaps on the lead armored personnel carrier went up and KGB troops machine-gunned the Afghans in a matter of seconds. The column then proceeded to the palace, where Boyarinov led a bloody assault.

The troops moved methodically through the palace, killing everyone inside. Moscow would later publicly proclaim that the troops had been invited into the country by the Afghan president. But Boyarinov made sure that story could never be confirmed. Moments after the Soviet commandos entered the palace, they killed the Afghan president and his mistress. Boyarinov was under strict orders to leave no witnesses alive.

With the presidential palace secure, an Afghan Communist and KGB agent named Babrak Karmal broadcast a statement over Afghan radio from a safe position inside the Soviet Union. Claiming that he was taking over the government, he explained that his predecessor had been executed on orders of a "revolutionary tribunal" and he appealed immediately for Soviet "military assistance." Moscow, of course, graciously agreed to the request, and more troops were soon on their way.[12]

The Soviet decision to invade Afghanistan had been made by a Special Politburo Commission weeks earlier. Made up of KGB chief Andropov, Foreign Minister Andrei Gromyko, Defense Minister Ustinov, and Boris Ponomarev, the commission had concluded that military intervention was needed because the pro-Soviet government in Kabul was weak. According to the available transcripts of its deliberations, the commission dismissed the possibility that the Carter administration would strongly condemn the move or take action. The Americans had too much at stake in détente, and Carter wanted an arms control agreement.

Back in Washington, President Jimmy Carter sat in the Oval Office in stunned disbelief. Only days earlier, in a top-secret meeting with his advisers, he had expressed his commitment to détente and arms control with Moscow. Inform the Kremlin, he had told Secretary of State Cyrus Vance, that he would "go to the mat for the SALT agreement" to get ratification in the Senate.[13]

For its part, the State Department had dismissed the idea of a Soviet invasion in a secret cable written earlier in the year. "A Soviet invasion would probably redound to the disadvantage of global strategic interests," the cable read. "It would deal a severe blow to détente with the West."[14]

Carter took the Soviet move personally; to him it was a breach of trust. He had agonized early in his administration about making sure Brezhnev did not view him as antagonistic. Now, along with the fall of the Shah of Iran, the taking of American hostages, and Soviet victories in Nicaragua, Ethiopia, and Grenada, America was in retreat. Carter's disbelief was quickly replaced by anger, and he assembled his national security team. Despite the boldness of the Soviet move, there were bitter divisions about how to respond. Vance called for moderation, perhaps a verbal rebuke, but a continuation of détente and arms control. National Security Adviser Zbigniew Brzezinski, on the other hand, recommended a strong course of action. In a top-secret memo to the president, he argued that a firm response was crucial because American credibility was so low: "One of our basic problems with the Soviets, as has been the case with all our recent predecessors in office, is maintaining actions. Since we have not always followed these verbal protests up with tangible responses, the Soviets may be getting into the habit of disregarding our concern."[15]

Carter wrestled with the conflicting advice, but not for long. Moscow had gone too far this time, he believed, and he followed Brzezinski's lead. Vance resigned shortly thereafter.

The day after the invasion, Brzezinski suggested that the United

States begin secretly shipping arms to the Afghans who were resisting the invasion.[16] He was not under any illusion that the Afghans would actually thwart the invasion. The resistance, reports told him, was fragmented and lacked good leadership. "[They] certainly cannot force a Soviet withdrawal," Brzezinski said. And America's ability to help them was limited. The CIA's covert capabilities had been dramatically curtailed in recent years. So when President Carter authorized a covert plan of lending assistance to the Afghans, he did so with the simple goal of "harassing" Soviet troops.[17]

A secret arms pipeline was set up that ran through Egypt. But it had little immediate effect on the ability of the Afghan rebels to fight. Six months after the covert aid began, a government study concluded that the resistance still didn't have enough weapons. Instead, the Afghans had to resort to ingenious means to attack their enemies. They filled iron cooking pots with locally fabricated explosives to make land mines, for example, and they used Molotov cocktails against tanks.[18]

The Kremlin closely monitored the covert assistance program. Military intelligence reported that a hundred U.S. instructors had been sent to Pakistan to train Afghans and that shipments of weapons were arriving.[19] But the Soviets remained confident that their forces could be withdrawn within a year.[20]

In January, Carter took several steps to signal his anger at the Soviet move. He postponed Senate ratification of the SALT II treaty and placed a partial embargo on grain sales to the Soviet Union. He also tightened the U.S. ban on exports of military-related technology to the Soviet Union. The defense budget was boosted by 5 percent and he announced the Carter Doctrine, declaring that the United States was prepared to resist any further Soviet encroachment in the Middle East—by force if necessary.

But while Carter's steps were clear and bold, America's allies in Europe were uncertain; they vacillated between condemning the Soviet action and trying to ignore it. In early 1980, German chancellor Helmut Schmidt and French president Valéry Giscard d'Estaing met in Paris to discuss what they described as a "deteriorating situation." They were concerned about the Soviet move, but they also didn't want to abandon détente. The best they could do was issue a statement about how the pursuit of détente would be "more difficult" as a result of the "Afghanistan incident." But they steadfastly refused to condemn the Soviet move, saying only that "détente would probably not be able to withstand another shock of the same type."[21]

Throughout 1980, much of Europe acted as if the Afghanistan invasion had not happened. On March 19, without advance consultations or even notification of his allies, Giscard met with Brezhnev in Warsaw, Poland. At the end of June, Schmidt visited Moscow. Carter may have declared sanctions against the Kremlin, but throughout the year France, West Germany, Italy, and Japan continued to hold high-level talks on expanding trade with Moscow.

With NATO divided, Moscow was less concerned about Carter's actions. Gromyko, the glum Soviet foreign minister, told the Central Committee that Carter's actions amounted to "a ruckus." But it was in a "weakened form," he told them, because most of NATO was not behind them.[22]

As Reagan watched the divide between Washington and her European allies grow, he was saddened but not surprised. He had been concerned about the mood in Europe when he had visited the continent a year earlier. In February he had written a longtime friend, Lorraine Wagner, about his concerns. "The national leaders I met in England, France, and Germany could not hide their concern about us," he said. Europeans "want the solid dependable United States, including the solid dependable dollar they once knew. They are very fearful, and I'm afraid that if we don't begin showing some muscle soon, they are going to begin making overtures to the Soviets in self-defense."[23]

CHAPTER XI

WORD AND DEED

FOR REAGAN IT WAS AN OFTEN BRUISING PRIMARY. A crowded field of ten Republicans had announced their intention to take on Jimmy Carter in 1980. But as the campaign continued the field thinned, and with a critical win in New Hampshire, Reagan broke free from the pack. All the while, he kept his rhetorical guns pointed firmly at Carter.

For his part, Carter made clear his belief that Reagan was a warmonger. Reagan was going to set off "a massive nuclear arms race against the Soviet Union" that would pose a "serious threat to the safety and the security and the peace of our nation and of the world." Reagan did not "believe in peace," he told voters. Indeed, Reagan's radical views on the Cold War meant that the election would determine "whether we have peace or war."

Then came the commercials. Earnest-looking people appeared on TV expressing their fears of Reagan because he "shoots from the hip," along with a review of past Reagan statements on the use of force.[1]

Some members of the news media seemed to share that opinion of Reagan. John Chancellor began his August 18, 1980, broadcast with these words: "Good evening. Ronald Reagan said today that the Vietnam War was a noble cause in which the United States tried to help a small country newly freed from colonial rule against a totalitarian neighbor bent on conquest." On another occasion, the NBC network introduced a story about Reagan's views of war and peace with the headline "Reagan Rages." Coverage like this led *Washington Post* media critic Tom Shales to declare that there was a "network news campaign against Ronald Reagan." Reagan's views on the Cold War were often taken out of context, said Shales, and this was meant to cast doubt on "his fitness as a leader, if not, by implication, on his sanity."[2]

But despite these criticisms, Reagan was all too willing to speak out candidly about his strategic vision. One of his more interesting discussions was with Robert Scheer, a former editor at the radical *Ramparts* magazine who was now with the *Los Angeles Times*. Scheer recorded his long interviews with Reagan, which were conducted on the campaign airplane, and they reveal a candidate with a well-thought-out strategic vision.

They discussed wars from the past. Scheer asked about the Korean War, and Reagan declared that it had been poorly handled. "When you have a no-win war, there is no punishment for aggression. . . . I think it would have been far better if we'd won the war and there had been a united Korea, a democratic Korea."[3]

They discussed Vietnam. Reagan saw multiple failures on the part of LBJ, but he was particularly scornful of how naive the President had been in conducting the war by being up front with the enemy. "I don't think nuclear weapons should have been used in Vietnam," he said. "I don't think they were needed; but when somebody's out there killing your young men, you should never free the enemy of the concern he might have for what you might do." The first law of war was to keep your enemy guessing.[4]

They talked about the nuclear stalemate and American nuclear strategy. Would Reagan ever consider a preemptive nuclear strike against the Soviet Union? "What I'm saying is that the United States should never be in a position, as it has many times, of guaranteeing to an enemy or a potential enemy what it won't do."

Reagan explained to Scheer that the Soviet Union believed it could win a nuclear war. He outlined his views about the growing

Soviet margin of superiority in the arms competition. But he also made a point of telling Scheer that America could not be paralyzed in the face of the Soviet threat. The Soviets were not ten feet tall. He had recently finished a book called *Command Decision* that described mistakes made during World War II, he told his interlocutor. There were a "number of times in which we overestimated the Germans and did not take the actions we could have taken. How many people know that we had such an awe of the Wehrmacht, the great German military force, that it was invincible? How many people know that the Germans actually sent soldiers to the Russian front in summer uniforms, that they had a drive in Berlin asking women to contribute fur coats to send to the troops on the Russian front? . . . Do you know that if the French and the British had advanced at that point, they could have gone right to Berlin because the Germans had now used kind of militia-type troops on that front and had a very thin line?" The Allies had become paralyzed, fearing the Nazis were invincible, and "we didn't make that decision that should have been made."[5]

Reagan was determined not to make the same mistake during the Cold War. Despite Carter's criticisms, Reagan remained open and determined about his plans for boosting the defense budget and squeezing the Russians. He had first proposed the idea back in 1963, and he repeated it during the presidential campaign. Much to the chagrin of some nervous campaign advisers, he also told *Washington Post* editors and writers about his idea. "I think there's every indication and every reason to believe that the Soviet Union cannot increase its production of arms. Right now we're hearing of strikes and labor disputes because people aren't getting enough to eat. They've diverted so much to military [spending] that they can't provide for the consumer needs. [It] would be of great benefit to the United States if we started a buildup."[6]

These were themes and ideas Reagan had been enunciating since the 1950s. But far from indicating a lack of imagination, they spoke of his tenacity. As Reagan once explained to Landon Parvin, "You have to keep pounding away with your message, year after year, because that's the only way it will sink into the collective consciousness. I'm a big believer in stump speeches—speeches you can give over and over again with slight variations. Because if you have something you believe in deeply, it's worth repeating time and again until you achieve it."[7]

Reagan's rhetoric caught the attention of Moscow. He was already a known entity to the KGB, which had tried to undermine him in 1976 with a disinformation campaign. Now he was within striking distance of the Oval Office, and KGB residents in the United States were ordered to gather more information on the man.

The KGB began monitoring everything Reagan said, and put some choice quotes in his dossier. In San Francisco, a KGB officer met secretly with an old Reagan enemy from the politician's Hollywood days. Harry Bridges, the head of the International Longshoremen's and Warehousemen's Union and a secret member of the Communist Party, had tutored Herb Sorrell in how Sorrell might take over the Hollywood labor movement; Reagan had stopped him. Now the KGB was asking Bridges everything he knew about Reagan.

They also talked with dozens of unsuspecting friends and acquaintances of Reagan. The result was an extensive dossier that was made available to Soviet-bloc leaders. It was part personal history, part analysis of Reagan's political acumen.

The dossier made special note of the fact that when Reagan had been in Hollywood, "he proved himself as a dyed-in-the-wool anticommunist in that he actively participated in the campaign to drive progressive persons out of the film industry and the unions." It was proof, the report noted, that he took ideas seriously.

Reagan's 1980 campaign positions were "typical for a conservative Republican," but also different in that "he has called for regaining the 'international leadership position' which the United States had forfeited." The report gave grudging respect to Reagan's political skills, describing him as a "firm and unbending politician for whom words and deeds are one and the same," and went on to say that "people who know him better say that he is pragmatic and resourceful and has a feeling for the political balance of power on which he built his tactics."

The report also offers proof that the KGB had a detailed knowledge of Reagan's personal life. Alas, there proved to be no skeletons that could be exploited. "His fortune, which he acquired through real estate speculation, is estimated at between 2–4 million dollars. . . . He does not smoke and seldom drinks. He loves horses and riding and maintains a stable on his ranch. He is superstitious and is interested daily in his horoscope."[8]

At the Kremlin, KGB chief Andropov decided to keep a wary eye on Reagan. At one point, according to KGB officer Boris Yuzhin, operatives working in the United States were brought together to talk about Reagan with a senior official. "He told us that the day could come when we might be asked to get rid of Reagan."[9]

For the Kremlin, the presidential election had all the markings of a lose-lose situation. Carter, who had started out so promising for Moscow, was now seen as wildly unpredictable. After acquiescing to Soviet moves in Ethiopia, Yemen, Grenada, and Nicaragua, he had suddenly become hawkish with the thrust into Afghanistan. Reagan, on the other hand, had a long record of committing himself to battling communism. Some in the Kremlin clung to the hope that Reagan might turn out to be another Nixon, the committed anti-Communist who had become the father of détente.

In the waning days of the campaign, fearful that Carter might lose the election, the White House dispatched Armand Hammer to the Soviet embassy for a secret meeting with Ambassador Dobrynin. Hammer had done business with every Soviet leader since Lenin. He had dined with Stalin, laughed with Khrushchev, and spent time with Brezhnev in his dacha. He was also a longtime KGB asset.[10]

The two men sat in Dobrynin's office at the Soviet residence and chatted like old friends. Hammer bluntly told Dobrynin that the President was "clearly alarmed at the way things stood in the election campaign." Then Hammer asked if Moscow might be willing to help.

Could the Kremlin expand Jewish emigration to bolster Carter's standing in the polls? Hammer asked. Such a gesture might make a critical difference in several key states. It would also bolster Carter's image as a man who could deal effectively with Moscow. If Moscow performed such a favor, Hammer told Dobrynin, "Carter won't forget that service if he is reelected."

Dobrynin couldn't promise anything. But as he recalls, after the meeting he fired off a memo to the Politburo in Moscow outlining Hammer's request. Whether the Kremlin ever seriously considered the proposal is difficult to say. In the end, however, the Soviets decided to let Carter sink. The presidential election was close, and it would be wise to keep open lines to both sides.[11]

Casting an enormous shadow over the election was the ongoing hostage crisis in Iran. Fifty-two Americans had been held hostage in Tehran for more than a year in what many considered the ultimate proof of America's impotence. A hastily organized rescue mission had ended in disaster. Carter was engaged in painstaking discussions with the Iranians to secure the hostages' release. Reagan, on the campaign trail, was calling the Iranians "barbarians" and "kidnappers." Some in the Reagan campaign feared that Carter might cut a deal with the Iranians in the final month of the campaign to save his political life. Reagan campaign manager William Casey, adviser Ed Meese, and vice presidential nominee George Bush's older brother Prescott collectively worked to ensure that Carter did not pull an October surprise. Later, charges would be made that these efforts included a campaign to delay the release of the hostages. But these claims would be disproved.

★   ★   ★

ON ELECTION DAY, RON AND NANCY REAGAN WAITED ANXiously for news about the returns. In the past, Reagan had spent election nights dining at a friend's house before going to campaign headquarters to await the final returns. He had done this for both gubernatorial elections, which he had won handily, so of course he didn't want to do anything different for this, the most important night of his political career. In the late afternoon, he got into the shower to get cleaned up for his night out, when Nancy walked into the bathroom.

"Telephone call," she said. "It's Jimmy Carter."

Reagan got out of the shower, dried off, and picked up the phone. Carter was conceding; the race was over.

"Thank you, Mr. President," Reagan said before hanging up.[12]

★   ★   ★

REAGAN'S MARGIN OF VICTORY WAS A LARGE ONE, PARTICULARLY in terms of electoral votes. The KGB took note and sent an analysis to the Kremlin, trying to explain what the victory meant and what Reagan might try to do with his mandate.

The serious deterioration of the American economy was considered the biggest factor in Carter's defeat. But "the weakening of the position of the USA throughout the world, including the regions on which the economy of the USA is substantially dependent," was also important. Add "the obvious incompetence and the clear weakening of Carter, who according to a widespread feeling in the USA was not able to secure a firm leadership of the country at a difficult period" and it was clear that national security was a big factor as well. Throughout the campaign, "Reagan, whose reputation as a 'consequent conservative' has never been questioned by anyone in the U.S., banked on his promise to provide 'strong leadership' and branded Carter as having been responsible for economizing the U.S. 'down to the level of a second-rate power.' "

So Reagan had a mandate not only to deal with economic malaise but also to act forcefully on the world stage. What was the KGB expecting from Reagan? He was going to dramatically boost the defense budget and speed up the development of new weapons systems. He was also expected to increase the effectiveness of American intelligence with the goal of "undermining the positions of the socialist countries and progressive forces."

The KGB report concluded, "It can be expected that Reagan, who tackles all problems in an absolute pragmatic way, will pursue a foreign policy of a hard, but at the same time an essentially consistent line."[13]

Even with Reagan's victory and his commitment to be more assertive on the world stage, there were grounds for optimism in Moscow. The widespread feeling was that Soviet military superiority was now a reality. The buildup of strategic nuclear weapons had continued unabated, and at the same time the Soviets had begun deployment of the SS-20 missile. The SS-20 had three warheads and was feared throughout Western Europe.

"The SS-20 was a breakthrough, unlike anything the Americans had," recalls General Danilevich. "We were immediately able to hold all of Europe hostage."

The Soviet General Staff believed they "had amassed a superior first-strike arsenal" and had "achieved superiority" over the United States, recalls A. S. Kalashnikov, a chairman of the Strategic Rocket Forces.[14]

That sense of confidence was not limited to those in uniform. At the Kremlin, Leonid Brezhnev had proclaimed that for the first time the correlation of forces—the combined economic, political, and military might—had "irrevocably shifted in favor of socialism." This was more than idle talk intended for public consumption. In the corridors of power, Ambassador Oleg Grinevsky recalls, there was talk that "the United States is losing the arms race." Indeed, there was the widespread belief that "the Soviet Union had reached the peak of its power."[15]

★   ★   ★

ONLY DAYS AFTER HIS ELECTION VICTORY, REAGAN WENT TO work, getting extensive intelligence briefings from the CIA's Office of Current Operations. These briefings were more extensive than those any previous president had ever received. This was in part because Vice President–elect George Bush, who had served as CIA director, believed the briefings would be highly valuable. "Bush knew from firsthand experience that filtering went on as an intelligence product moved through the White House staff and on to the President," recall Richard J. Kerr, the former deputy director of Central Intelligence, and Peter Dixon Davis, a senior member of the CIA Intelligence Directorate. "He also knew that to make intelligence relevant the Agency needed regular feedback from its key customers."

Beginning in late November, CIA officers were dispatched to California to begin the briefing process. The briefers met first with Ed Meese, Reagan's close aide, and then presented the president's daily briefing (PDB) to Reagan, who was often in his bathrobe, during the morning at his home in Pacific Palisades. The same procedure went on almost daily up until the inauguration.

At the same time, the CIA officers provided Reagan with intelligence on areas he was most interested in. Using a secure communication facility, CIA analysts would put together a classified briefing, and photo interpreters and technical experts in the Office of Science and Technology would gather information gleaned from satellites. Most of the intelligence concerned hot spots like Iran, Poland, and Afghanistan.

"He read the PDB carefully, asking an occasional question, and then read the other material," recall Kerr and Davis. "Reagan was a studious reader, going over each item deliberately and with considerable concentration." After the morning briefing, the CIA officers would meet with Reagan's aides. There Richard Allen, Reagan's national security adviser, Bill Casey, his choice for CIA director, and Ed Meese would review the material and ask probing questions.

The entire procedure had a profound effect on Reagan. He was intrigued by the material and he became a heavy consumer of intelligence. He insisted that not only he receive the top-secret PDB, but also Vice President George Bush, the secretaries of state and defense, and the national security adviser. This all had the effect of elevating the importance of the CIA in the Reagan administration. As Kerr and Davis recall, "The Agency had finally obtained the continuing, high-level access it had been seeking since 1961."[16]

CHAPTER XII

THE HAND OF GOD

RONALD REAGAN STOOD AT A PODIUM DRAPED WITH FLAGS
and red, white, and blue bunting on the west side of the
Capitol grounds. Tens of thousands of people had gathered on the gently sloping lawn on a cold January afternoon to observe the transfer of power.

Reagan was standing stiffly, his right arm raised. His left hand
rested on his mother's Bible, opened to the seventh chapter, four-
teenth verse of Second Chronicles: "If my people, which are called
by my name, shall humble themselves, and pray, and seek my face,
and turn from their wicked ways; then will I hear from heaven, and
will forgive their sin, and will heal their land."

The economy was in bad shape. The prime interest rate was 21
percent, unemployment was high, and inflation was in the double
digits. So Reagan devoted a good deal of his inaugural address to the
state of the economy. He spoke only briefly about foreign policy;
delicate negotiations aimed at returning the American hostages from
Iran to the United States were taking place and he didn't want to disrupt the process.

Reagan had played an unsuspecting role in securing the hostages'
release. As Carter aides would later admit, Reagan's pending arrival

as the new commander in chief, along with his strong talk, had been an important factor in the negotiations. It seems the Iranians, like the Soviets, had their fears about Reagan.[1]

The weight of his job as commander in chief was resting heavily on Reagan's shoulders—and, literally, in his coat pocket. There sat a plastic-coated card that contained the codes he would use in the event that he needed to launch America's nuclear arsenal. And always standing nearby was a young military officer carrying "the football," the small bag that contained the directives to begin the nuclear launch sequence.

A few days earlier he had been briefed on the procedure; now the tools of Armageddon were in his possession. He learned quickly just how razor thin his window of opportunity for making the difficult decision would be. Moscow regularly positioned nuclear submarines off the East Coast, he was told. If they launched, he would have six or eight minutes to decide how to respond.

Pushing the button in the face of a Soviet launch was an issue that every president since Eisenhower had grappled with. Each president would make his own decision. But a clear plan had been developed under Ike about how to protect the president once the bombs started falling. The president would be taken immediately to the helicopter pad on the South Lawn. He would board a helicopter with the football on board and be transported to a secret and protected site. This was the so-called continuity-of-government plan, and every president since Ike had chosen to adopt it.

Reagan was briefed on the plan by two old friends. Judge William P. Clark was a quiet, gentle lawyer and rancher who had come to work for Reagan in Sacramento. Reagan later appointed him to the California Supreme Court, and in Washington, Clark would serve as undersecretary of state, national security adviser, and finally secretary of the interior.

Tom Reed had been a nuclear physicist at Lawrence Livermore, had joined Reagan's gubernatorial campaign in 1966, and had gone on to serve as secretary of the Air Force under President Ford. He was now Reagan's special assistant for national security affairs.

Reed was very familiar with the plan and did most of the talking. He explained in intricate detail just how the continuity-of-government plan would work, how communications and command-and-control were expected to be preserved after a first strike. Both Clark and Reed could sense Reagan's discomfort, particularly the part about being hustled on a helicopter to a safe location. When Reed was finished, Reagan shook his head.

"No, I'm not going to do that," he told them. "If it happens—God forbid—I'm not going anywhere. I'm staying here at my post."

The two men left and a new plan was drawn up. In a nuclear emergency, Reagan would stay in the White House.[2]

Reagan abhorred the prospect of nuclear war. But he was mindful of how Moscow used "fear of the bomb," as he had put it in the 1950s, to put the West at a psychological disadvantage. "The ultimate determinant in the struggle now going on for the world will not be bombs and rockets," he had said back in 1964, "but a test of wills and ideas—a trial of spiritual resolve."[3]

Now that he was president, those were more than mere words; it was a reality to be faced every day. And he appeared determined not to blink.

In one of his first press conferences, he set the tone. The Kremlin's goal, he said, was "the promotion of world revolution and a one-world Socialist or Communist state. The only morality they recognize is what will further their cause, meaning they reserve unto themselves the right to commit any crime, to lie, to cheat, in order to attain that [end]."[4]

Clearly, Reagan was not going to be another Nixon; no one had spoken about the Kremlin in such a manner since the early days of the Eisenhower administration. Reagan was determined to change the psychological climate of the Cold War, and he wanted to go beyond mere words.

In mid-April 1981, a group of Soviet ships was cruising in the murky waters of the Mediterranean just off the Italian coast. Aboard the flagship was Admiral Gorshakov, the iron-willed founder of the modern Soviet Navy. No one was more responsible for the Soviet Union's growth as a world power than Gorshakov.

As the small flotilla proceeded on its way, several U.S. Navy P-3 Orion reconnaissance aircraft began following. They shadowed Gorshakov for close to an hour and then suddenly, without warning, one of the P-3s pulled away from the squadron and dove at the Soviet fleet. It flew in close, buzzing Gorshakov's flagship, before banking in the sky and returning back to base.

The flight of the P-3 was no random act. A few months later, the USS *Conolly*, a destroyer based out of Norfolk, Virginia, intentionally sailed through a Soviet anti–submarine warfare exercise in the Atlantic, forcing several of the smaller ships to scatter. Weeks later, a U.S. Navy ship proceeded into the Sea of Okhotsk, which was dotted with sensitive military installations on nearby Sakhalin Island and the Kamchatka peninsula. The Soviet Union claimed the Sea of Okhotsk as its own, but the United States was putting that belief to the test. The Soviets scrambled several aircraft and ships before the U.S. Navy vessel returned to open waters. On August 19, a Soviet destroyer operating in the Mediterranean reported being buzzed, this time by U.S. Navy S-3 and SH-2 helicopters.

Incidents like these accumulated in a steady trickle, just enough to send a message. And they continued for the next couple of years. In May 1982, the frigate USS *Lockwood* performed maneuvers in the Sea of Japan and in Peter the Great Bay, which the Soviets claimed were internal waters. Soviet ships and aircraft challenged the *Lockwood*, but the ship's captain stayed on course.

In April 1983, six U.S. Navy fighter aircraft were launched from carriers and flew low over the remote Zeleny Islands, where Moscow had military installations. The sound of their jet engines rattled the windows of the officers' quarters.

Throughout the Cold War, American presidents had been reactive, responding to Soviet probes and provocations around the world. Reagan wanted to be less reactive and more aggressive, taking the initiative away from Moscow.

As the Navy probed the edges of the Soviet empire, the Air Force did the same in the skies.

"Sometimes we would send bombers over the North Pole, and their radars would click on," recalls General Jack Chain, the former Strategic Air Command commander. "Other times fighter-bombers would probe their Asian or European periphery. During peak times, the operation would include several maneuvers a week. They would come at irregular intervals to make the effect all the more unsettling.

Then, as quickly as the unannounced flights began, they would stop, only to begin again a few weeks later."[5]

Just to get the point across, simulated attacks were performed. In the frigid waters surrounding Alaska's Aleutian Islands, the military carried out Operation Kernal Potlatch, war games in which amphibious assaults were rehearsed. Supported by a battle ground centered on the aircraft carrier USS *Carl Vinson*, Navy F-14 fighters would lift off from the island of Adak to intercept and escort Soviet maritime patrol planes flying in the Pacific. After the F-14s were airborne, A-6E attack bombers would take to the air and fly directly toward the Soviet Pacific Fleet base at Petropavlovsk to stage a mock attack. They were practicing and sending a message. On more than two dozen occasions, Soviet radar operators at Petropavlovsk detected the American bombers, which would turn away only a hundred miles from the Soviet shoreline.[6]

These operations, which were part of a so-called psychological operation (PSYOP), had their intended effect. "Reagan is unpredictable," Yuri Andropov confided to Soviet ambassador Dobrynin after the operations began. "You should expect anything from him."[7]

★   ★   ★

ON MARCH 30, 1981, RONALD REAGAN WAS LEAVING THE WASH-ington Hilton Hotel on a cool afternoon after having given a speech to the Business Trades Council of the AFL-CIO. Accompanied by four Secret Service agents and a couple of aides, he stepped out onto the sidewalk and headed toward the presidential limousine.

Reporters who were gathered nearby shouted questions at him, and he waved before reaching the car. Mike Putzel, a reporter from the Associated Press, fired off a question about Poland. Reagan turned to answer. . . .

Pop. Pop. Pop.

There were screams and yelling. Someone shoved Reagan from behind, forcing him into the back seat of the limo.

"Get us out of here!" screamed Jerry Parr, a Secret Service agent, who was lying on top of Reagan. The limo sped off.

Reagan was feeling a sharp pain. Parr got off him, and Reagan thought maybe he had hurt a rib. Blood started pouring out of the president's mouth. It took a while to determine that Reagan had in fact been shot.

Lodged under his left arm was a .22-caliber "Devastater" bullet, which was designed to explode on impact. It was one of six bullets that had been fired by a deranged young gunman named John Hinckley Jr. One of the shots had ricocheted off the bulletproof limo before penetrating Reagan's chest muscles.

The limo arrived at George Washington University Medical Center, and Reagan soon found himself lying flat on his back. Doctors huddled over him, trying desperately to pump blood into him as he bled from the bullet wound.

"I focused on the tiled ceiling," he recalled later. "And prayed."

By 3:24 P.M., less than an hour after the assault, doctors were operating to remove the bullet. Reagan's tremendous physical strength, which had given him the confidence to overcome physical threats in Hollywood and Sacramento, now proved to be something of a hindrance. It took doctors more than half an hour to cut through his chest, because there was so much muscle.

"I have never in my life seen a chest like that on a man his age," one doctor reported.[8]

The doctors snatched the bullet from Reagan's body and his chest was closed at 5:20 P.M. With blood transfusions his condition stabilized. He remained unconscious.

In the days that followed, Reagan lay in bed with Nancy seated at his side. He met with advisers and was briefed on any significant developments. But perhaps more than anything, he contemplated what had happened. In his shooting and survival, there were what he later came to call "miraculous factors" that had protected him.

The question shouted by the AP reporter, which had caused him to turn just before the gun discharged, may have saved his life: If his torso had not turned at that moment, the bullet might well have penetrated his heart. Jerry Parr, the quick-thinking Secret Service agent who had pushed him into the limo and out of harm's way, was in the Secret Service because of Reagan. As a young boy, Parr had seen a movie called *Code of the Secret Service* about a superagent named Brass Bancroft. The story entranced him and led him to join the Secret Service. The young star who had played Bancroft in the film was Ronald Reagan.[9]

★ ★ ★

REAGAN HAD LONG BELIEVED THAT EACH INDIVIDUAL HAS A DI-vine purpose in life. He was a "mystic," he explained in 1974. "I've always believed that we were—each of us—put here for a reason, that there is a plan, a divine plan for all of us."[10]

He had been spared an assassin's bullet. What further proof did he need that his divine purpose was not yet fulfilled?

"I know it's going to be a long recovery," he wrote in his diary after leaving the hospital and returning to the White House. "Whatever happens now I owe my life to God and will try to serve him every way I can."

These were not thoughts that he kept to himself. To his pollster and friend Richard Wirthlin he explained that coming "close to passing through the portal of death" and being spared meant "there was something the Lord wanted him to accomplish." To his longtime friend Bill Clark he explained quite simply, "I was protected for a reason."

On Good Friday, April 17, barely two weeks after he had been shot, Reagan met with Cardinal Cooke of the Archdiocese of New York. The cardinal had come at the President's request, and they sat together in the White House residence talking for several minutes. Reagan was wrestling with the emotions of having survived. Cooke assured him that "the hand of God was upon you."

"I know," Reagan responded. "And I have decided that whatever time I have left is left for Him."[11]

A little over two years later, Reagan paid an emotional visit to Cooke in a private chapel at St. Patrick's Cathedral in New York. Cooke was dying of leukemia. The two men prayed together.[12]

★ ★ ★

IF EVERY PERSON IS GIVEN A DIVINE PURPOSE, AS REAGAN BELIEVED, he knew what his was to be. He had battled communism for close to forty years now. What could be more abhorrent to God than a system that denies God? This was perhaps the greatest crime of communism, a "godlessness" that denigrated the nobility of man in the name of exalting mankind. As Reagan told a reporter in 1980, it was atheism that made the critical difference. Under communism a child was taught "from the beginning of his life that it is a human being whose only importance is its contribution to the state—that they are wards of the state—that they exist only for that purpose, and that there is no God, they are just an accident of nature. The result is they have no respect for human life, for the dignity of an individual . . . the Communist party has substituted Karl Marx for God."[13]

Faith was more important than life itself. During the early 1960s, Reagan was a frequent speaker at anti-Communist rallies and meetings. After one of these speeches, a man stood up on stage next to him to speak. "I love my little girls more than anything," the man explained with tears in his eyes. *Uh-oh,* Reagan thought. "But I would rather see my little girls die now, still believing in God," the man continued, "than have them grow up under communism and one day die no longer believing in God." Reagan was struck by the emotion in the man's words, and he would recount this particularly poignant moment often, even more than twenty years later.

Only ten days before the attempt on his life, Reagan had given a speech in Washington on the false hope of communism as compared with real faith in God. "The Marxist vision of man without God must eventually be seen as an empty and a false faith—the second oldest in the world—first proclaimed in the garden of Eden with whispered words of temptation: 'Ye shall be as gods.' The crisis of the Western world, Whittaker Chambers reminded us, exists to the degree in which it is indifferent to God."

He went on to say, "Evil is powerless if the good are unafraid." Now was the time for "renewing our spiritual strength. Only by building a wall of such spiritual resolve can we, as a free people, hope to protect our own heritage and make it someday the birthright of all men."[14]

He had also believed for some time that not only individuals but some nations are part of a "divine plan." Since the 1950s he had voiced his belief that America had such a mission, and he always expressed it in terms of demonstrating an "abiding love of freedom and a special kind of courage."[15]

Now he came to see his escape from death as a reminder from God about his purpose as president. And it infused him with an even greater desire to defeat communism, the great false God of the twentieth century.

★ ★ ★

FOR ONE OF HIS FIRST MAJOR SPEECHES AFTER HIS RECOVERY, Reagan took to the podium at the U.S. Military Academy at West Point to speak to graduating cadets. He repeated his view that under atheistic communism people were taught that their "only importance" is in their contribution to the state, "that there is no God, they are just an accident of nature." But he went on to draw parallels between Soviet communism and Nazism, the belief system most identified with evil in the popular mind. America's military power and spiritual resolve during World War II had "prevented what could have been a retreat into the Dark Ages." But the job was not yet done. As the Western world sought freedom and tranquillity after the war, "another great power in the world was marching to a different drum beat, creating a society in which everything that isn't compulsory is prohibited. The citizens of that society have little more to say about their government than a prison inmate has to say about the prison administration." Today's challenge was every bit as important as the victory against the Nazis. "Today you are a chain, holding back an evil force that would extinguish the light we've been tending for 6,000 years," he told cadets.[16]

CHAPTER XIII

THEY CAN'T KEEP UP

ONE OF REAGAN'S MOST IMPORTANT CAMPAIGN PROM-
ises had been to restore American military might, and
less than two weeks after entering office, he approved
an immediate defense-budget increase of more than
$32 billion. To oversee the buildup, he tapped a longtime friend and
former aide from his Sacramento days, Caspar Weinberger. A cor-
porate attorney with a Harvard law degree who had served under
General MacArthur during World War II, Weinberger was a tenacious man. In California he had run Reagan's budget office with a
firm hand. Later, as President Nixon's director of the Office of Management and Budget and secretary of Health, Education and Welfare,
Weinberger was just as vigorous in cutting government waste and reducing program budgets. They called him "Cap the Knife."

Weinberger's appointment was initially seen by Moscow as a positive sign. The Soviet health minister, an academician named Petrovsky, had worked with Weinberger when he was head of HEW.
Even though Weinberger was known as a conservative, Petrovsky
"was charmed by him," recalls Dobrynin. "Having learned about his
appointment as secretary of defense, Petrovsky repeated to everybody in Moscow that there would be 'a friend of his' in the Reagan
administration."

Dobrynin shared Petrovsky's warm feelings. "I regarded Weinberger as a balanced man, judging by his past record," Dobrynin recalls. "But it was not long before we all were strongly disillusioned."[1]

What Kremlin leaders failed to understand was that while Weinberger was an enemy of big government, he had always been a strong advocate of increased defense spending. And as Reagan's secretary of defense, he had ambitious plans.

It would not be easy; there were deep divisions within the newly formed cabinet about how much to spend on defense. Along with restoring American military strength, Reagan was promising to cut taxes and reduce the budget deficit. White House Budget Director David Stockman said large increases in Pentagon spending would bust the federal budget. Soon Weinberger and Stockman were engaged in a running debate over the matter at just about every meeting.

Weinberger had the support of Vice President George Bush, CIA Director William Casey, White House Counselor Ed Meese, UN Ambassador Jeane Kirkpatrick, and National Security Adviser Richard Allen. But the majority of the cabinet was opposed to his plan. The secretaries of commerce, treasury, health and human services, and education, favored only modest increases, arguing instead for shoring up social programs. And there were critics outside the administration. Richard Nixon had sent Reagan a memo shortly before the inauguration offering his advice. When it came to budget cuts, the Department of Defense "should not be considered off limits," the former president wrote. "The Pentagon should not be a sacred cow."

Matters finally came to a head at a cabinet meeting in the White House.

"Mr. President, you have double-digit inflation and double-digit unemployment," warned one cabinet member. "You can't spend all of this money on the military. We have to spend it on social programs."

Another cabinet member explained that it would create bad publicity to boost spending on guns while cutting the butter. Congress would probably object; it might bust the budget. The debate raged on until Reagan leaned forward and raised his hand to halt the discussion.

"Look, I am the President of the United States, the commander in chief; my primary responsibility is the security of the United States. . . . If we don't have our security, we'll have no need for social programs. We're going to go ahead with these programs."

The matter was now settled. Going against the advice of the majority in his cabinet, Reagan commenced the largest peacetime military buildup in American history.[2]

With the President now firmly committed to defense matters, Weinberger began working with tremendous zeal. On the wall behind his Pentagon desk rested a framed quotation from Winston Churchill: "Never give in, never give in, never, never, never, never; in nothing great or small, large or petty, never give in."

Weinberger fought tenaciously with members of Congress who wanted to trim his budget requests. As one domestic critic put it, he "defended nearly every tank, missile, and machine gun, every weapon system that has come across his desk." At the Pentagon, one former admiral called him "one of the few genuine anticommunist cold warriors in Washington."[3]

Several miles away from the Pentagon, at the Soviet embassy in Washington, Soviet ambassador Dobrynin watched these developments in horror. Weinberger "never seemed to tire of leading the Pentagon charge" and "supported all of Reagan's statements on foreign policy without reservation, except that he tended to make them sound even tougher."[4]

On his first trip overseas, Weinberger met with his counterparts in Europe and was blunt. "If the movement from the Cold War to détente is progress," he said, "we cannot afford much more progress."

Following Weinberger to the Pentagon were a group of resolute defense intellectuals who shared Reagan's vision. Fred Ikle, who had served in the Ford administration and had written extensively on strategic matters, was brought in as the undersecretary of defense for policy. For the important post of assistant secretary of defense, the administration turned to Richard Perle, a familiar figure on Capitol Hill as an aide to Senator Scoop Jackson. Together with the leadership of all the military branches—Army, Air Force, Navy, and Marines—these Pentagon officials pieced together a budget. Reagan's objective was to increase the military budget as a share of federal spending from one-fourth to one-third in three years.[5]

Reagan wanted to restore American power and might, but he also wanted to squeeze the Kremlin. As he told one reporter in an interview, "They cannot vastly increase their military productivity because they've already got their people on a starvation diet. . . . If we show them [we have] the will and determination to go forward with a military build-up . . . then they have to weigh, do they want to meet us realistically on a program of disarmament or do they want to face a legitimate arms race in which we're racing. Up until now, we've been making unilateral concessions, allowing ours to deteriorate, and they've been building the greatest military machine the world has ever seen. But now they're going to be faced with [the fact] that we could go forward with an arms race and *they can't keep up*."[6]

The mood in Moscow quickly turned gloomy. "During my long career as ambassador the collective mood of the Soviet leadership had never been so suddenly and deeply set against an American president," recalls Dobrynin.[7]

Reagan had first expressed the idea of squeezing Moscow with an arms race back in 1963. But how could it be done with maximum effect? In early 1981, the Pentagon convened a group of specialists to come up with a new top-secret military strategy that could answer such questions. Under the direction of Fred Ikle, they hammered together a "defense guidance," the most secretive and authoritative statement of Pentagon strategy, resource planning, program development, and force planning. Indeed, the document is so sensitive that it remains classified twenty years later. (The author has obtained a copy.) What they came up was a radical break with the past.

The top-secret document defined American "national security objectives" and spoke of the all-important need to prevent the outbreak of war and to protect American interests. But new objectives were added:

"Reverse the geographic expansion of Soviet control and military presence throughout the world, in particular where such presence threatens the geostrategic position of the United States.

"Encourage long-term political and military changes within the Soviet empire that will facilitate building a more secure and more peaceful world order."[8]

Rolling back and changing the Soviet system would be no easy

task. But there were fissures in the Soviet edifice, "political and economic weaknesses in the Soviet Union and Warsaw Pact allies which
are emerging." And those weaknesses needed to be exploited.

A major chink in the Soviet armor was the nation's moribund
economy, which was burdened by a heavy military budget. The
growing Soviet military budget was sucking down the overall economy, because it was claiming "a large, undiminishing, or even rising
burden on the Soviet economy."

With dramatic increases in American defense spending on the
way, Moscow would be forced to respond, and it wouldn't be easy.
The United States needed to press its advantage. "We should use this
opportunity to help shape the future competition in ways which are
advantageous to the United States."

Back in 1967, Reagan had said that Russian communism was an
inefficient form of serfdom and could not compete with the more
efficient capitalist system. Now, as president, he would see the
United States put his view to the test. The defense guidance declared
that it was time to "exploit and demonstrate the enduring economic
advantages of the West to develop a variety of systems that are difficult for the Soviets to counter, impose disproportionate costs, open
up new areas of major military competition and obsolesce previous
Soviet investment or employ sophisticated strategic deception options to achieve this end."

The key was to play to American strengths—technology and innovation—and exploit Soviet weaknesses in an arms race. "An inherent advantage of our system is the ability to combine managerial
skills and technology to solve difficult military problems," the defense guidance said. "Competing with the Soviets more effectively
will require that the United States use its advantages to develop an
overall strategy." The United States needed to "take advantage of the
enemy's weaknesses."[9]

In short, the defense buildup was as much about economic warfare against the Soviets as it was about restoring American military
power.[10]

As Reagan recovered from his wounds, he also faced a shaky domestic economy. He worked hard to secure passage of his economic
program of tax cuts and deregulation, but he actually devoted more

time to national security and defense questions during his first year in the Oval Office. He chaired fifty-seven meetings of the National Security Council, more than one a week. One-third of his time in the Oval Office was spent mulling over security and defense questions in meetings and briefings, or reading reports. Few presidents, none in peacetime, had sustained such a pace of involvement in national security affairs.[11]

When he wasn't meeting with aides, Reagan was reading intelligence reports about the Soviet bloc. In his pre-presidential days, he had relied on newspaper clippings, special reports, or verbal accounts from friends for news about what was going on behind the Iron Curtain. He had been speaking about the failings of the Soviet economic system for more than twenty years. But his views were controversial, and they were ridiculed by scholars who believed he was fooling himself about the weakness of communism. Seweryn Bialer of Columbia University flatly rejected his views. "The Soviet Union is not now nor will it be during the next decade in the throes of a true system crisis," he wrote in 1982, "for it boasts enormous unused reserves of political and social stability that suffice to endure the deepest difficulties."

Massachusetts Institute of Technology economist Lester Thurow went a step further, claiming that the Soviet Union was "a country whose economic achievements bear comparison with those of the United States." As for Reagan's talk about trying to liberate Eastern Europe, Thurow announced that "it is a vulgar mistake to think that most people in Eastern Europe are miserable." John Kenneth Galbraith of Harvard concluded as late as 1984 that "the Russian system succeeds because, in contrast to the Western industrial economies, it makes full use of its manpower."

Historian Arthur Schlesinger took a trip to Moscow in 1982 and later declared that Reagan's vision of pushing the Kremlin over the brink was nonsense. "I found more goods in the shops, more food in the markets, more cars on the street—more of almost everything, except, for some reason, caviar." He was dismissive of "those in the U.S. who think the Soviet Union is on the verge of economic and social collapse, ready with one small push to go over the brink. . . . Each superpower has economic troubles; neither is on the ropes."

Reagan knew better. As president, he was fond of reading detailed intelligence reports while sitting in the Oval Office or up in the residence. He had become hooked after the unprecedented number of briefings the CIA had given him at his home in Pacific Palisades after being elected. Now he couldn't get enough, and he mostly enjoyed field reports or rough intel that had not been sifted through by analysts.

"He enjoyed looking at all of it," recalls David Wigg, the CIA liaison to the White House. "He particularly enjoyed information about the economic troubles they [the Soviets] were experiencing."[12]

Communism was not an abstract enemy to Reagan. The threats against his family in Hollywood had come from a human voice; the attempted firebombing in Sacramento was carried out by real perpetrators; his name had been scraped on the bullet at SDS headquarters by human hands; the alleged plot to kill him using a Cuban agent involved real people with real names. So when he thought about the Soviet empire and the menace it represented, he wanted to put a human face on it.

"What are they saying about the Pope in Warsaw?" he would ask, recalls Bill Clark. "What is Brezhnev thinking about in Europe? How are they dealing with losses in Afghanistan?"[13]

Reagan was also given a steady stream of intel that confirmed his view that his arms buildup was causing Moscow fits. "Soviet economic growth is stalling while the price of military research and technological innovation is skyrocketing," read a National Intelligence Estimate that crossed his desk in July. "Those advantages the USSR has won over the West in some aspects of general purpose forces are likely to be ever more expensive to sustain in the face of aroused US defense interests."[14]

Using human intelligence sources inside the Soviet bloc, CIA analysts determined that the Kremlin was very concerned about Reagan's defense plans. The Soviets were expressing these concerns in both public and private meetings.

Matching the Reagan buildup would not be easy for Moscow, said another NIE. Soviet leaders would "confront increasingly difficult economic choices." Cutbacks in the civilian economy would become necessary. "Cutbacks in consumer goods and services could have two unpalatable consequences: a worsening of already poor prospects for improving labor productivity and an increase in worker discontent."[15]

★   ★   ★

ONE AREA IN WHICH THE DEFENSE BUILDUP WAS NOT PROCEED-
ing apace was in strategic nuclear arms. Moscow had continued to add to its arsenal; but in Washington, it was impossible to get
approval from Congress for any new strategic missiles. In late 1982,
Reagan lost a critical vote in Congress for funding the MX missile.
It was the third time in the past eighteen months that the Pentagon
had proposed a new basing mode for intercontinental missiles and
Congress had said no.

"The bottom line," recalls Robert McFarlane, "was that we
weren't putting any missiles in the ground."[16]

A certain hysteria seemed to be developing in the country concerning the prospects of nuclear war. In June 1982, 750,000 people
marched in New York's Central Park calling for an immediate nuclear freeze. It was the largest political demonstration in American
history, larger than anything Nixon had seen during Vietnam.

In Hollywood, antinuclear activists organized into small groups
to figure out how they could translate their fears onto the screen. A
film produced for television, called *The Day After*, portrayed the fate
of nuclear holocaust survivors in the American Midwest. Edward
Hume, the film's scriptwriter, explained that he wrote the story because "most people have no sense of the enormity of these weapons
and just how suicidal they are."[17]

As children heard the debate unfold, they became frightened
about the future. "A lot of kids are scared they might not have a future because of nuclear war," an eleven-year-old told a congressional
committee. "I want a future, too."

Surveys conducted by the American Psychiatric Association
concluded that roughly half of all high school students had fears
about nuclear conflict and were changing their plans as a result. At
Brown University, students passed a nonbinding referendum asking
the college to stockpile cyanide pills to facilitate suicide in the event
of a nuclear war. Other schools passed similar measures.[18]

In Massachusetts, the State Health Commission produced television commercials about the evils of a nuclear holocaust. "When I grow up, I want to be alive," a child said in one of these commercials.[19]

This was hardly an isolated movement; it even cut into Reagan's own political base. A *Los Angeles Times* poll of delegates to the 1984 Republican Convention found that a stunning 62 percent supported the concept of a freeze in the development of nuclear arms.[20]

As it was so often in his war against communism, this matter became highly personal for Reagan. His youngest daughter, Patti Davis, embraced the nuclear-freeze cause with gusto. She worked on behalf of the California Nuclear Freeze Initiative (which passed in 1982) and lobbied her father on the cause. She telephoned him several times and asked him to meet with two of his strongest critics. Always the happy warrior, he readily agreed.

Harold Wilens was a California businessman who had organized protests against the Vietnam War in the 1960s and had evolved into a disarmament activist. He was a board member of the Center for Defense Information, which had been highly critical of Reagan, and a large contributor to antinuclear causes.

Wilens met with Reagan in early February 1983 and challenged the President to support a freeze as the only way to avoid a nuclear holocaust. Reagan listened politely and then challenged Wilens's thinking. "The problem you and your friends don't understand, Mr. Wilens, is that the Soviets are way ahead of us."

The businessman left, declaring that he understood Reagan better now and considered him a reasonable—if ill-informed—man.

More intriguing was a private meeting with Boston antinuclear activist Helen Caldicott. Again, it had been a phone call from Patti Davis that led to the encounter.

A medical doctor based at the Children's Hospital Medical Center at Harvard Medical School, Caldicott was an alarmist of the sort that personified where Reagan believed "fear of the bomb" could lead. As she once explained to a group of fellow doctors: "What is the point of keeping these children alive for another five, ten, or twenty years . . . when during this time they could be vaporized in a nuclear war?"

Caldicott came to the meeting with Reagan filled with despair and righteous anger over his course of action. For more than an hour, Reagan sat with his daughter and Caldicott discussing nuclear war. Caldicott told him that it was the film *On the Beach* that had first propelled her into peace activism. Don't believe everything you see in the movies, the former actor advised her.

The meeting turned awkward at one point when Reagan explained that the Soviets were financially supporting the peace movement. Caldicott rejected the charge. But she was cochair of International Physicians for the Prevention of Nuclear War, along with Dr. Evgeni Chazov, Brezhnev's personal physician. Unknown to Caldicott, the group's deliberations were reported to the KGB.[21]

Caldicott and Patti Davis left the meeting upset that they had not changed the President's thinking. Reagan wondered whether he might lose his daughter's support over this issue. "She seems like a nice, caring person," Reagan wrote about Caldicott, "but she is all steamed up and knows an awful lot of things that aren't true. I tried but couldn't get through her fixation. For that matter I couldn't get through to Patti. I'm afraid our daughter has been taken over by that whole gang. . . ."

His relationship with his daughter, which had been rocky for several years, became even more strained. Patti believed that because her father wouldn't embrace the freeze, he might very well cause a nuclear holocaust. "I shared Caldicott's fear about what the remaining years of my father's administration would bring," she later recalled. "I sat at the dinner table that night drinking too much wine. . . . I felt like I'd let down an entire movement."

Despite the difficulties with his daughter, Reagan stood firm.[22]

★   ★   ★

SHORTLY AFTER THE FAILED MX VOTE, ADMIRAL JOHN POINDEXter, who was working on the National Security Council staff, approached Robert McFarlane with an idea. Poindexter, who had graduated at the top of his class at the Naval Academy and was a scientist by training, suggested that the administration explore the possibility of researching and even deploying a strategic defense system. The Defense Science Board had already come to a similar conclusion. And General Daniel Graham, head of a private group called High Frontier, had already met with the President and proposed such a plan.

McFarlane told Poindexter that he liked the idea and had in fact been thinking along similar lines. "It had seemed to me for about ten years, since the Nixon and Ford years, that we were competing with the Russians militarily on the wrong terms," he recalls. "Our comparative advantage was in quality and technology. It really caused me to pause and look back. I asked myself, How could we reorient our investment strategy? How do you spend your resources? It seemed to me that spending on offensive systems and numbers was less effective than investing in our comparative advantage—technology. And I began to look at what were the areas in which we could invest and that we needed an investment strategy for high technology that could be played out."[23]

Poindexter pulled together some of the brightest strategic minds in the U.S. military science community to talk about a resource shift from the traditional emphasis on nuclear weapons to a high-tech system in strategic weapons. The group included Bob Lenhart, an aide on the NSC; General Richard Bovery; Al Keel of the Office of Management and Budget; John Foster of the high-tech company TRW; and Richard DeLauer, a scientist and engineer. Also included was Dr. George Keyworth, President Reagan's science adviser. "We met in the Situation Room and brainstormed for a while," Poindexter recalls. "The conclusion of the meeting was that the technology had progressed so much since the days of the ABM that the idea of strategic defense deserved a lot of research."[24]

As Poindexter proceeded with these consultations, McFarlane broached the idea with Paul Gorman of the Joint Chiefs of Staff. Gorman told him that the JCS had an interest in the concept, thanks largely to Admiral James Watkins, a serious student of science who believed that technology had progressed to the point where the United States could shift from mutual assured destruction (MAD) to a strategic defense posture.

After getting a green light from members of the science community and the JCS, Poindexter and McFarlane went to Bill Clark, who was the President's national security adviser. They explained

In 1946, Ronald Reagan was living the good life in Hollywood with a new $1 million contract. He spent weekends playing golf with Jack Benny or George Burns, followed by dinner at the trendy Beverly Club. Though superstardom eluded him, a Gallup poll ranked him with Laurence Olivier in terms of audience popularity.

A strike erupts in Hollywood in September 1946. Reagan and other stars are soon required to pick sides.

Violence marred the 1946 strike. Warner Brothers security advised performers to sneak onto the studio lot through a drainage ditch to avoid injury. Reagan refused and drove through the gauntlet in a car.

The Hollywood strike of 1946 was organized by Herb Sorrell (r.), who hoped to take over film industry unions. Supported by money from the Communist Party and the organizational help of Soviet agents, Sorrell warned those who opposed him, "There may be men hurt, there may be men killed before this is over."

Ronald Reagan with his family—
Maureen, Michael, and Jane
Wyman in 1946. His opposition to the
communist-backed strike brought death
threats, forcing him to sit up at nights with
a pistol to guard his family.

Following his divorce from Jane
Wyman, Reagan fell in love with
actress Nancy Davis. Unlike Wyman,
she shared many of his views about
politics and the world.

While working as a spokesman for General Electric, Reagan began thinking about how to defeat the Soviet Union. Instead of arms control, he suggested an intensified arms race. "In an all-out race our system is stronger," he told audiences. If Moscow tried to keep up, the communist system would become "unhinged."

R onald Reagan and
Lauren Bacall onstage
with Harry Truman in Los
Angeles, 1948. Concerned
that Henry Wallace was soft on
communism, Reagan launched
and served as chairman of the
League of Hollywood Voters.
He encouraged stars such
as Humphrey Bogart, Desi
Arnaz, and Gregory Peck to
support Truman.

B y 1967, California
governor Ronald Reagan
was telling voters that we
needed to go further than
Truman's policy of containment.
Only by changing the communist system itself would peace
be possible.

As governor, Reagan was outspoken on issues ranging from campus radicalism to Fidel Castro. His views landed him on a hit list for the Weather Underground. The group kept a bullet with Reagan's name on it at their headquarters.

Reagan visiting Lawrence Livermore National Laboratory, 1967. The first governor to visit the weapons lab, he also made visits to Los Alamos.

Governor Reagan and his family at home in Sacramento. In 1969, radicals angered by his views came within inches of firebombing his house as the children slept inside.

George C. Scott in the title role in *Patton.* "I told you once," Reagan wrote the film's producer, Frank McCarthy, "I would hate anyone who ever played that role other than myself." For Reagan, Patton was the type of leader America sorely needed in the Vietnam era.

February 1973: American POWs return home from Vietnam. America lost the war because of a lack of political leadership, Reagan believed. On the advice of General Omar Bradley, Reagan proposed winning the war by invading North Vietnam.

Ronald Reagan and Henry Kissinger, 1978. Reagan was a strong critic of détente and argued for economic warfare, cranking up the arms race, and actively supporting dissidents behind the Iron Curtain.

March 1981: the assassination attempt. The bullet came within inches of killing Reagan. He believed his life had been spared by God for a reason.

Ron and Nancy Reagan meet with Pope John Paul II. God had spared his life, Reagan told the Pontiff, so he could defeat communism.

Reagan's military buildup and hard line toward Moscow were highly unpopular, according to the polls. But Reagan vowed to stay the course, even if it cost him reelection.

From 1981 to 1983 Reagan signed a series of top-secret directives to wage an economic and political war against the Kremlin.

Reagan at a cabinet meeting, 1983. At critical junctures, he rejected the advice of most of his cabinet and charted his own course.

onald Reagan at the Berlin Wall, 1982. Reagan visited the wall more than any other president, and the Stasi worried when he did, fearing he was encouraging dissident activities. Even a private visit he made before he was president brought heavy surveillance by Stasi cameras and agents.

eagan at the Korean Demilitarized Zone in 1983. North Korea had plans to kill him during the visit.

Reagan and Gorbachev meet for the first time in Geneva, 1985. Reagan told Gorbachev that when it came to an arms race, "I assure you we won't lose."

Ronald Reagan confronts Mikhail Gorbachev at the Reykjavík Summit. Russian transcripts of the meeting show Reagan did more than hold his own against the Soviet leader.

Reagan asks Gorbachev to "tear down this wall" in 1987. Reagan had first suggested the gesture in 1967.

Ronald Reagan looks over his Soviet-bloc intelligence file on his eighty-first birthday in February 1992. John Koehler (r.), a long-time friend and AP reporter, discovered them in the Stasi archives.

Reagan left office confident in how history would judge him. When he visited newly freed Central Europe a year after leaving office, he was greeted in Berlin by a love song written in his honor, titled "The Man Who Made Those Pussyfooters and Weaklings Feel Ashamed." In Poland, Solidarity leader Lech Walesa's parish priest gave him a sword. "I am giving you the saber for helping us to chop off the head of communism."

what they had found, and Clark decided to act immediately. In December 1982, he arranged for members of the Joint Chiefs to meet privately with President Reagan.

There was a tremendous snowstorm that day and Clark was out of town, so McFarlane ended up running the meeting. The roads in Washington were so covered with snow and ice that the the Joint Chiefs had to be brought to the White House in tracked military vehicles. McFarlane raised the subject first, and the Joint Chiefs immediately announced their belief that the United States should consider ending its complete dependence on MAD and move toward research and development of a strategic defense initiative system. Reagan sat and quietly listened.

For Reagan, the idea was nothing new. He had first heard about fantastic laser systems with military applications while visiting Lawrence Livermore as governor and during his freewheeling conversations with Maxwell Hunter. And he was aware of how vulnerable America was to a missile strike. Only a couple of years earlier, before he was elected president, Reagan had traveled with an aide, Martin Anderson, to NORAD in Colorado, where it was laid out in no uncertain terms that America could do nothing to stop even a single missile.

The military brass finished their presentation in the Oval Office, and Reagan took to the idea almost immediately. He did so, according to most of his advisers, out of strong conviction. "He thought MAD was quite simply immoral," recalls Secretary of State George Shultz.[25]

Shortly after the meeting with the JCS, Clark sat down with McFarlane and Poindexter to determine how to proceed. It was McFarlane who suggested that the President mention the idea in a speech—a sort of public affirmation of the shift in the American strategic vision.

The plan to explore a strategic defense system was kept low-key for a while. Shultz, Weinberger, and certain members of the JCS were not consulted about the speech until two days before it was made. McFarlane worked feverishly to hammer out a speech, using his own typewriter—no secretaries—to maintain secrecy. Reagan made edits that toughened the speech considerably.

Where McFarlane had written that the plan was to "try harder at lowering the level of arms . . . we simply must succeed in this endeavor," Reagan edited it to read that there was a need to follow a "course to lower the level of arms. . . . We are engaged right now in negotiating with the Soviet Union to bring about a mutual reduction of all weapons." Where McFarlane had written that strategic defense "will not be rapidly or easily obtained," Reagan struck the phrase completely.

But on the eve of the speech, many top advisers started to get cold feet. Robert McFarlane consulted with people at DOD and the State Department. Secretary of State George Shultz and several Pentagon officials, Ron Lehman in particular, apparently did not want him to give the strategic defense speech. Many people, wrote McFarlane in a memo, "have expressed their most extreme concern at the uproar which the initiative will cause among the European Defense and Political Community." One adviser he quoted in the memo said his speech would "create a furor from which we will never recover."[26]

Clark went to Reagan and briefed him on these concerns. Reagan listened and expressed his determination to proceed anyway.

In late March 1983, Reagan addressed the nation: "Wouldn't it be better to save lives than to avenge them? Are we not capable of demonstrating our peaceful intentions by applying all our abilities and our ingenuity to achieving a truly lasting stability? . . . Let me share with you a vision which offers hope. It is that we embark on a program to counter the awesome Soviet missile threat with measures that are defensive. . . . Current technology has attained a level of sophistication where it's reasonable to begin this effort . . . to give us the means of rendering these nuclear weapons impotent and obsolete."[27]

The day after the speech, Reagan signed a directive that called for research into the program to begin.[28]

★   ★   ★

Moscow's response to the SDI speech was a mix of shock and horror. Aleksandr Bessmertynkh, who was working in the Foreign Ministry at the time and later became Soviet Foreign Minister, recalls, "For the first weeks, that announcement seemed a little bit fantastic. But then it started to come to the minds of the leaders that there might be something very, very dangerous in that."[29]

Yuri Andropov, who had replaced Brezhnev as General Secretary, declared that Reagan's move was an attempt to achieve global superiority. SDI was "a bid to disarm the Soviet Union," he declared in a public speech. "Should this conception be converted into reality, this would actually open the floodgates to a runaway race of all types of strategic arms, both offensive and defensive." A booklet by the Soviet military publishing house warned that SDI signified an American effort to achieve "world supremacy."[30]

Almost immediately, Moscow began a propaganda campaign to undermine the SDI program. A month after Reagan's speech, a group of two hundred Soviet scientists wrote a letter, which was published in the New York Times, denouncing the Reagan administration's initiative. The letter, which repeated many of the criticisms made by Andropov, set off a firestorm of criticism in the United States. Other scientists joined in the protest. CIA analysts noted in a report that, ironically, many of the Soviet scientists who signed the letter to the Times had "been instrumental in the development of both conventional and exotic missile defense systems."[31]

More quietly, however, the Soviet leadership began to think hard about how serious the SDI challenge might be. The Kremlin arranged for a group of scientists, headed by Yeveniy Velikhov, Vice President of the Academy of Sciences, to analyze SDI technology and determine if it could actually work. A physicist by training, Velikhov was a leading figure in the Soviet laser and particle-beam weapons effort. He also had signed the New York Times letter.

"A team was organized around him which contained our best specialists who could help answer these questions," recalls General Nikolai Detinov. "Around these academics a group of our best professionals was also gathered to help answer these questions." The group met for several months, evaluating the military, economic, and strategic implications of Reagan's programs. It presented its conclusions to the Kremlin at the end of 1983.

While asserting that the SDI program would fail to produce a leak-proof defense system over the next fifteen to twenty years, the group was troubled by the general thrust of the program. The Soviet Union's best and brightest believed that the SDI program could lead, in the words of General Detinov, "to the development of a whole line of new technologies in the United States that were not completely devoted to defending against a strike from the Soviet Union but to a certain degree still constituted an anti-missile defense. This was the danger of the program."

In short, the Kremlin came to believe that the United States might not be able to develop a defense system to protect against a first strike by the Soviet Union. But it could, in the words of General Detinov, "create some kind of system that would be able to defend against a Soviet retaliatory attack. . . . This understanding alarmed us. It also alarmed scientists and our general staff and a number of the leaders of our country."

General Vladimir Slipchenko, a leading military scientist who served on the Soviet General Staff, recalls that SDI put the military "in a state of fear and shock because we understood that this could be realistic due to the economic and financial capabilities of the United States." Compounding this fact was the military's view that because of its weak economy, the Soviet Union "was not ready or prepared to respond adequately."[32]

Reagan quickly became aware of Soviet fears over SDI, and of Soviet economic vulnerability if the nation attempted to compete in this area. Months after Reagan's Star Wars speech, CIA Director William Casey authorized a secret study to determine how Moscow might respond to the SDI program. Moscow was "not confident that, over the long haul, they could match US technology if the United States makes a high-level sustained effort, and they would be reluctant to be drawn into a technological 'race' with the United States."

If Reagan hung tough, the report said, Moscow would be faced with a vexing, expensive choice. The Soviets could try to match Reagan's program or they could try to circumvent it. Either option would require enormous changes that they probably could not afford.[33]

CHAPTER XIV

A PLAN

I N A 1967 VETERANS DAY SPEECH TO A JUNIOR HIGH SCHOOL IN Albany, Oregon, Reagan had explained his views on the origins of war. "In all of history, one can find few, if any, instances where people have started a war. War is the province of government, and therefore the more autocratic government is, the more centralized, the more totalitarian, the more government can direct and control the will of the people—the greater the chance of war."

Focusing on weapons, diplomatic niceties, and dialogue meant you were looking only at symptoms. You needed to look instead at the nature of the Soviet system. If you wanted peace, you needed to change the Soviet system. As he told the students, too many people were of the opinion that " 'there are no simple answers to these complex problems.' Is it possible that the answer is, in truth, simple, but one that demands too much, one that is simply too hard for too many of us to accept?"[1]

As the Pentagon began developing the top-secret defense guidance, work began at the White House on how to reshape America's national defense strategy. Reagan had been a longtime critic of America's foreign policy. As a member of the Crusade for Freedom, he had been a passionate supporter of liberating the "captive nations." When it came to wars in Korea and Vietnam, he believed American presidents had failed to make victory their chief goal. And détente had been a failure because, far from mellowing the Soviets, it had instead given them a new lease on life.

Two trusted longtime Reagan friends were put in charge of shaping the new strategy—William P. Clark and Tom Reed, the same men who had spoken with Reagan about the continuity-of-government program. The process was to be supersensitive. "All matters relating to this . . . will be classified Top Secret," read the directive that began the process.[2]

Clark and Reed pulled together a team that included Fred Ikle from the Pentagon, who was piecing together the defense guidance; Richard Pipes from the National Security Council; and Lawrence Eagleburger from the State Department. This small group, along with a select group of their aides, met and debated, disagreed and cajoled, trying to craft a new strategy. They went through nine interagency segments to hammer the document together. The whole process was less science than art, as ideas were adopted and abandoned depending on whether Reagan approved of them during his reviews.

Reagan received updates in the form of memos, and he would sit at his desk in the Oval Office, scribbling notes in the margin of a memo before firing it back to Clark. The Joint Chiefs of Staff were even brought in a number of times to look at various parts of the study.

"But when it was done," Clark said, "the study and the decisions were the President's."[3]

The study led to a National Security Decision Directive, which laid out several top-secret global objectives, among them:

Global objective #3: "To contain and reverse the expansion of Soviet control and military presence throughout the world, and to increase the costs of Soviet support and use of proxy, terrorist and subversive forces."

Global objective #5: "To foster, if possible in concert with our allies, restraint in Soviet military spending, discourage Soviet adventurism, and weaken the Soviet alliance system by forcing the USSR to bear the brunt of its economic shortcomings, and to encourage long-term liberalizing and nationalist tendencies within the Soviet Union and allied countries."

No American administration had ever pledged to go so far in seeking to undermine the Soviet system. Reagan understood this, and he knew his radical approach was not without risks. Given Soviet military superiority and American attempts to regain it, the possibility of war in the 1980s was the greatest "since World War II," said the directive Reagan signed. But if the United States stuck to this policy, Reagan declared, it "could result in a fundamentally different East-West relationship by the end of the decade."[4]

Precisely *how* to force change in the Soviet system was the critical question. Reagan had written and spoken out on this subject numerous times over the past two decades. In 1963, he conceived a plan to squeeze the Soviet economy with a military buildup and a cutoff of trade. In 1972, after reading Laurence Beilenson's book *Power Through Subversion*, he grew fond of the idea of supporting insurgents and subversives trying to undermine communist regimes. During détente, he had spoken about the need to form common cause with people behind the Iron Curtain. What was now needed was someone to connect all the dots with a detailed plan or strategy.

The task fell to Richard Pipes, who had been recruited to join the NSC to handle the Soviet folio. Pipes was a first-rate intellect, a Baird Professor of History at Harvard and author of scholarly works on the formation of the Soviet Union and the life of Peter Stuve, the intellectual founder of Russian social democracy. Where Reagan was intuitive in his thinking, using instinct and natural insight to sift through the issues, Pipes was a meticulous scholar. The two men gathered, processed, and stored information differently. And yet both had arrived at the same conclusions about the Soviet Union.

Like Reagan, Pipes had been arguing for years that the Soviet Union was doomed to face disruptions and would probably collapse if proper pressures were applied. In 1976, he explained to an interviewer that Moscow could not compete with the United States in an arms race. Reagan had arrived at that conclusion through intuitive insight, whereas Pipes made reference to the memoirs of Khrushchev, where the Soviet leader declared "that vast military expenditure is all very well for the Americans who can sustain it and profit from it, but it spells the ruin of the communist world." Pipes went on to quote Khrushchev's conclusion that if a real arms race took place, it might "bring about the collapse of socialism and a restoration of capitalism in our country."[5]

For his views, Pipes had faced what Reagan had experienced in Hollywood—ostracism by his colleagues. Many of Pipes's colleagues considered him an anti-Communist ideologue who was out of step with the times, and were scornful of his appointment to the NSC. The *Washington Post* declared that "for rank hysteria in scholarly garb, it's hard to top Harvard prof Richard Pipes." But Reagan stood by him.[6]

After being given his assignment by Clark, Pipes began laboring away in his cramped third-floor office at the Old Executive Office Building. The result of several months of work was a stunning forty-three-page secret paper that largely confirmed what Reagan had been saying for twenty years.

Pipes began with the notion that détente had been a mistake because it attempted to deal with the Soviet leadership in the hope that the Soviets would change their policy. Pipes argued that, instead, Soviet aggressiveness was inherent in the system and therefore what was necessary was to change the system—basically, what Reagan had said in 1967. "U.S. policy toward the Soviet Union proceeds on the assumption that the maintenance of power by the Soviet regime rests ultimately on force and that Soviet external aggressiveness stems in part from the nature of the Soviet political system," Pipes began.

For that reason, the United States needed to pursue three key objectives: "The decentralization and demilitarization of the Soviet economy; (2) the weakening of power and privileged position of the ruling communist elite; (3) gradual democratization of the USSR." Nothing quite so bold had ever been proposed before.

Pipes painted a picture of a Soviet Union stretched to its limits, vulnerable to ethnic strife, and lacking in political legitimacy. Behind this view was the fact that a huge military budget was straining the resource base of the Soviet Union. "To maintain the military build-up, it has lowered the rate of growth for consumption and capital investment. If these priorities continue, however, the living standard will hold steady and may decline and investment will be squeezed. . . .

This would sharply restrict the resources available to non-military claimants and heighten political tensions over allocation decisions." Pipes predicted that in the face of Reagan's defense buildup the Soviet Union would be under greater pressure to reduce the growth in military spending in order to free up the labor and capital resources urgently needed in the civilian economy.

But Soviet vulnerabilities went beyond economics. Economic problems were causing "growing malaise in Soviet society," Pipes wrote, leading to strikes, a flourishing black market, and widespread corruption. This struck at the heart of the system, because "the malaise in Soviet society is symptomatic of an underlying loss of commitment to the system and to the political order."

Pipes also expected more upheaval in Eastern Europe, like what had been happening in Poland. The Soviets had been trying to buy political stability there but could no longer afford it. "In the coming decade slow economic growth in Eastern Europe will threaten regime stability in bloc countries. The downfall of a corrupt and incompetent party leadership in Poland, precipitated by the protests of a popular workers' movement, and the use of the military to fill the gap, also raise disquieting questions about the legitimacy and effectiveness of Communist party rule throughout the bloc."

These were truly radical ideas in 1982. But Pipes went further. Three years before a young man named Mikhail Gorbachev entered the scene, he predicted a new reformer would emerge in Moscow. This new leader would "favor a more accommodating foreign policy stance in order to increase trade with the West and ease domestic economic problems." However, his goal would be saving the Soviet system, not fundamentally changing it.

Given these realities, Pipes proposed that the United States adopt a strategy that would "exploit the vulnerabilities in Moscow's global situation." The decade ahead presented a unique opportunity for the United States in this regard. "The Soviet system has never undergone the kind of passage it will be taking in the 1980s and the West has not in the post-war period made change in the Soviet Union an explicit objective of its dealings with the USSR, and taken steps to give practical meaning to that objective.

"The increasing attraction that some Western values hold for the

Soviet people will cause the regime to expend considerable effort to protect them from foreign contagion and to prevent the development of a strong dissident movement. The Soviet economy also will be hard pressed to keep pace with rising consumer expectations, probably resulting in more leadership attention to work stoppages, strikes, and other manifestations of social unrest." Therefore, Pipes argued, the United States should "exacerbate weaknesses in Soviet foreign and domestic policy."

Pipes laid out the policy with staggering clarity. "U.S. policy toward the Soviet Union must therefore address both the requirement to contain and reverse Soviet expansion and the need to strengthen and sustain a process of promoting change within the USSR itself that will reduce the Soviet threat to U.S. interests and those of our allies. This second track of U.S. policy toward the Soviet Union is not designed to preserve the status quo, but to assist internal forces that might lead to constructive change.

"By identifying the promotion of evolutionary change within the Soviet Union itself as an objective of U.S. policy, the United States takes the long-term strategic offensive. This approach therefore contrasts with the essentially reactive and defensive strategy of containment, which concedes the initiative to the Soviet Union and its allies and surrogates."

Critical to this effort was not only sustaining the Reagan military buildup that would drain the Soviet economy, but also restricting Soviet access to Western technology. The goal should be "to avoid subsidizing the Soviet economy or unduly easing the burden of Soviet resource allocation decisions, so as not to dilute pressures for structural change in the Soviet system."

Along with economic pressure, the Pipes study also called for aggressive political action. There was a battle of ideas taking place, and the United States needed to be engaged. "U.S. policy toward the Soviet Union must have an ideological thrust which clearly demonstrates the superiority of U.S. and Western values of individual dignity and freedom, a free press, free trade unions, free enterprise, and political democracy over the repressive character of Soviet communism. We should state openly our belief that people in communist countries have the right to democratic systems."

Pipes argued that this battle of ideas should also include efforts to covertly support democratic movements. The Reagan administration should "encourage democratic movements and forces to bring about political change inside these countries. In this connection, the U.S. must develop the means to extend U.S. support to individuals and movements that share the U.S. commitment to political democracy and individual freedom. Long-term political cadre and organization building programs, long a strongly emphasized instrument of Soviet policy, must become a regular, and more developed, part of U.S. policy."[7]

★   ★   ★

THE PIPES STUDY WAS DELIVERED TO THE OVAL OFFICE IN EARLY December 1982. Reagan read through it and examined a top-secret National Security Decision Directive that was attached. The directive would order senior officials in his administration to pursue several new objectives toward the Soviet Union, among them: "To contain and over time reverse Soviet expansionism" and "To promote, within the narrow limits available to us, the process of change in the Soviet Union toward a more pluralistic political and economic system in which the power of the privileged ruling elite is gradually reduced."[8]

Reagan set the study and the directive down on his desk. Having reviewed the study for NSSD 11-82, he was making it policy. He lifted his pen and signed his name.

Reagan's war, now spelled out in detail, was secretly official U.S. policy.

CHAPTER XV

THE CHANCE OF
A LIFETIME

I N EARLY SEPTEMBER, EIGHT HUNDRED POLISH WORKERS GATH-
ered in a modern sports complex on the outskirts of the port
city of Gdansk. This was the first congress of the Solidarity
movement, and the workers had gathered to determine the
next stage in their campaign for greater freedom behind the Iron
Curtain. As the meeting convened, there were real reminders of just
what they were up against: Only a few miles away, more than
100,000 members of the Soviet Army were practicing maneuvers
along the Polish border.

Poland had been chafing under Soviet rule from the beginning,
when the Red Army had occupied the country in 1945. Throughout the Cold War period there had been strikes, protests, and small
opposition movements. But in the summer of 1980 matters got
alarmingly worse for the Kremlin when increases in food prices set
off a wave of labor unrest.

Workers at the Lenin Shipyard in Gdansk had gone on strike in
mid-August, led by a plucky electrician named Lech Walesa. They
occupied the shipyard and issued far-reaching demands for labor reform and greater civil rights. Solidarity, the first free trade union behind the Iron Curtain, had been born. Within less than a year,

membership in the movement had swelled to 10 million people, or more than one of every four people in the country.

Moscow's reaction to these startling developments had been predictable. Leonid Brezhnev, now aged and a whisper away from death, called up Soviet Army reserves and increased the combat readiness of the Soviet Northern Group of Forces stationed in the area. Soviet warships were dispatched for a "friendly" visit to Polish ports, a show of force that was expected to intimidate the Polish public.

More quietly, the Kremlin established a special commission to explore how to deal with the growing problem in Poland. Headed by Mikhail Suslov, a party functionary who had risen quickly through the ranks under Josef Stalin and was now the party's chief ideologist, the commission included KGB head Andropov, Foreign Minister Andrei Gromyko, and Defense Minister Dmitri Ustinov.[1]

Moscow was not the only communist power concerned about events in Poland; Solidarity was a threat to the entire Soviet empire. East Germany's Erich Honecker and Czechoslovakia's Gustav Husak, who shared a border with Poland, wanted immediate military action to be taken. Working with Warsaw Pact commanders, the Kremlin drew up plans for the invasion of Poland: Soviet, East German, and Czech troops would enter the country under the pretext of military maneuvers. Fifteen Soviet divisions, one East German, and two from Czechoslovakia would breach the border and deploy in the proximity of big cities and industrial centers. Polish military units would be ordered to stay in their barracks and not interfere. Plans called for the use of violence if necessary.[2]

But as the delegates met at the Olivia sports complex near Gdansk, events were taking a dramatic turn. Going beyond their initial calls for reform, the delegates now demanded free elections. They also issued a call for workers in other Soviet-bloc countries "who made up their mind to fight for the free trade union movement" to meet with Solidarity leaders. It was nothing less than a call for unified action against communist authorities throughout the Soviet bloc. The appeal was so direct and stunning that it sent Yuri Andropov into a rage during one Politburo session.[3]

Other Soviet-bloc leaders were equally angered and concerned. The Hungarian leader János Kádár declared in a confidential letter to

Stanislaw Kania of Poland, "The provocative message of the Solidarity congress directed to the workers of the socialist countries . . . is
evidently a step suggested by international reactionary forces to divide and set the people of the socialist countries against one another."[4]
In Bulgaria, communist authorities feared that events in Poland
would quickly spin out of control. Force needed to be used. "A delay
in delivering a blow [against the counterrevolutionaries] will result in
loss of power and the restoration of capitalism," declared Foreign
Minister Mladenov in secret consultations. "It should be clear that if
new elections were to be held, anti-socialist forces take power."[5]

In East Berlin, Erich Honecker said that if Solidarity was not
stopped he would soon face "German imperialism in front of us, and
the possibility of a capitalist Poland behind us."[6]

This was not simple paranoia. Solidarity's ideas were spilling over
into other communist countries. Czechoslovakia, East Germany, and
Hungary were seeing a rise in dissident activities. Even the Soviet
Union itself was not immune to the infection. According to a KGB
report for 1981, Solidarity activists "who were inciting strikes among
Polish workers employed at construction sites in the Soviet Union"
had been expelled from the country. And there were labor strikes in
neighboring Estonia.[7] Major General Ya. L. Zhuk, head of Soviet
military counterintelligence in the Baltic Military District, noted in
one report that "many Soviet servicemen are displaying politically
hostile and nationalist sentiments and, on this basis, are intending to
commit treacherous and other hostile acts. . . . They approve of the
subversive activity of Solidarity."[8]

The time for hoping that the problem would disappear or solve
itself was rapidly coming to an end; it was time for action.

Moscow quietly began placing an array of specialists in Warsaw
to coordinate a brutal crackdown inside Poland.[9] The hope was that
the Polish government would be able to handle it by itself. Marshal
Viktor Kulikov, commander in chief of the Warsaw Pact, told senior
Polish officials in a private meeting that they had to try to solve the
problem of worker unrest themselves. Kulikov hastened to add,
however, that if they did need help the Warsaw Pact armies would
come to their assistance.[10]

In Washington, President Reagan was following events in
Poland closely. He had watched emotionally in 1979 when the pope

visited his native land and had remained optimistic that Poland would someday be free.

But there were signs that trouble lay ahead. Throughout the late summer and early fall of 1981, Warsaw Pact troops moved along the Polish border. State Department cables reported that the Soviets were quietly closing the border between Poland and Lithuania.[11] There were also remarkable feelers being sent out by some Polish officials who were sympathetic to Solidarity. Approaching U.S. diplomats, they explained their fear that Reagan, like previous presidents, would abandon Poland if the Soviets cracked down and simply leave the Polish people to their fate. According to a secret State Department cable, one senior Polish diplomat "expressed some concern about the possibility that the U.S. and the USSR had discussed or agreed upon new 'spheres of interest,' such as those agreed upon at Potsdam and Yalta, to Poland's detriment." He was quietly assured that no such agreements had been made.[12]

Reagan was determined not to do anything of the sort. He had championed the Crusade for Freedom goals in the 1950s and had been critical of both Eisenhower's inaction after the Soviet invasion of Hungary in 1956 and of LBJ after the crushing of the Prague Spring in 1968. It was clear that those feelings had never left him. On the thirtieth anniversary of the Hungary uprising, he pointedly asked: "Can anyone truly say it was in fact in our interest to stand by, hands folded at the dying of light in Hungary?"[13]

Reagan was kept apprised of events in Poland thanks to several senior Polish military officers who were spying for the CIA, the most important of whom was Colonel Ryszard Kuklinski, an aide to the Polish national defense minister. Kuklinski was a particularly capable and efficient spy who smuggled out more than thirty thousand pages of classified Soviet and Warsaw Pact documents to the CIA. His cache of information included war plans, military maps, allied command procedures, summaries of exercises, blueprints of command bunkers, electronic warfare manuals, military targeting guidelines, and Warsaw Pact nuclear doctrine. Kuklinski also provided detailed information on Polish plans for martial law; he just wasn't sure when it would happen.

Kuklinski communicated with the CIA through a contact codenamed Daniel in a series of notes and letters. He expressed fear among some pro-Western officers that the United States might abandon the country to the Soviet Union just as it had done after World War II. "In this extremely gloomy atmosphere," he wrote on April 26, 1981, "one of the most committed officers openly said that Poland had to undertake far-reaching political reforms. General XXX [not identified in the letter] bitterly accused 'the Americans [of having] sold us out to Russia. Without the Americans' silent assent, the "comrades" would not dare to act in this way.' "

Kuklinski himself struggled with this question and concluded: "We Poles realize that we must fight for our own freedom, if necessary making the ultimate sacrifice. I remain convinced that the support your country has been giving to all who are fighting for that freedom will bring us closer to our goal." He signed himself, "With heartfelt greetings. Yours, PV."[14]

CIA Director William Casey was monitoring these reports closely. Like Reagan, he was determined not to abandon the Poles. The stakes were high; the outcome of events in that country could determine the fate of the entire communist system.

On December 4, 1981, Casey received a secret memo from his assistant, Robert Gates, about the need to keep the Solidarity experiment alive. It was in America's interest to see a continuation of the Polish experiment. There were signs that it was spilling over into other Soviet-bloc countries. "I believe it is not going too far to say that the successful implantation of pluralism in Poland would represent the beginning of the end of Soviet-style totalitarianism in Eastern Europe, with extraordinary implications for all Europe and for the USSR itself."[15]

Bill Casey certainly needed no convincing. In a top-secret memo of his own, Casey wrote that Solidarity was a bold experiment in the heart of the Soviet empire, whose "very survival will contribute to the long-term unraveling of the Soviet position in Eastern Europe."[16]

★   ★   ★

ON DECEMBER 9, A HEAVILY FORTIFIED SOVIET MILITARY TRANSport plane escorted by fighter aircraft descended onto a secret military air base near Warsaw. Onboard was Marshal Kulikov, the

Warsaw Pact's commander in chief. He was greeted by heavily armed Soviet security agents, who bundled him into the back of a black sedan and drove at high speed to a nearby Soviet military installation.

Three days later, Operation Springtime began. In the middle of the night, Polish security forces, supported by Polish military units, in effect invaded their own country. Tanks rolled into the streets of Warsaw; roadblocks were set up throughout the country. Simultaneously, 3.4 million private telephones went dead. Five thousand Solidarity activists were rounded up in one night; borders were sealed with Poland's neighbors. The Polish internal security apparatus mobilized its force of 250,000, including motorized police units (ZOMO) and paramilitary forces under the command of the Interior Ministry. The resistance, or so officials thought, had collapsed without a fight. At 6:00 A.M., General Jaruzelski went on radio and television to announce that a "state of war" had been declared and that authority now rested with the newly formed Military Council of National Salvation.

Reagan was at his ranch in California when he got the first reports out of Poland. While many in the White House were numb at the news, Reagan was furious. He got on the phone with aides to discuss the situation.

"The President was absolutely livid," recalls Richard Pipes of the NSC. "He said, 'Something must be done. We need to hit them hard, and save Solidarity.' The president was gung-ho, ready to go."[17]

Reagan immediately returned to Washington to determine his next move. At the CIA, Bill Casey worried about the broader implications of martial law. "If the Polish government makes martial law work and settles Poland," he asked agency analysts, "will it allow the Soviets additional freedom of action elsewhere?"

CIA analysts wrote back that if martial law worked it would have a strong psychological effect because it would "enhance Soviet credibility" and encourage allies such as Syria, Libya, and Cuba. A lot seemed to be resting on exactly who won in Poland.[18]

★ ★ ★

REAGAN CONVENED AN EMERGENCY MEETING OF THE NSC. "THE Soviet-backed action must not stand," he declared. As his advisers discussed the situation, Reagan jotted a note to himself. His goal was nothing short of free elections in Poland.[19]

As Reagan recorded in his diary: "I took a stand that this may be the last chance in our lifetime to see a change in the Soviet empire's colonial policy re Eastern Europe. We should take a stand and tell them unless and until martial law is lifted in Poland, the prisoners were released and negotiations resumed between Walesa and the Polish government, we would quarantine the Soviets and Poland with no trade or communications across their borders. Also tell our NATO allies and others to join us in such sanctions or risk an estrangement from us."

It quickly became apparent that whatever Reagan planned to do, he was probably going to have to do it alone. In Europe, the Socialist International, an influential body that included political leaders and heads of state from Social Democrats and Socialists in Germany, France, Great Britain, and a smattering of other Western European countries, issued a bland statement. Comparing the human rights situation in Poland to that in Turkey, it went on to equate the Soviet occupation of Afghanistan with the civil war in El Salvador. (The group never explained how ninety thousand occupying troops were the same as fifty-five American military advisers.)

On orders from Washington, U.S. diplomats in West Germany met with officials to gauge the German position. What they discovered was more than a bit disturbing. According to U.S. State Department cables, West German officials were less concerned about martial law than about American remarks. German officials said they were taking a wait-and-see attitude as to whether Jaruzelski would succeed or not. They even proposed extending economic assistance to Poland because it might help Jaruzelski succeed in his "national renewal" efforts. West German officials emphasized that whatever happened in Poland, they didn't want it to affect relations with the Soviet Union.[20]

The response from many other allies was similar, so Reagan decided to act alone.

"We can't let this revolution against Communism fail without offering a hand," he wrote in his diary. "We may never have an opportunity like this in our lifetime."

On December 29, Reagan took to the airwaves to announce an embargo against Poland and the Soviet Union for the declaration of martial law. Poland would now lose its most favored nation (MFN) trading status and face high tariffs on its exports to the United States. Reagan would work to prevent any new financial credits from being extended to the Polish government. Most important, he issued a decree banning the sale of oil and gas technologies to the Soviet Union. It was a decision that would cost the Kremlin billions.

The sanctions were hard-hitting and designed to target critical sectors of the Soviet-bloc economy. Reagan wanted to use the sanctions as a tool to keep the freedom experiment in Poland alive. "If the Polish government will honor the commitments it has made to basic human rights in documents like the Gdansk agreement, we in America will gladly do our share to help the shattered Polish economy, just as we helped the countries of Europe after both world wars."[21]

As a weapon the sanctions were well targeted; Poland was vulnerable to Western economic pressure. "Poland is largely dependent on the West, above all on the German Federal Republic and the USA," said one Warsaw Pact report. "Its capital debt is some $27 billion." Without an infusion of capital from the West or the opportunity to export goods to the United States, Poland's economy would be in shambles.[22]

Poland exported large amounts of natural resources and other goods to the United States. Sanctions meant that Poland now had little access to the American market, cutting off access to critically needed hard currency. As General Czeslaw Kiszczak, then Polish interior minister and cocreator of martial law, told me, "Economic sanctions caused enormous losses in the economy."[23]

★   ★   ★

REAGAN'S FIRM LINE LEFT HIM ALONE AMONG WESTERN LEADERS. The most critical Western power with ties to Poland was West Germany. Washington tried to convince Bonn to support at least some of what Reagan was doing. But Chancellor Helmut Schmidt was offering at best only grudging support. In a private meeting with East Germany's Erich Honecker, according to a secret East German transcript, Schmidt declared that martial law was "necessary."[24] In a meeting between German foreign minister Hans Dietrich Genscher and the Polish vice premier, Genscher likewise justified the imposition of martial law.[25]

Schmidt arrived in Washington in early 1982 to discuss the situation in Poland and met with Secretary of State Al Haig. The two sat for breakfast and engaged in a wide-ranging discussion. Schmidt was frank and blunt.

He declared that the Soviets viewed Poland as "theirs," and that it was ridiculous for Reagan to think he could "overthrow the post–World War II division of Europe," according to a secret State Department transcript of the meeting. Schmidt actually chided Haig about the idea that political freedom was possible in Poland.

"The West needs to be realistic regarding the possibilities for change in Eastern Europe," he said. Reagan was suffering from "illusions" if he expected Moscow to honor the Helsinki Final Accord guaranteeing basic individual rights. He even went so far as to justify martial law because he had "continuing doubts regarding the organizational skills of the Polish people, given their inclination to romanticism."

Haig pressed Schmidt to support some form of sanctions against the Soviet Union, because "we had to find ways to keep pressure on the Soviets." Schmidt responded that West Germany "would not stick its neck out."[26]

Nor, it seems, would anyone else. In Canada, Prime Minister Pierre Trudeau declared his "impartiality" over what was going on in Poland and refused to support sanctions or other measures. NATO ally Greece would not publicly criticize the crackdown at all, and while Italy criticized martial law, it said it would simply "pause to reflect" on economic relations with the Soviet bloc. Norway said Reagan's sanctions were a mistake "because they exacerbate tensions and offer no real promise of economic or political gain." France strongly condemned the imposition of martial law and pledged to hold consultations regarding new credits to Poland. But privately officials professed to understand the "difficulties and escalation" that had led to martial law. Even Reagan's erstwhile ally, Margaret Thatcher in London, would go only so far. Denouncing martial law as barbarous and declaring her support for sanctions against Poland, she was skeptical of sanctions against the Soviets. Reagan, it seemed, was all alone in his efforts to keep the Solidarity movement alive.[27]

Reagan dispatched Haig and Defense Secretary Weinberger to Europe to try to convince the U.S. allies. Ministers from all the NATO countries gathered in January for a special session of the North Atlantic Congress (NAC) to consider how the West should deal with the crisis. Haig and Weinberger haggled with their counterparts for several days and hammered out a compromise. While no one was willing to consider the kind of hard-hitting sanctions Reagan had put in place, alliance members did commit themselves to the goal of encouraging reform in Poland. As general as it was, this action was a long way from Schmidt's mild endorsement of the crackdown.

Reagan, however, made clear that he was firmly committed to liberating Poland. "What is at stake in Poland is freedom," read the official U.S. statement following the NAC meeting. "We in the west have a *responsibility not only to preserve our own freedom but to nurture it where it does not exist.*"[28]

Reagan's commitment to nurturing freedom in Poland won him criticism from many who believed he was risking conflict with the Kremlin. George Kennan, who had first formulated containment in 1947, declared that demands for freedom in Poland were "inevitably self-defeating," and that Reagan was undermining détente.[29]

★   ★   ★

IN MOSCOW, KREMLIN LEADERS TOOK COMFORT IN THE MILD words emanating from Western Europe. They applauded Europe's "realism" and "genuine concern," as opposed to the "wild accusations" coming out of Washington.[30] In Warsaw, martial law officials went a step further. With morale low among their own military officers, they circulated quotes by Schmidt made to Polish officials that "General Jaruzelski acted in the best interests of the nation."[31]

But Reagan was clearly throwing down the gauntlet. Sanctions against Poland were a major drain on Soviet resources. "We already are stretched to the limit in our capacity to help the Poles, and they are still making more requests [for money and food]," Brezhnev told the Politburo somberly after the sanctions were announced. "Perhaps we can do a bit more, but we certainly can't give a lot more."[32]

Of even greater concern was the fate of what Soviet officials routinely called the "deal of the century." The Kremlin had plans to construct a three-thousand-mile pipeline from the Urengoi gas fields of Siberia through Eastern Europe, to link up with the Western European gas grid. It was a financial dream: Billions of cubic feet of Russian natural gas would flow to West Germany, France, Italy, and Belgium, and tens of billions of dollars in desperately needed hard currency would flow back to Moscow. Making the deal even sweeter was the fact that the equipment and machinery needed to build the pipeline was being financed by the Western Europeans at interest rates well below market.

The Soviet Union had an estimated 40 percent of the world's proven natural gas reserves. The project was, in short, a cash cow.

But the massive turbines needed to make the pipeline work were made by General Electric. Now the deal was in jeopardy because of Reagan's sanctions on oil and gas technology.

For Reagan and his advisers, this was precisely the point. Sanctions were targeted on oil and gas technologies because these were needed by Moscow to keep the weakening economy upright. A report issued several months before martial law had been declared laid it all out: "With extensive Western assistance in energy (particularly gas) development Soviet hard currency earnings could rise substantially by the end of the decade. In the worst case scenario, with little or no Western assistance, Soviet exports of energy for hard currency would disappear by 1990." The future strength of the Soviet economy hinged on Moscow's ability to get access to Western technology. If Moscow failed to do so, the results could be disastrous. "This would have repercussions for the countries of both the Western alliance and the Eastern bloc. Such an outcome would certainly place strains on the economies of the U.S.S.R. and Eastern Europe, strains which would have both domestic and foreign policy consequences." Because the stakes were so high, cutting off these technologies "would be tantamount to pursuing a policy of economic warfare against the U.S.S.R."[33]

Moscow could try to go it alone and build the turbines by itself. But that would delay the project by several years. And as Soviet economist Abel Aganbegyan admitted, "Each month's delay costs us millions of rubles."[34]

Moscow, feeling the squeeze, took its complaints directly to Washington. In February, Ambassador Dobrynin had lunch with Al Haig at the State Department. Dobrynin "complained bitterly about the economic burden which had been placed on Moscow because of American trade sanctions." He also denounced what he called the administration's efforts to "isolate the Soviet Union." But he got nowhere.[35]

Moscow was not the only one who wanted the deal. Most of Western Europe saw the pipeline as a chance to create jobs and find a new source of energy. Helmut Schmidt publicly rebuked Reagan for imposing sanctions and declared that his country would proceed with the project. Much of Europe followed.

Three Western European companies—John Brown of Great Britain, AEG-Kanis in Germany, and Italy's Nuovo Pignone—produced the GE turbines under license. The allies declared that they would produce the turbines without U.S. approval. In Congress, a bill was introduced to overturn Reagan's sanctions. American industry groups and major corporations such as GE, Dresser Industries, and Caterpillar lobbied to overturn the decision. But Reagan stood firm.[36]

"They can build their damn pipeline," Reagan told his aides. "But not with our technology."[37]

Invoking the terms of the Export Control Act, Reagan announced that he was extending the sanctions to include any foreign companies that were using U.S. licensed technology. If the European firms proceeded with the pipeline deal, they would be risking a trade war with America and would be denied access to the U.S. market.

The Europeans responded swiftly. Margaret Thatcher declared that British companies would not have to comply with Reagan's order, and the French did the same.

With neither side willing to back down, it appeared that a trade war might be pending. Reagan was looking for opportunities to use the situation to defuse the crisis but still impose strong sanctions on Moscow. Was there a way out of this fix?

A young banker named Roger Robinson had recently joined the National Security Council staff. Robinson knew the Soviet economy well, having served as a vice president at Chase Manhattan Bank with responsibility for loans to the Soviet Union.

Robinson went to work and drafted a plan that would mollify

the Europeans and get them thinking in terms of applying pressure on Moscow. In consultation with the allies, a bargain was struck. In exchange for ending the pipeline sanctions, the Europeans admitted that it was not in their interest to subsidize Moscow. It was a stunning concession on the part of the Europeans, who had continued to trade and provide loans to the Soviet bloc even after the invasion of Afghanistan.

Specifically, the allies agreed "not to sign or approve any new contracts for the purchase of Soviet gas" until discussing it with Washington. They would strengthen the effectiveness of controls on transfer to the USSR of high technology, including critical oil and gas equipment. The Europeans also committed to changing their bank lending practices by "substantially raising interest rates to the USSR" in any loan agreements that were signed.[38]

The Reagan administration did not succeed in ending the pipeline project. But the sanctions did delay the project by some eighteen months. At the same time, the project was effectively cut in half: One strand would be built, but not the other. More important, perhaps, the allied agreement would lead to a more coherent economic strategy with regard to the Soviet Union. Within a few years, a more restrictive Western policy on loans and technology would be in place, severely undermining the Soviet economy.

The great deal Moscow had imagined had become tainted, and uncertainty about East-West relations meant that some banks were unwilling to proceed with the project. The fact that only one strand of the pipeline was completed severely undermined the Kremlin's financial position. Project delays and the political baggage connected with the deal effectively froze Soviet currency earnings. What Moscow had once hoped would yield dramatic increases of some $15 to $30 billion per year barely proved to be a moneymaker. According to a secret State Department assessment of Soviet energy exports to Western Europe, sales actually declined during the period. In 1981, Moscow exported 78 million cubic meters (mcm). By 1984, when the large pipeline was expected to be on-line, sales had dropped to 74 mcm.[39]

Reagan had wanted to do more than punish the Kremlin; he wanted to help the opposition in Poland. The Crusade for Freedom, of which he had been such a big part back in the 1950s, was all about helping the captive nations free themselves, and the people of Poland seemed to be trying to do just that.

As sanctions began to bite the Polish government, the CIA was tracking the activities of the opposition, looking for opportunities to help. Despite the brutal crackdown, opposition to the government was continuing. A CIA report in early February 1981 noted that work stoppages and street demonstrations were still taking place.

Especially important in resisting communist power was the Catholic Church. Pope John Paul II, himself a Pole, insisted that the communist government and not Solidarity needed to make concessions for Poland to find peace. The Church had an extensive network in the country, composed of local parish priests who were supporting the "underground resistance." Using this network, the Church could move supplies in and out of the country secretly.[40]

Reagan was certainly mindful of the role the Church could play in bringing freedom to Poland. In the summer of 1981, before martial law had been declared, he exchanged letters with an old friend named John Koehler. A longtime reporter for the Associated Press and now the AP's assistant general manager in New York, Koehler had taken an extensive trip through Central Europe. What struck him most, he reported to Reagan, was the strong religious sentiment he found among the people. It was something that greatly surprised him.

Reagan read the letter and wrote Koehler back, thanking him for his account. "I was particularly interested to read your comments about the resurgence of religion. I have had a feeling, particularly in view of the Pope's visit to Poland, that religion may very well turn out to be the Soviets' Achilles' heel. I've had some reports that it is even going on in an underground way in Russia itself.

"I know I'm being criticized for not having made a great speech outlining what would be the Reagan foreign policy. I have a foreign policy; I'm working on it. I just don't happen to think that it's wise to always stand up and put in quotation marks in front of the world what your foreign policy is."[41]

At the suggestion of his senior advisers, Reagan phoned Pope John Paul II in the days after imposition of martial law to make it clear that the U.S. government was strongly behind the Solidarity movement and planned to do all it could to sustain it. A few weeks later, State Department Special Envoy Ambassador Dick Walters was quietly dispatched to Rome to brief the Pope.

In a sense, Walters was the perfect man for the mission. A devout Catholic, he was a career army officer and a gifted linguist who spoke eight languages and many dialects. This gift for languages, as well as his ability to maneuver through difficult political waters overseas, led to his use as a special envoy by Presidents Johnson, Nixon, and Ford. Walters had also served as Deputy Director of Central Intelligence at the CIA, and had seen more than his share of action. He was involved in the 1953 coup that overthrew the left-wing government of Premier Mohammed Mossadegh in Iran. He had been in Brazil when Brazilian military officers staged a coup in 1964.

To develop a closer working relationship with his foreign interlocutors, Walters often arrived a day before his secret meetings so he could ride the buses around and pick up local slang and intonation.[42] His gift for language helped him to develop a near-perfect imitation of the Pope after only a few meetings.[43]

Walters arrived in Rome with a stack of secret material, including classified satellite intelligence and electronic intercepts, among them detailed photos of the Soviet gulag and of Soviet missile bases targeted at the United States. Walters explained the U.S. position on Poland, which was similar to John Paul's view, and shared classified information on Poland, Lithuania, Central America, terrorism, Chinese military power, and even the nuclear ambitions of Pakistan. He asked the Holy Father "not to criticize the U.S. defense budget," explaining the necessity of meeting the Soviet military challenge. He also proposed cooperation on issues related to Poland. The Holy Father agreed. The meeting went well, because there was "a staggering conversion of interests" in what the United States and the Pope wanted to occur in Poland and the Soviet Union.[44]

★ ★ ★

WHAT THE SOLIDARITY UNDERGROUND NEEDED MORE THAN anything was material support from the West. Some private organizations were willing to provide such support, and in the days following the declaration of martial law a series of confidential cables were sent from the State Department to diplomatic posts across Europe. Written by John Lenczowski, who was working at State and who later moved to the National Security Council, the cables were an effort to drum up moral and financial support for the underground in Poland.

The cables alerted diplomatic posts that "American labor, church and other private groups" were declaring "a day of Solidarity with the Polish people." The organizers envisioned "rallies and fundraising" for private assistance to Poland.

The cables included a directive from Secretary of State Haig to contact heads of governments in various countries to request their support in the effort. Ambassadors were also encouraged to ask foreign governments to use their national television and media outlets, such as the BBC in London and national television in West Germany, to cover the events. By spreading the word, the U.S. government was hoping to boost private charity efforts that were already under way in support of Solidarity.[45]

Reagan wanted to make sure that the issue of Poland remained in the public eye, and his efforts angered Warsaw. He was leading a "slanderous propaganda campaign against Poland," complained the Polish Ministry of Internal Affairs in a confidential report. In contrast with the restrained statements being made by the European governments, Reagan was causing "the humiliation of the Polish state in the eyes of world opinion with all of its consequences, as well as bringing out in the society attitudes of uncertainty and anxiety."[46]

How the U.S. government would support the Solidarity Underground was left to CIA Director William Casey. A staunch Catholic, Casey had spent the past forty years subverting totalitarian governments. During the Second World War, he served in the Office of Strategic Services (OSS), with responsibility for placing agents behind enemy lines and supporting resistance movements in occupied Europe. After the war, he served on the board of the International Rescue Committee (IRC), a refugee organization.[47] This group, headed by a close friend of Casey's, Leo Cherne, was committed to helping anti-Communist refugees fleeing the Soviet bloc. But IRC was not your typical refugee organization. Because it had access to

Soviet-bloc refugees and had good contacts behind the Iron Curtain, the IRC was considered a valuable resource for the CIA. When Allen Dulles was appointed director of the CIA by President Eisenhower, Casey sent Dulles a series of reports concerning the IRC's activities. Dulles made a note that the group's work was important and there needed to be cooperation.[48]

In 1956, when street battles raged in Budapest, Hungary, the IRC became a focal point for fund-raising and the distribution of supplies to the anti-Soviet forces. Bill Casey contributed to these efforts, and the IRC sent representatives to Vienna to purchase food and medical supplies. Cherne and another IRC member crossed the border into Hungary with a large supply of food and medicine. There they were met by Marcel Faust, a member of the Committee's European staff. Faust was a political refugee from Austria who had worked for the OSS with Casey during World War II.[49] As Cherne later told the IRC board, no supplies went through "any agency of the Communist government," but "only through organizations representing the anti-Communist patriots of Hungary." After the Hungarian uprising was smashed by Soviet tanks, the IRC continued supporting the resistance using clandestine methods. The committee had "ways and means to penetrate the Soviet blockade," they said.[50]

In the 1960s, the IRC turned its activities to the situation in East Germany, cooperating with West Berlin officials on a very secretive tunneling project. West Berlin was the epicenter of the Cold War at the time. The Berlin Wall had just been built, and tensions were high. In January 1963, the group secretly provided funds to build tunnels under East Berlin. Leo Cherne, with the support of William Casey, raised funds to construct tunnels throughout the summer of 1965. The project appeared destined to work until East German border guards discovered the entrance to a large tunnel. The West Berliners guarding the entrance opened fire and one of the border guards was killed; the project had to be canceled.[51]

In 1968, when the Soviet Union crushed the Czechoslovak experiment in internal reform, Bill Casey flew with Cherne to Austria and tried to cross the border with food and supplies for the opposition. Soviet troops, however, prevented them from entering Czechoslovakia.

In addition to his work for the IRC, Casey lent his support to an organization called American Friends of Russian Freedom. Smaller than the IRC, American Friends was a private committee set up to assist in the defection of Russian troops in Berlin. The organization worked to provide jobs and visas to assist in the defection and to "drive a propaganda wedge between the Russian people and their Leninist overlords."[52]

So the dilemma of aiding the Solidarity Underground was not a new challenge for Casey. But precisely how he did it remains difficult to say. Private organizations, including labor organizations, ethnic groups, and Catholic charities, were getting money into the country. He was probably commingling the money.

According to detailed files from Polish internal security, there was a steady flow of CIA money beginning in mid-1982. Polish intelligence had informants inside the Solidarity movement with access to the organization's financial records, and they tracked the flow of money from west to east. Agents reported that some of the private organizations helping Solidarity "are only intermediaries in the transfer of money" that in reality was coming from the CIA. In several instances agents stole documents from Solidarity offices in the West that allowed them to trace the flow of money through the Solidarity Bureau in Brussels.[53]

Polish interior minister Kiszczak was also tracking the flow of money. Intelligence indicated that the CIA was "hiding behind some labor unions and various charitable organizations, some very respected," to get aid into the country. This support was vital, Kiszczak told me. "We realized that a successful fight against the underground structures will be possible if we maximally limit Western aid in the form of money, printing equipment, printing ink and paper."[54]

So the battle for Poland was on. Backed by Reagan, the courageous people of that country were desperately standing up to the repressive actions of the military government.[55]

CHAPTER XVI

THE CRUSADE

I N EARLY JUNE 1982, RONALD REAGAN BOARDED *AIR FORCE One* for an intensive ten-day trip to Western Europe. He was seventy-one years old, but his itinerary looked to be one for a man half his age: summit with Western leaders; visit with the Pope; trip to Germany; trip to Great Britain; three major speeches to deliver.

When asked about it, Reagan simply said that his mission as president was to carry on "the task of world leadership that this country never sought, but has been thrust upon it."

Air Force One took off from Andrews Air Force Base and six hours later arrived at France's Orly Airport amid tumult and fear. French authorities had been expecting violence, and shortly after the plane touched down, a bomb ripped a hole in the side of an American school in the Paris suburb of St. Cloud. A Marxist terrorist group, Action Direct, claimed responsibility for the attack and threw down a marker. "Close the school during the visit of the reactionary President Reagan or else watch out," read graffiti scrawled on one of the school's walls.

Along with the attack came threats to other Americans in France: the American College, the American Cathedral, the American

Church, and the American Legion building all had to be evacuated because of bomb threats during Reagan's first two days in France.

The main order of business was the Versailles Economic Summit. But there were also trips planned to Bonn, Berlin, Rome, and London. The continent was simmering with antiwar and anti-American feelings. Reagan had been warned about this before *Air Force One* lifted off, and aides had advised that he cancel some appearances (particularly in Berlin) because of the possibility of a confrontation with radical protesters. But Reagan insisted on sticking to his plans.

Shortly after he arrived, Reagan and his wife enjoyed a private party in Paris. Among those attending was actress Olivia de Havilland. With Reagan, she had battled the Communists as a member of the Hollywood Independent Citizens Committee. De Havilland recounted with a laugh her suspicions about Reagan back then. "At first," she said, "I thought you were one of them."

Reagan chuckled. "And I thought you were one."[1]

The summit meeting in Versailles brought Reagan together with the leaders of the major Western powers. It was a difficult meeting; there were discussions about the gas pipeline that Moscow wanted to build, and concerns about the strength of the American dollar, trade issues, and interest rates. Reagan pushed hard for an agreement to limit the flow of technology and credits to Moscow. The summit ended with mixed results.

On June 7, Reagan traveled to Rome for a meeting with Pope John Paul II. It was the first meeting between the two men, who were so different yet seemed to share a certain bond. Both had recently survived an assassin's bullet, and both shared a revulsion over the scar the Iron Curtain had placed in the heart of Europe. For Reagan, it was about freedom: The Soviet empire was a menace and an abomination. For the Pontiff, it was a matter of both faith and identity: A devout man who had grown up in wartime Europe, he had seen his people cast off the Nazis only to be conquered by oppressors from the East.

The two men met for six hours, including a forty-five-minute private session in the gilded Papal Library. As they sat, Perugino's *Resurrection* peered at them from the wall.

Reagan told the Pope how he felt that his life had been spared for a purpose: to deal with the evil communist system. He also recounted how he had watched, teary-eyed, when John Paul made his triumphal return to Poland in 1979. Then they went on to discuss the present situation.

"Hope remains in Poland," Reagan told the Pontiff. "We, working together, can keep it alive."

The Pope nodded in agreement.

At the end of the meeting, Reagan applauded the Pope for supporting "freedom and compassion in a world that is still stalked by the forces of evil." Then they sat together as a group of American seminarians and priests sang "America the Beautiful" and "God Bless America." Reagan brushed away tears.[2]

As the two men talked, the nearby streets were teeming with protesters. "Reagan Brings War to Italy," read one of the signs. "Reagan Executioner," said another.

The event had been organized by the Italian Communist Party (PCI), and protesters numbered in the tens of thousands. Despite its occasional public denunciation of Moscow, the PCI was secretly receiving millions of dollars in subsidies from the Kremlin. And party members were being secretly trained in Moscow by the KGB's "illegals" directorate.[3]

The protests in Italy were only a harbinger of things to come. After his visit with the Pope, Reagan ventured to West Germany, ground zero in the burgeoning antiwar protest movement that had taken root across Western Europe.

Back in 1977, German chancellor Helmut Schmidt had called for NATO to do something about the deployment of Soviet SS-20 missiles. NATO responded with a decision in 1979 to begin the deployment of U.S. Pershing II and cruise missiles. The plan, which was widely supported in the alliance and had been strongly backed by President Carter, called for negotiations with Moscow over these so-called intermediate nuclear forces (INFs). If those talks failed, the plan was to go ahead with the deployment of the Pershing II and cruise missiles in 1983.

The planned deployments were unpopular among many in Western Europe, particularly in West Germany, where most of the missiles would be stationed. Reagan's forceful denunciations of the

Soviet Union and his commitment to radically boosting defense spending only fanned the flames of protest. The vast majority of people in the streets were sincerely fearful of the prospects of war. And as they had for several decades, the Soviets were cultivating that fear and using it to their advantage.

In a 1976 Politburo meeting, Leonid Brezhnev had extolled the value of encouraging the peace movement. It would prove useful in weakening Western resolve, he declared. When demonstrations erupted in 1977 over plans to deploy the neutron bomb, Moscow secretly funded some of the protest groups. Those demonstrations succeeded: President Carter canceled the deployment.[4]

When Reagan arrived in Bonn and then later in Berlin, tens of thousands filled the streets to hang him in effigy and protest his policies.

Leading the protests in Bonn were Petra Kelly and her boyfriend, General Gert Bastian, retired from the German Bundeswehr. Kelly was a Green Party leader who exuded a kind of innocence that young people found disarming. Bastian, who had left the army in 1980, was a rugged, handsome, and articulate leader who could speak with real authority. He was cofounder of an organization called Generals for Peace.

Both Kelly and Bastian were already well-known in American circles and had flown to the United States in December 1981 to speak out against Reagan's policies. In a media tour arranged by the disarmament group SANE, Bastian made appearances on *The Today Show,* National Public Radio's "All Things Considered," and numerous other radio shows.[5] As Reagan arrived in Bonn, it was Bastian who rallied the crowd on the streets.

Unbeknownst to most of the protesters, Bastian was in fact on the East German Stasi payroll. Generals for Peace was receiving a hundred thousand German marks per year, and he was supplying information to his paymasters.

Also organizing in the streets was KFAZ, the Committee for Peace, Disarmament and Cooperation. Headed by Martin Niemöller, a Protestant clergyman and former head of the World Council of Churches, this was one of the largest and most effective umbrella groups in the European peace movement. Much of the group's authority rested on Niemöller, who had been an articulate critic of Germany's conduct in World War II and the failure of ordinary Germans to stand up to Fascists.[6]

But like Bastain's Generals for Peace, KFAZ was secretly receiving cash payments from the East German Stasi and using the funds to rent buses, print signs, and conduct mass protest appeals. By the time Reagan arrived, KFAZ had already made its presence known to his administration. When Al Haig arrived in Berlin in early 1981, it had taken to the streets, and when Caspar Weinberger visited Bonn a few months later, it had organized protests. (Not surprisingly, when Leonid Brezhnev arrived in Bonn in November 1981, KFAZ did not organize any protests and the streets were relatively quiet.)

Yet another peace organization that was leading protests was the German Peace Union (DFU). Headed by Joseph Weber, a former colonel in the West German Army, the DFU was getting 5 million deutchse marks per year from the Stasi.[7]

The East Germans were not the only ones pouring money into the peace movement. As Sergei Grigoriev, a former senior official in the Communist Party of the Soviet Union International Department, recalls, his department "led an active campaign in Western Europe," funding dozens of peace groups "through various public organizations and a number of communist parties. Millions of dollars were injected into the creation of all sorts of ad-hoc groups and coalitions."[8]

When Reagan arrived in Bonn, there was tear gas hovering above the streets and a chain of German police offers was holding back the crowds. Reagan traveled to the German Bundestag to deliver a major speech on war and peace. Inside the chamber there was about as much division and deception as there was outside. Shortly before his arrival, fifty-nine left-wing members of the Social Democrats had signed a petition attacking his policies, particularly the "massive arms buildup with mass-destruction weapons such as the ones that your defense minister [Caspar Weinberger] has enforced."

Some from the left and center opposed the INF deployment out of genuine conviction, others for less pure motives. Seated in the gallery as Reagan took to the podium was William Borm, a former member of Parliament and now chairman emeritus of the Free Democrats (FDP). Borm was a fierce critic of Reagan and a champion of warmer relations and détente with the East. He was also, since 1973, an East German spy who had let many of his speeches and articles denouncing Reagan be authored by Stasi agents. (He would be decorated a year later by Stasi spy chief Markus Wolf for his valuable service.)[9]

Seated near Reagan was Social Democrat floor leader Herbert Wehner. Considered a moderate compared to some of the more radical members of his party, Wehner nonetheless was concerned about what Reagan was doing. The Soviet military was "defensive rather than aggressive," he had said, and Reagan was exacerbating problems. Like Borm, Wehner was on the Stasi payroll.[10]

As Reagan began his speech, one member stood up and heckled him. "What about El Salvador?!" yelled Karl-Heinz Hansen. "What about El Salvador?!"

Reagan paused from reading his text. "Is there an echo in here?" he asked with a wry smile.

There was thunderous applause, and he continued.

"The nuclear threat is a terrible beast," he said, recognizing as he had in the 1950s that "fear of the bomb" was Moscow's most potent weapon. "Perhaps the banner carried in one of the nuclear demonstrations here in Germany said it best. The sign read, 'I am afraid.' "

But Reagan declared that peace was possible only if the West remained strong and showed fortitude. Despite the rancor inside the Bundestag and out on the streets, he was interrupted eighteen times by applause.

From Bonn, Reagan traveled to Berlin, the divided city he had gone to three years earlier. Unlike the last time, this visit included a plethora of television cameras as he drove up in his limousine to Checkpoint Charlie. The trip had the feel more of a pilgrimage than of a normal appearance. As he stepped out of the car, he was obviously repulsed by the tall, gray edifice in front of him.

"What do you think of the wall?" shouted a reporter.

"It's as ugly as the idea behind it."[11]

★   ★   ★

FOR REAGAN, THE WALL WAS CONSTRUCTED NOT ONLY OUT OF brick and mortar but also ideas. And while he could not tear down the wall itself, he could puncture, rip, and destroy the ideas that helped to hold it up. He did just that when he arrived in London on June 8 to address the British Parliament.

The invitation had come at the suggestion of British Prime Minister Margaret Thatcher, the strong-minded Iron Lady with whom he shared so many ideas. The setting was grand and regal; he would speak at the Royal Gallery of the House of Lords, with oil paintings of British military victories lining the walls and guards in their red beefeater uniforms standing behind him. He wanted to fill up the room with equally grand ideas about dealing with the threat to freedom.

He spoke about a Soviet empire that was both strong and weak, a world-class military power backed up with fourth-rate ideas and a limping economy. It was destined for the "ash heap of history," he said.

"Around the world today, the democratic revolution is gathering new strength. . . . In the communist world as well, man's instinctive desire for freedom and self-determination surfaces again and again . . . optimism is in order, because day by day democracy is proving itself to be a not-at-all fragile flower. From the Stettin on the Baltic to Varna on the Black Sea, the regimes planted by totalitarianism have had more than thirty years to establish their legitimacy. But none—not one regime—has yet been able to risk free elections. Regimes planted by bayonets do not take root."

Then he announced the launch of what would later be called "Project Democracy," a bold effort to not simply protect freedom but advance it. In it there was plenty that tied in with his secret strategy. He wanted to "foster the infrastructure of democracy, the system of free press, unions, political parties, universities, which allows a people to choose their own way." This would be a "crusade for freedom," a break from the traditional strategy of containment. "We have forged the beginning of a fundamentally new direction in American foreign policy," he declared.

The chamber was deeply divided by what Reagan said. Many criticized him for uttering platitudes while failing to outline a specific plan to negotiate with Moscow. Margaret Thatcher, however, was enthusiastic.

After the speech, the Prime Minister took Reagan to 10 Downing Street for a private reception. With a glass of wine in her hand, she offered a toast, praising Reagan "for putting freedom *on the offensive* where it belongs."[12]

How to structure this crusade was critical. Certainly there was a covert side to it; Bill Casey was working on that aspect at the CIA. But Reagan had only limited faith in a covert approach. The United States had used covert action in the past in an effort to advance democracy, and had met with limited results. Doing it covertly was sometimes necessary, but it seemed to signify a lack of confidence in the mission or its goals. Freedom was worth fighting for and advancing; that had been the way the Crusade for Freedom had operated in the 1950s. And during Reagan's stint on the MPIC in Hollywood, the belief had always been that open competition between the ideas of freedom and the ideas of oppression meant freedom came out on top.

Three weeks after his speech in London, Reagan convened a cabinet-level meeting to discuss precisely how Project Democracy would be carried out. Seated around the table were National Security Adviser William Clark, Defense Secretary Weinberger, Secretary of State George Shultz, UN Ambassador Jeane Kirkpatrick, and CIA Director Casey.

The cabinet discussed the state of the world and the mechanics of how the new initiative could be launched. The meeting included discussions on how to find wiggle room for covert operations under current law and on using more overt political action to push the Soviets back.[13]

The cabinet deliberated on how the ideas of freedom could be spread to the people of Eastern Europe and how dissident groups behind the Iron Curtain could be supported most successfully.

When the subject of CIA involvement came up, there was almost immediate opposition to direct Agency involvement. Some of that opposition came from CIA Director Bill Casey himself, who understood the tinge that might be associated with any dissident groups connected with the CIA. In the end, the United States Information Agency was put in charge of the project.

In many ways it made sense that USIA would run Project Democracy. The agency was headed by Charles Wick, a longtime

Reagan friend who had direct access to the President. USIA was already managing Voice of America, which was beaming radio broadcasts into the Soviet bloc, and it also had representatives at embassies who could provide important information.

★   ★   ★

As USIA TOOK OVER MANAGEMENT OF THE EMBRYONIC PROJect, White House Counselor Ed Meese heard of a proposal for a "Democracy Program" written by Georgetown University professor Allen C. Weinstein. The proposal called for the creation of a National Endowment for Democracy, which would provide money to overseas organizations working to develop democracy in their respective countries. Weinstein suggested that the organization be quasipublic, with taxpayer funds being funneled through a private organization to advance the interests of democracy. Meese was intrigued by the idea and took the proposal to others in the White House, including National Security Adviser William Clark. Eventually it reached the President, from whom it received immediate support.

The Reagan administration pushed hard to get funding on Capitol Hill, and a bipartisan coalition got behind the idea. Carl Gershman, an aide to UN Ambassador Jeane Kirkpatrick, was picked to serve as the endowment's president. An assortment of organizations from across the political spectrum participated in the formation and operation of the organization, including the AFL-CIO and the U.S. Chamber of Commerce.[14]

The NED proved to be an important tool in the effort to undermine Soviet power. It was very much a CIA-like subversive operation—without the risks and baggage. There were no spies. But as Allen Weinstein put it, "A lot of what we do today was done covertly 25 years ago by the CIA."[15]

There was a lot of work to do, particularly in Poland. In late 1982, the CIA was very concerned about the future of the Solidarity movement. Bill Casey was receiving secret reports that martial law was working. Authorities were seizing underground printing presses and arresting scores of activists. To survive, the CIA concluded, Solidarity would have to concentrate on creating a structure less vulnerable to penetration by the security services. The secret report also noted, "The underground Solidarity organization is clearly handicapped by lack of funds (the union's assets were seized by the authorities), [and] by slow and cumbersome means of communication among the various units."[16]

There were already government and private efforts under way to support Solidarity. Trade unions, Catholic charities, and Polish ethnic organizations were sending money and supplies, as was the CIA. Now the NED offered another channel for doing the same. The NED had a mandate to support democratic movements all around the world. But given the gravity of the situation in Poland, it was clear where the focus would be: "The Polish non-violent massive resistance movement should be accorded the highest priority."[17]

Early NED grants went to Polish political prisoners and their families for food, clothing, and medicine. The endowment also funded an "East European Democracy Project" to publish books and materials that could be smuggled into Poland, thereby reducing the level of government control over information. U.S. taxpayer funds were also used to "purchase paper, equipment, spare parts and printing supplies, and to pay salaries, authors' fees and distribution costs" for numerous underground publications operating inside Poland.[18]

This was the sort of subversive operation that the Crusade for Freedom supported in the 1950s, with Reagan's enthusiastic support. But getting money and material into martial-law Poland wasn't easy. As one contact wrote to NED headquarters, how the money was being transferred would not be known by the NED, but they would receive a receipt signed by a dissident and a report of how the funds were used. Money going to underground publications would be acknowledged with a secret code printed on one of the pages.[19]

Money and supplies for the Solidarity Underground would sometimes be transferred through Sweden, where the Independent Polish Agency in Lund provided everything from printing presses to radio equipment.[20]

The endowment supported underground movements in other Soviet-bloc countries as well. One grant funded efforts to publish a Russian version of George Orwell's *Animal Farm*, among other anti-totalitarian books. Distributing such material, which was considered "subversive" by communist governments, was not easy. "No one method of distribution can be successful indefinitely; sooner or later, each channel will be more or less completely blocked," noted the recipients of the funds. "Consequently, it is necessary constantly to seek new possibilities and to test them in practice."[21]

At times, getting material behind the Iron Curtain required innovative thinking. At one point, some ten thousand balloons carrying containers of anti-Soviet, pro-Solidarity propaganda leaflets were released from Bornholm Island, Denmark, to ride the wind currents into Poland.[22]

In Czechoslovakia, funds were given to the Charter Seventy-seven Foundation, which supported dissidents inside the communist country. The money went for "a program of technical assistance to encourage free speech and communication." The endowment also transferred several hundred thousand dollars to an organization to set up a communications system so independent groups in several Soviet-bloc countries could pass subversive material to one another.[23]

The NED was government funded and had no direct ties to the Reagan administration. But unofficially it enjoyed backing inside the Reagan White House and received valuable advice and support. NED officials once wrote to officials at the U.S. embassy in Czechoslovakia to determine whether supporting a project to produce antigovernment videos in that country would be worthwhile. A diplomat wrote back, declaring it "seems to me to be a pretty good idea."[24]

★ ★ ★

IN THE FALL OF 1982, HAVING LAUNCHED PROJECT DEMOCRACY, Reagan was eager to press ahead with broader action. He signed another National Security Decision Directive laying out his plans for Eastern Europe. There was cautious optimism that a breakthrough might be possible in this, the heart of the Soviet empire. As with his other directives, this one was classified secret and given to advisers on a strictly need-to-know basis.

Reagan's primary goal in Eastern Europe was to "loosen the Soviet hold on the region." He wanted to undermine Soviet military capabilities there, lessen the region's dependence on the Kremlin, and reinforce the pro-Western orientation of their peoples.[25]

These were broad-based and ambitious goals, easy to write down. But precisely how were these objectives going to be achieved? In the Carter administration, National Security Adviser Zbigniew Brzezinski had tried to lure the countries of Eastern Europe out of the Soviet orbit by cultivating closer relations with communist governments using incentives such as trade and cultural exchanges. The hope had been that these governments would drift into a more pro-U.S. position and away from Moscow.

Reagan continued this practice in a limited sense, by reaching out diplomatically but not promising many economic incentives. Diplomats were sent to the region with a blunt message. As John Whitehead, Assistant Secretary of State, recalls, "I was assigned to go off to the Warsaw Pact allies and to try to explain to them that it might be in their interests not to be so dependent on the Soviet Union and to make a little better friendship with the United States. That's the first time I've ever put it that way . . . but that was my assignment."

At first, the meetings were confrontational as Reagan pressed the governments on human rights and declared in clear terms that their relationship with the Soviet Union was not in their best interest. But over time, as the economic situation continued to deteriorate, the governments began to warm to these diplomatic overtures.

Moscow watched nervously, well aware of what Reagan was up to.

"In our department of the Central Committee of the Communist Party of the Soviet Union, which dealt with relations with the socialist countries, we knew about Mr. Whitehead's mission," recalls Georgy Shakhnazarov. "We believed that he undermined the socialist camp, but there was nothing we could do against it."[26]

But far more important than this dialogue with East European communist elites was Reagan's effort to forge a bond with the people of the region. They were, after all, the big losers in the communist system. Reagan wanted to speak past the governments to the general public, which he considered a potential ally.

Reagan believed that ideas reinforced the bricks and mortar that held up the Iron Curtain. And he already knew that when he attacked the legitimacy of communism, it set off aftershocks inside the Soviet empire. AP reporter John Koehler had written him in June 1981 confirming this, soon after a speech Reagan delivered at Notre Dame University.

"The years ahead will be great ones for our country, for the cause of freedom, and the spread of civilization," Reagan had told the students. "The West will not contain communism, it will transcend communism. We will not bother to renounce it, we'll dismiss it as a sad, bizarre chapter in human history whose last pages are even now being written."

Koehler wrote Reagan:

"By coincidence, I was in Prague on the day you made your speech at Notre Dame, and within hours, word had gotten around on your statements about communism and there were expressions of glee and I detected some hope over your remarks that it [communism] was a passing phenomenon."[27]

As he had for more than thirty years, Reagan spoke about communism in stark black-and-white terms that resonated with many behind the Iron Curtain. He went on Radio Free Europe/Radio Liberty and in an on-air interview said he hoped to "show the captive nations that resisting totalitarianism is possible."[28]

Reagan took special care to be tough and unequivocal about communism. When his speechwriter, Tony Dolan, sent him a draft of the now-famous "evil empire" speech, Reagan took pen in hand and made it even tougher. Dolan, for example, had written "surely historians will see they are the focus of evil in the modern world." Reagan changed it to "they are the focus of evil in the modern world."

Reagan's strong language was denounced in many quarters. Anthony Lewis of the *New York Times* called the "evil empire" speech "simplistic" and "sectarian." Strobe Talbott of *Time* magazine explained that no one really took the speech seriously because it was riddled with pure ideology. Many on Capitol Hill complained that it would set back relations with Moscow.

But in a dark, damp cell housing political prisoners in Russia, word started to spread. The prisoners tapped on walls and quietly talked through toilets to share what Reagan had said. Natan Sharansky remembers feeling energized and emboldened; Reagan had given them hope.[29]

★　★　★

REAGAN'S SPEECHES OFTEN REACHED PEOPLE IN THE SOVIET BLOC through radio broadcasts. Shortly after his return from Europe, Reagan signed another secret directive, this one on international broadcasting.

Reagan had enormous faith in the power of the radio. As a young man he had worked at WHO radio in Iowa, where he mastered the technique of reaching people over the airwaves and saw the powerful intimacy it could create between broadcaster and audience. Later, he came to see the cold war as a "battle of ideas . . . a test of wills," as he had put it in 1957. So radio broadcasts beamed behind the Iron Curtain were vitally important and were given the same priority as other programs deemed vital to national security.[30]

Since the 1950s, the United States had been beaming radio signals into the Soviet bloc via Radio Free Europe (RFE) and Radio Liberty (RL). The Crusade for Freedom, Reagan's old group, had raised money for RFE. But the stations were often controversial in the United States. Many people questioned their value and found their mission to be unsavory. This had particularly been the case during the era of détente. Senator William Fulbright, chairman of the Foreign Relations Committee in 1972, had declared, "These radios should be given an opportunity to take their rightful place in the graveyard of cold war relics," and he attempted to pull the plug.

Needless to say, Fulbright's efforts were welcomed in Moscow. He was called a man "known to the American and world public as a man who judges events with a sober realism." As a sign of their support, the Kremlin even published a Russian translation of his book-length critique of U.S. foreign policy, *Arrogance of Power.*[31]

The radios survived Fulbright's efforts, and during the Carter years funding for them grew because of Zbigniew Brzezinski's personal interest in the program. But they struggled through troubled management and fuzzy thinking about their mission and purpose. Early in his administration, Carter appointed John Gronouski, a former postmaster general and ambassador to Poland under Lyndon Johnson, to manage the radio stations. Gronouski was supportive of the radios but failed to grasp how they should be used. Caught up in the good feelings of détente, at one point he even proclaimed his desire to offer the Soviet Union and the governments of Eastern Europe a "right of reply" to any broadcasts they felt were inaccurate.[32]

For Moscow, the radios were a nagging problem. As early as 1965, Soviet authorities had conducted a large survey of "basic public attitudes" and discovered that 40 to 60 million people regularly listened to radios. Of these, 50 to 75 percent learned of major public issues mainly through foreign radio broadcasts, not the official Soviet media. The effect of these broadcasts on the Soviet political system was stunning. Soviet researchers discovered that 20 to 30 percent of the population, perhaps more, doubted the credibility of all Soviet information sources and the basic ideological legitimacy of the system.[33]

Given these facts, it is no surprise that Soviet authorities considered the radios a threat, and they were prepared to do what they had to do to deal with them.

On February 21, 1981, shortly before 10 P.M., a violent explosion rocked Munich. Caused by twenty kilos of plastic explosives, the blast carried such force that windows were broken in buildings up to a mile away.

The bomb was part of a sensitive operation code-named Munich Tango, which, according to East German Stasi files, was organized and carried out by the notorious terrorist "Carlos." Equipped with explosives provided by Romanian intelligence and radio detonators from East Germany, a terrorist cell group had used detailed intelligence from a Soviet KGB agent working undercover in Munich to determine where to plant the bomb. Once they completed their task, the culprits returned to a safe house in East Berlin.

The target was not a secret NATO military facility or a weapons command post, but the headquarters of Radio Free Europe/Radio Liberty. The station was what KGB agent Oleg Tumanov called "everything that constituted a deadly threat to the existence of the

Soviet state." The attack was approved and carried out, says Tumanov, because the Soviet Politburo feared radio broadcasts "more than any other American weapon."[34]

Reagan had long known of the broadcasts' value. He had learned from Soviet dissident Vladimir Bukovsky that the radios encouraged dissidents in their activities, giving them a sense of confidence and hope that they were not alone. During the 1980 presidential campaign, he had spoken about "our neglected ability of communications" and the need to use them to advance American national strategy.[35]

Communist regimes needed to control information in order to monopolize power, Reagan said, and the radios represented an alternative. "The truth is mankind's best hope for a better world," he said publicly. "That's why in times like this, few assets are more important than the Voice of America and Radio Liberty."[36]

With the goal of bringing change to the Soviet empire, Reagan ordered a review to determine how the radios could be used more effectively, exposing Soviet crimes and detailing Soviet failures. Senior administration officials put high value on upgrading the radios and believed that they could fundamentally weaken the Soviet system. As Reagan foreign policy adviser Ken Adelman put it, radios could not cause dissatisfaction with a regime, but they could make dissatisfaction politically significant. "Radio can be contributory, but it can never cause a particular situation; it can help propel events. In this way, radio can help destabilize a regime."[37]

Reagan clearly believed so too. So he wanted more stations, sharper programs, and an extensive effort to combat Soviet jamming.[38]

The hope was to integrate the radio broadcasts into the broad strategy of rolling back Soviet power and transforming the Soviet system. This was a new approach. In the words of Brigadier General Walter Jajko of the Department of Defense, the Reagan administration was "the first to recognize the need to wield information abroad as a weapon."[39] Colonel Alfred H. Paddock, an expert on psychological warfare for the U.S. Army, explained that Reagan's approach indicated that the President understood the psychological dimensions of the Cold War better than any previous president did.[40]

Reagan's initiative brought about the greatest programming expansion and radio modernization in the history of international broadcasting. A massive six-year, multibillion-dollar upgrade was launched, including the renovation and enhancement of the world's largest shortwave system. One hundred existing shortwave transmitters were doubled in power. Old transmitters, "so old they belong in museums," according to counselor of USIA Stanton H. Burnett, were replaced entirely. New transmitter relay sites were added to strengthen frequency reception.

USIA Director Charles Wick put together a team to figure out how to overcome Soviet jamming of the broadcasts. Moscow was spending $1.2 billion a year to suppress the broadcasts with what listeners derisively called "Soviet jazz." Using groundwave jammers for local metropolitan areas and skywave jammers elsewhere, they were trying to keep a lid on the number of people who could listen in.[41]

Wick funded the development of new technologies under Hugh Fallis, vice president of engineering at Radio Free Europe/Radio Liberty. They tested an antenna that was resistant to jamming and then published and distributed the design to dissident groups in Eastern Europe. They also used the new transmitters in their arsenal to engage in a sort of "arms race" with Soviet jammers. When jamming intensified, engineers would schedule almost twice as many transmitters as usual to carry the signal to counteract the interference.[42]

As important as boosting the power of the radios was sharpening their message. In the early months of the Reagan administration, officials were shocked to discover that at times the Soviets were being given broadcast time. Wick was outraged when he discovered on August 17, 1981, that Voice of America was broadcasting excerpts from an interview with Soviet spokesman (and KGB agent) Georgi Arbatov. The radios were supposed to be counteracting the Soviet media, not providing the Soviet government with another news outlet. Wick demanded that the practice be halted immediately, pointing out that Radio Moscow had its own broadcasts and that American spokesmen had yet to be asked to appear on its programs.

The sharper ideological focus that Reagan desired was highlighted in a 1981 internal memo from the director of policy at the Voice of America, Phillip Nicolaides:

The USIA is justified because it is the primary psychological arm in a global struggle against a powerful, determined, implacable foe, bent on burying our system. . . . Merely refuting Soviet canards is not enough. We must portray the Soviet Union as the last great predatory empire on earth, remorselessly enslaving its own diverse ethnic populations, crushing the legitimate aspirations of its captive nations and ever seeking, by all means, from subversion to military intervention, to widen its subjects. . . . We must strive to destabilize the Soviet Union and its satellites by promoting disaffection between peoples and rulers, underscoring the lies and denials of rights, inefficient management of the economy, corruption, indifference to the real wants and needs of the people, suppression of cultural diversity, religious persecution, etc. We should seek to drive wedges of resentment and suspicion. . . . We should fan the flames of nationalism. . . . We should counter Soviet propaganda . . . we should extol the merits of our system . . . we should not expatiate endlessly on stories which tend to put us or our allies in a bad light while glossing over stories which discredit the leadership of communist nations.[43]

The sharpness of the memo set off a firestorm among many longtime VOA employees. Nicolaides eventually left USIA as a result, but Wick agreed with the thrust of what was said in the memo. "Too many of our people have felt they were covered by the First Amendment and should not have any editorial direction," he told employees. "I feel we have to be pro-American."[44]

Soon after, reporting at VOA began to change. Gone were interviews with Soviet officials. Instead, more stories began to appear concerning the thousands of Soviet dissidents who had been committed to mental hospitals in "the most shocking abuse of human dignity." There was an interview with an Afghan government defector, who spoke about Soviet human rights abuses in his country. Another story examined the use of chemical weapons in Southeast Asia.[45]

VOA also took several other innovative steps. Recognizing the strong religious desires of the Polish people, the Voice of America began broadcasting Catholic masses from American churches for the benefit of worshipers in Poland. At the same time, another spiritual program, "Religion in Our Lives," was launched. Produced by Rev. Potapov, chairman of the Committee for the Defense of Persecuted Christians, the program was broadcast six times a week in seven languages to ethnic groups throughout the Soviet Union. The program discussed religious freedom and persecution in the Soviet bloc.[46]

Suddenly millions who before could never have heard the broadcasts because of jamming could get the signal, and millions more who before could hear only a faint voice through a heavy screen of static could now get a clear signal. Hundreds of hours of new Russian, Polish, and Ukrainian broadcasting were now available over the airwaves.[47]

The audience was large and, with the stronger signal, growing even larger. Working through independent European survey research organizations, the Reagan administration collected information on the listening habits and patterns of individuals behind the Iron Curtain. These surveys indicated that by 1984, Voice of America was reaching 14 to 18 percent of the USSR's adult population at least once a week. Radio Liberty was listened to by 8 to 12 percent of the population.

In Eastern Europe the numbers were even higher. According to surveys from 1982 and 1983, Western radio was listened to at least once a week by 68 percent of Poles, 64 percent of Romanians, 58 percent of Hungarians, 37 percent of Czechs, and 33 percent of Bulgarians. The audience was for the most part young, well-educated, and urban.[48]

★   ★   ★

A S THE EFFORT TO REACH PEOPLE BEHIND THE IRON CURTAIN continued, Reagan and his advisers constantly looked for stress fractures in the Soviet bloc. At the CIA, Bill Casey ordered a series of top-secret studies on the stability of the Soviet empire. In April 1983, the CIA's National Intelligence Council issued a "Top Secret" report titled "Dimensions of Civil Unrest in the Soviet Union." It was a subject of enormous interest to Reagan, who had written about it himself in the 1970s. Based on the reporting of human intelligence (HUMINT) sources, the report concluded that the Soviet Union was not necessarily an "effectively repressed society."

There was plenty of social ferment behind the Iron Curtain. Industrial workers, coal miners, bus drivers, and construction crews had been involved in civil unrest, which was clearly "on the rise" and not limited to a few isolated instances. These were large protests and strikes, sometimes including up to ten thousand people. Dissatisfaction with the regime was so high that there had been two assassination attempts on Brezhnev.

"The real significance of popular unrest is its potential to disrupt political stability in the USSR," advised the CIA. "Soviet leaders apparently are sensitive to this danger."

Instead of just reporting on instability, the report noted that the Reagan administration could actually encourage unrest. The key factor was ensuring the flow. "Great public awareness of popular unrest could lead to more of it."[49]

Another secret CIA report, titled "Domestic Stresses on the Soviet System," explained that the radios were an important tool in encouraging dissent. They enjoyed a large audience and could "undermine regime credibility."[50]

Buoyed by such surveys and research, steps were taken to reach the far corners of the Soviet empire. The National Security Council implemented plans to broadcast to Islamic audiences and other nationalities in the Soviet Union. Fifty-five new positions were added to broadcast in Georgian. The administration also added new language groups, including Azerbaijani (for the Islamic Soviet Union).[51]

★   ★   ★

ON THE GROUND IN EASTERN EUROPE, THE BROADCASTS HAD A palpable effect. There was greater activism by opponents of communism. General Kiszczak, the Polish interior minister, could see the latent effect from his office in central Warsaw.

"A large importance of RFE for intensifying political ferment in Poland was derived not from how many people listened but what kind of people they were," he told me. "Above all, these listeners were people active in the opposition. Furthermore, RFE was assisting the political communication inside opposition centers, and the subject of some of the programs was frequently the inspiration for their actions."[52]

The broadcasts bred boldness and melted away some of the fear of the regime. Colonel Henryk Piecuch, a senior official in the Polish Interior Ministry, saw the transformation before his eyes. "Under its influence people simply stopped being afraid, and this is always the beginning of the end of all sorts of tyrannies," he told me. "There wasn't a single coordinating meeting of the special services of the Soviet bloc which did not include consideration of matters relating to the radios."[53]

In the Soviet Union, dissident Anatoly Marchenko listened to the broadcasts for encouragement when he was behind bars—and noticed that his guards were listening, too.[54] Ludmilla Alexeyeva, a veteran Soviet dissident and cofounder of the Moscow Helsinki Watch Committee, saw the broadcasts as not only encouraging individual dissidents but also spawning a much larger movement inside the Soviet Union. "While our own authorities ignored our calls to dialogue and reform, the West wanted to know all about us. . . . Without foreign broadcasts, neither the human rights movement nor the religious rebirth in our country would have been possible on anything like the scale which they have attained."[55]

In Poland in particular, the radios proved to be valuable in sustaining the underground movement. Martial law had limited the ability of Solidarity to get a message to the people. But with the boosted power of the radios under Reagan, the underground leadership had a new voice. The programs often included interviews and features on Polish dissident writers; millions of Poles could listen. All this had the effect of "broadening the circle" of Polish citizens willing to collaborate with the underground movement.[56]

The value of the broadcasts was not simply in spreading the word; they also served as a means of sending coded messages to Solidarity leaders. Sometimes it would be a warning of pending government action, or confirmation of plans for a secret meeting. A special song might be played or certain code words used at a certain time.

When a request was made for a message to be sent, Charles Wick always approved it. "Because it was in the national interest, so long as it didn't hurt the integrity of the radios, we would broadcast it," he told me.[57]

Martial law authorities were aware of this tool and were befuddled at what to do about it. These broadcasts were "creating a system of communications" for the Solidarity Underground, one that they could not undermine.[58]

The radios also advertised planned protests or other forms of social action. "RFE was assisting the political communication inside opposition centers, and the subject of the programs was frequently the inspiration for their actions," General Kiszczak told me. "For example, RFE would give instructions that on day X at 8 P.M., in Warsaw at points A, B, C, D people will gather to march to Zamkowy Square, to protest against this or that. National opposition activists did not have to do anything, because a large demonstration was organized in their stead and for them by RFE."[59]

For Kiszczak, who was tasked with keeping a lid on Solidarity, this all presented a daunting challenge. Reagan was a difficult adversary with clear and defined goals. As he put it in a speech to security officials, "The main objective set at the time by the Reagan administration is to exploit the situation in Poland for purposes of struggle against the socialist system in strategic terms, to let the influence of anti-socialist forces in Poland spill over to other socialist countries too."[60]

This was something new for the communist leaders in Warsaw. Reagan had abandoned détente and come to office with a new strategy that was unlike anything they had seen before or during the cold war. Kiszczak correctly surmised that economic sanctions, the radio broadcasts, Project Democracy, and support for Solidarity were part of a broad-ranging strategy: "Reagan's activity in foreign affairs is not an improvisation, is not a chain of spontaneous initiatives, but a carefully planned and coordinated action, something of an integrated front of action under the slogans of world advocacy of the idea of freedom."[61]

When it came to Reagan, his enemies understood him perhaps better than anyone.

CHAPTER XVII

REVERSAL
OF FORTUNE

O N A HOT AFTERNOON IN AUGUST 1981, REAGAN SAT down with his cabinet for a briefing by the military. The United States Navy was conducting maneuvers near the Libyan coast, and Colonel Muammar Qaddafi was sending his planes out into international airspace to harass American pilots. The Libyans would cut across the Americans' flight path, pull up close, and make threatening maneuvers. The Navy was getting worried that there might be combat in the skies over the Gulf of Sidra.

An admiral asked Reagan a simple question: "If we are fired on, what are the orders?"

"Anytime we send an American anywhere in the world where he or she can be shot at, they have a right to shoot back," Reagan responded.

Defense Secretary Caspar Weinberger asked what the orders would be if the Libyans fired on U.S. Navy aircraft and then returned to Tripoli. "What about hot pursuit? How far can we go?"

Reagan pondered the question, but only for a minute. "All the way into the hangar," he responded.[1]

For more than a decade the United States had been on the retreat in the developing world. Allies had collapsed in Asia, the Middle East, and Latin America, and the Vietnam syndrome seemed to have paralyzed presidents into inaction. At the same time, Moscow had advanced, picking up new allies around the world.

Reagan had spoken and written about the battle for the developing world for more than two decades. The war in Vietnam had been a noble cause, even if the strategy had been poorly planned; anti-Communists in Angola, Southeast Asia, and Central America were worthy of American support. America was too much on the defensive and not thinking about how to advance.

Back in 1972, Reagan had sat in his study reading the book *Power Through Subversion* by his old friend Laurence Beilenson. Beilenson argued that the Communists were using guerrilla armies against the West to gain victories in the developing world. The strategy was risk-free and cheap, said Beilenson. And rather than fighting the insurgents, America needed to develop some guerrilla armies of its own. "If you can't beat the Soviets, join 'em" was his basic strategy.

Reagan read the book with great interest and declared that it was "must reading in the State Department."

Now that he was commander in chief, Reagan could do more than simply praise the book. If he was serious about "reversing Soviet expansionism," as his secret strategy declared, insurgents could be a powerful tool. And using that tool would fall to Bill Casey, the energetic director of the CIA.

During the Second World War, Casey had carried out covert operations against the Nazis as a member of the OSS. Later he had worked with several private organizations to roll back communist advances. Casey's wartime experience had convinced him that covert action could help defeat a totalitarian power. As he wrote in his book *The Secret War Against Hitler*, "I believe that it is important today to understand how clandestine intelligence, covert action, and organized resistance saved blood and treasure in defeating Hitler. These capabilities may be more important than missiles and satellites in meeting crises yet to come, and point to the potential for dissident action against the control centers and lines of communication of a totalitarian power."[2]

History taught that the Soviets were lousy at fighting insurgencies. It had taken the Red Army, the largest and most ruthless of World War II's victorious armies, some twelve years to defeat the isolated and ill-equipped Ukrainian Peoples' Army (UPA). After the war, the communist government in Poland took six years to defeat anti-Communist Polish guerrillas. Even antigovernment forces in the small Baltic republic of Lithuania had managed to fight on for more than ten years. The simple fact was that the Soviet military was incapable of running effective counterinsurgency operations. The Soviet military did not train for or believe in small-unit tactics, and there was no significant effort to win the "hearts and minds" of civilians. The Soviet policy had always been to seek the direct physical elimination of the guerrillas.

Casey believed these historical examples demonstrated that Moscow was vulnerable to insurgencies, and most important that they could *win*.

"History shows," he declared at one point, "that a combination of nagging insurgent military pressure and progressive withdrawal of domestic and international support is what brings down or alters an unpopular government."[3]

In early 1981, the Soviets were facing an insurgency in the remote mountains of Afghanistan. Seventy-five thousand troops were battling tribal rebels who were armed with vintage rifles and homemade hand grenades. President Carter had launched a modest covert aid program for the insurgents. But Casey wanted to do more.

He went to Reagan in March 1981 and asked for the authority to dramatically increase the number of weapons going to the rebels. Reagan signed off on the idea instantly. Armed with his new authority, Casey worked to carry it out with a vengeance. It would prove controversial later on.

★   ★   ★

A FEW WEEKS LATER A HUGE, BLACK C-141 STARLIFTER TRANSport lifted off from a secret airfield near Washington, D.C. The plane had no external markings, and the crew wore civilian clothes and were heavily armed. The massive cargo hold had been transformed into a flying hotel and communications center. Bill

Casey was in the plane's living quarters, which included couches, easy chairs, and a bed and bathroom. In the back there was a sophisticated communications center where he could speak securely with the President and receive intelligence updates.

The plane was bound for Europe and the Middle East. When it would touch down at a foreign airport, it would be night. And there would be no diplomatic personnel there to greet him.

The arms pipeline to the Afghan resistance ran from Egypt and China to Pakistan's port of Karachi or Peshawar Airport. There the weapons would be handed over to the Pakistan Intelligence Service (ISI), which would distribute them to the rebels. The arms, which were being paid for by the United States and Saudi Arabia, cost about $30 million per year.

Casey flew to Egypt to oversee the purchase of weapons and their shipment to Pakistan. Then he traveled to Saudi Arabia for a secret meeting with King Fahd. The two countries were splitting the cost of the weapons, but Casey wanted more from the Saudis. A few months later, Fahd sent an extra $15 million. Over the next five years Casey would pay repeated visits to Fahd asking for more money. In all, he would raise half a billion dollars from Fahd for the war in Afghanistan.

From Saudi Arabia, Casey went to Oman, a tiny Persian Gulf nation that Casey wanted to use as a transit point for weapons. Later he traveled to Beijing to meet with Chinese officials to discuss the war in Afghanistan. The Chinese were selling Soviet-designed weapons to the Afghan resistance. Casey asked them to open up the newly built Karokaram Highway, which ran from China to Pakistan, so more weapons could get through.

Casey labored like this for years, making the pipeline larger and more efficient. In a matter of a few years, the flow became so massive that it appeared as if it might burst. What had begun as a covert aid program of ten thousand tons of weapons in 1981 had mushroomed a few years later to sixty-five thousand tons. Crates that included assault rifles and grenade launchers now sat next to 122mm rocket launchers and antitank weapons.

Casey also thought of other ways to be useful. The resistance had very little intelligence concerning what the Soviet military might be planning in Afghanistan. Casey couldn't read their minds, but he did have spy satellites that could detail their maneuvers and tell what forces they had where. So he started handing supersensitive satellite intelligence over to resistance commanders.

As Casey raised the heat in Afghanistan, there were early signs that Moscow was concerned about where the war was going. A U.S. businessman traveling in Moscow who met with a senior Soviet official responsible for developing the five-year plan reported to U.S. officials about concern in the Kremlin that "the Soviet Union is now experiencing serious losses in Afghanistan."[4] In another instance, a Soviet Politburo member confided to the U.S. ambassador in Moscow, Arthur Hartman, that the war in Afghanistan was indeed more "costly" than anyone would have imagined.[5]

★   ★   ★

IF AFGHANISTAN PRESENTED THE BEST OPPORTUNITY TO DEFEAT the Soviets on the battlefield, Casey also saw the jungles of Central America as a land ripe with possibilities.

Reagan had been warning about the communist orientation of the Sandinistas in Nicaragua since before they had taken power. As a candidate in 1980, he had run on a platform that condemned the "Marxist Sandinista takeover of Nicaragua" and declared support for the efforts of the Nicaraguan people to establish a free and independent government.[6] Now that the Sandinistas were firmly in control of the country, they seemed to be leaving little doubt as to what their goals were. Links with the East Germans, Cubans, and Soviets were intensifying, even as the United States was sending economic assistance. The Sandinista army was growing out of proportion to the threat posed by its neighbors. And military advisers from the Eastern bloc and Cuba were arriving almost daily.

In early March, Reagan convened a meeting of his National Security Council to discuss several world hot spots. Casey came to the meeting anxious to do something about the Sandinistas. "If we can't stop Soviet expansionism in a place like Nicaragua," he asked, "where the hell can we?"

Reagan agreed, and days later he issued a secret "Presidential

Finding on Central America" authorizing a small covert operation targeting Nicaragua. A trickle of supplies went to a small army of Nicaraguan exiles that was being formed in the jungles of Honduras, along the Nicaraguan border.

Reagan then asked that a group be assembled to devise options for dealing with the problems of communist insurgents in Central America.

A secret deliberative body called the Restricted Interagency Group (RIG), including specialists from the CIA, the Pentagon, the NSC, and the State Department, laid out a number of options. Reagan could target Cuba with military action; he could cooperate with Argentina to support paramilitary action to overthrow the Sandinistas; or he could provide nonlethal aid to civic groups in the country. Reagan mulled over the options and eventually concluded that an insurgency was the best tool in his arsenal. Then he signed a secret directive authorizing the expansion of the covert aid program to $19 million.[7] Almost overnight, what had been a motley army of a few hundred began to grow. Eventually it would blossom into a force of some ten thousand.

Reagan's directive made it clear that he didn't simply want the CIA to build an army. He wanted to use American military muscle to send a clear message. The Pentagon "will provide maximum possible assistance to the Director of [Central Intelligence] in improving support to the Nicaragua resistance," read a secret memorandum. Caspar Weinberger embraced the role eagerly. "If it is proper and just that we should help those who wish to remain free," he said, "then we can hardly turn our backs on those who have lost their freedom and want it back."[8]

The most direct way the Pentagon could help was by flexing its muscles. Reagan had authorized the U.S. military to conduct maneuvers near the Soviet Union, and he wanted to do the same in Central America. Large-scale military exercises began occurring with regularity, including airborne assault operations and amphibious landings. The U.S. Navy brought NATO and Atlantic Fleet ships into the Caribbean to practice support operations for a potential land invasion.

These exercises proved to be highly controversial in the United

States. By a 50-to-29-percent margin, according to one poll, the American public expressed concern that Reagan was leading the country toward war in Central America. In Congress, a bill was introduced to stop them on the grounds that Reagan was usurping his authority as commander in chief. When reservists and National Guard units were included, more than a dozen governors refused to allow them to participate. "If the United States wants to send troops into Central America, that ought to be something that the President asks the Congress and the Congress debates and votes," said Massachusetts governor Michael S. Dukakis.

Visions of a new Vietnam were bandied about in Washington. Reagan knew "as much about Central America in 1983 as we knew about Indochina in 1963," quipped Senator Christopher Dodd.[9]

Reagan wanted to avoid a repeat of Vietnam, which he viewed as a one-sided war in which the United States had always been on the defensive. Much as he advised Nixon in the late 1960s to put North Vietnam under threat of invasion, he was now putting Nicaragua and Cuba on notice.

Images of the U.S. Navy off its coastal shores and marines practicing in the jungles of Honduras sent the Sandinistas into a panic. Daniel Ortega, the Sandinista president, became convinced that an invasion was imminent. He mobilized the population to defend the country, and thousands of Nicaraguans were pulled from their jobs to participate in emergency militia training. Fidel Castro became nervous, too, and he promptly withdrew a thousand advisers from Nicaragua. Ortega was furious.[10]

Castro, fearful that Reagan might target Cuba, dispatched his brother, Defense Minister Raúl Castro, to Moscow for consultations. There Raúl met with an ailing Brezhnev, Defense Minister Dmitri Ustinov, and Party Secretary Boris Ponomarev. After briefing the Soviet leaders on Reagan's "designs" in the region, Castro asked for assurances from the Kremlin. According to Castro, Brezhnev grimaced.

"We cannot fight in Cuba because it is 11,000 kilometers away," he said bluntly. "If we go there, we'll get our heads smashed."[11]

In both Managua and Havana, confidence was severely shaken. The Sandinistas, in particular, were facing an increasingly effective contra army and an American president who might be planning an invasion. In the face of it, their Soviet allies were backing down.

As the insurgency and Reagan's war of nerves went on, it began sapping the revolutionary fervor of some Sandinista leaders. Tomas Borge, the Sandinista interior minister who had warmed up to East Germany shortly after the revolution, kept a long running correspondence with Stasi chief Erich Mielke. You could see his confidence evaporate over time. In the early years, Borge signed off his letters with "revolutionary greetings" and the slogan "Free Fatherland or Death." But by 1988, apparently tired and worn down, Borge dropped the death pledge, signing off with "brotherly greetings." In his last letter to the Stasi chief on October 21, 1989, seventeen days before the fall of the Berlin Wall, Borge merely wrote "fraternally" above his name.[12]

The Kremlin was aware of the strains with their Latin allies and tried to placate them by shipping more arms. A second squadron of MiG-23 fighter aircraft was given to the Sandinistas. And the level of shipments to Cuba reached "the second highest annual total on record," said a CIA report, evidence of Havana's "anxiety." But this was not much of a substitute for allies who were looking for a superpower to back them up.[13]

Then an event occurred that changed the balance of power in the region decisively in Reagan's favor.

On October 12, 1983, martial law was declared on the Caribbean island of Grenada. Maurice Bishop, the dynamic Marxist prime minister, was under arrest and was being held by his more radical lieutenants. In charge was Bernard Coard, the defense minister with particularly strong ties to Cuba and Moscow. A week later, Bishop was shot by a firing squad and Coard declared a twenty-four-hour curfew. Trapped on the island were hundreds of Americans who were attending medical school there. With the curfew in place, they were under strict orders not to leave the island.

Grenada had been of interest to Reagan since early 1981, when intelligence indicated that it was serving as a transit point for Soviet arms bound for Marxist guerrillas in El Salvador. During the summer of 1981, the CIA had drawn up a covert-action plan designed to "cause economic difficulty for Grenada in the hopes of undermining the political control" of the Marxist government. But the Senate Intelligence Committee had rejected the idea.[14]

The Pentagon, with its mandate to rattle communist nerves in the region, began practicing military maneuvers in the area. A U.S. Navy exercise dubbed "Ocean Venture '81" included a scenario involving the rescue of American hostages on the fictional islands of Amber and the Amberdines. Many of the Navy officers involved in the maneuvers took this as a hidden reference to Grenada and the Grenadines.

In November 1982, Vice President George Bush, speaking before a Miami conference on the Caribbean, had said that Grenada's economy was bankrupt and the government was repressive. A few months later, Caspar Weinberger declared that Grenada was a Soviet surrogate in the region.

Now, in mid-October 1983, Reagan had a choice to make. The curfew was in place, trapping hundreds of Americans, and there was more bloodletting between the Marxist leaders on the island. Some were advising an invasion.

A few days earlier, a lieutenant colonel on the National Security Council staff named Oliver North had pointed out that a shipload of Marines had just left Norfolk, Virginia, bound for Beirut to relieve U.S. forces in Lebanon. Reagan ordered the flotilla diverted to the Caribbean.

Six neighboring countries were now stepping forward and formally requesting U.S. assistance to deal with a mounting crisis. Aides came to Reagan with the outlines of an invasion plan.

One mentioned that there would be political fallout; the invasion would be controversial and probably not very popular.

"I understand that. I'm prepared for that," Reagan said.

Another mentioned it might cause anxiety in Cuba, creating fears that that nation might be next.

"That's fine," he said. "They might be."

Reagan then asked how soon the invasion could take place.

In forty-eight hours, he was told.

"Do it," he ordered.[15]

★   ★   ★

O N OCTOBER 23, AMERICAN FORCES STORMED THE ISLAND OF Grenada. There were some fierce firefights with Cubans stationed on the island, but in a matter of days U.S. forces were in complete control. The American students were freed and returned to the United States, some dramatically kissing the ground upon their arrival.

In the United States, the military victory was greeted with an outpouring of patriotism. Inside the Soviet bloc, however, the invasion set off more alarm bells. Two days after the invasion, Nicaraguan defense minister Umberto Ortega phoned the U.S. ambassador in El Salvador. "Look, if you ever want to get your citizens out of here," he said meekly, "please call me. Here is my private number."[16]

In East Berlin, there was a mad scramble to find out about American war plans for Nicaragua. "Indications are intensifying regarding a possible U.S. military engagement in Nicaragua," read a secret Stasi memorandum. "It has been learned from leading circles close to J. [Jesse] Jackson that the Reagan Administration is preparing for a direct armed intervention in Nicaragua."[17]

In Havana, Fidel Castro, who had bragged to Erich Honecker back in 1980 that the Americans now would have to face three revolutionary governments, was again looking to the Kremlin for reassurances. "I believe that in the face of this new situation we must strengthen our defenses, keeping in mind the possibility of a surprise attack by the Yankees. The existing danger fully justifies our doing so."[18]

This time he went to Moscow asking for a large Soviet Navy flotilla to sail through the Caribbean as a sign of support. Moscow refused, fearing a confrontation with Reagan. Castro was so angered that he reportedly refused to attend the funeral of Soviet premier Chernenko a few months later.[19]

Moscow was forced to yet again cough up money to allay the fears of its anxious ally. This time it was to the tune of billions of dollars. Between 1974 and 1983, Moscow had sent Castro just over $3 billion in arms. In the four years following Grenada, the Kremlin sent him $7 billion.[20]

Reagan was advancing in the developing world, backing anti-Communist insurgents and using military might when necessary. This new assertive policy, which became known as the Reagan Doctrine, caused real concern in the Kremlin. "Although the immediate target of the policy of 'neoglobalism' [the Reagan Doctrine] now is mainly countries of the Third World, above all those with progressive regimes, its spear point is directed in practice against the Soviet Union and socialism as a whole," declared a top-secret Soviet Central Committee study on Reagan. His real objective, the study warned, was "not only to stop the further spread and consolidation of positions of socialism in the world, but also to 'exhaust' the USSR and its allies . . . wearing it down in conflicts in different regions of the world."[21]

Reagan was now turning the tables on the Soviets and exacting a price. For more than two decades, the Soviets had been ascendant on the world stage. Now Reagan was pushing them back and laying siege to their most important allies.

CHAPTER XVIII

STUBBORN
RESISTANCE

S OVIET DEFENSE MINISTER DMITRI USTINOV ROSE FROM HIS
chair and shuffled slowly over to the podium. Dressed in a
military uniform (though he was actually a civilian), Ustinov
slowly began delivering the keynote speech to the assembled
Communist Party functionaries who were seated in the Kremlin.

Ustinov, who had helped to build the Soviet nuclear arsenal, was
giving an address at the anniversary celebration of the Bolshevik
Revolution. Reagan had been in office less than a year, but a new
wind was already blowing through Moscow. In labored words, reading from a prepared text, Ustinov laid out the challenge. The new
American president was "seeking military superiority, imposing a
state of siege on the socialist countries, calling into question everything positive achieved in Soviet-U.S. relations, and exacerbating
tensions around the world."

It was a grim speech. Watching nearby were staff from the U.S.
embassy, who listened quietly and afterward spoke with some senior
party members. From what they heard, it was clear that the psychological climate of the Cold War was shifting.

Less than two years earlier, Leonid Brezhnev had confidently declared that the correlation of forces was moving "irrevocably in favor
of socialism." Now suddenly that confidence seemed to be shaken,

and much of it was due to an America that had seemingly been rein-vigorated. As a State Department cable reported, Ustinov was mak-ing "an admission of the seriousness of the challenge they feel they face from the west."[1]

Reagan was using blunt language to describe the Soviet bloc, condemning communism, comparing it with Nazism. It was the sort of language they had never before heard from an American presi-dent. Even during the coldest days of the Cold War, Truman, Eisen-hower, Kennedy, and Johnson had never been so direct and blunt. And as Reagan's strategic initiatives began to unfurl, it became clear that his actions matched his convictions.

"Two features of Reagan's policy toward the Soviet Union upset them [the Soviet leadership] most," recalls Soviet ambassador Do-brynin. "One was his apparent determination to regain military su-periority; the other, his determination to launch an ideological offensive against the Soviet Union, and foment trouble inside the country and among Soviet allies."[2]

Leonid Brezhnev declared, "The ruling circles of the United States of America have launched a political, ideological, and eco-nomic offensive on socialism and have raised the intensity of their military preparations to an unprecedented level."[3]

With Reagan's massive defense buildup in full swing, it did not take long for a siege mentality to take over the Kremlin. Aleksandr Bessmertynkh, who later served as Soviet foreign minister, recalls a Foreign Ministry in the early 1980s that felt as if it was being over-whelmed. "The thrust of the reports that were coming to the polit-ical leadership was that after a certain period of accommodation [détente in the 1970s] the United States had suddenly with a new President who had come to Washington, President Reagan, decided to change the course of defense policy and start an enormous build-up. All the leaks and all the reports that we were getting from our own intelligence in the United States . . . indicated that the United States was serious about overwhelming the Soviet Union in one basic strategic effort."[4]

Reagan was being aggressive and forceful. "He believes the So-viet Union and the United States are in a state of war," declared Leonid Zamyatin, head of the Central Committee International De-partment.[5]

The mood among the Soviet military brass was equally grim. The hard-fought and costly effort to gain strategic superiority now appeared as if it might be for naught. General Detinov, the stern-faced member of the General Staff, remembers that "the American defense spending increase, SDI, and other defense programs greatly troubled the Soviet leadership."[6]

To express their concern, four leading generals wrote books explaining the need to rise to Reagan's challenge.[7]

But Soviet resolve seemed to be weakening. Secret cables sent by the American embassy in Moscow reported: "One Soviet contact came away from a recent speech to a select group by Soviet military and foreign ministry officials on the domestic and international situation visibly shaken by the message." The economy was bad, but in the face of the U.S. defense buildup, "more sacrifices by the Soviet people will be required." Surprised diplomats even encountered support for Reagan's policies among the Soviet intelligentsia. "One hears [Soviet] intellectuals praising the U.S. Administration's foreign policy, since 'toughness is the only thing the Soviet leaders understand.' "[8]

Some feared that war was imminent and that Reagan was preparing for an attack. In May 1981, KGB stations in London, Washington, New York, and Western European capitals received orders to be alert for indications of an imminent American attack. Andropov believed that a first strike was being planned, and he prepared the secret services for war.[9]

But few bought into such paranoia. The military brass, according to General Detinov, never took the threat of an American attack seriously. Neither did the aged Defense Minister Ustinov.[10]

Likewise, Foreign Minister Gromyko dismissed such paranoia, explaining that the Americans would never strike first, but only "in response to aggression."[11]

The real concern was not over a surprise attack but Reagan's stubborn efforts to regain superiority and undermine Soviet power.

★ ★ ★

IT WAS A SOMBER AND DEJECTED YURI ANDROPOV WHO ROSE TO speak before a secret session of the Warsaw Pact's Political Consultative Committee in Prague, Czechoslovakia. The gathering of the senior Soviet-bloc leaders would have the chance to hear about the East-West struggle through the eyes of the KGB chairman and an ironclad Communist. It was the world according to Andropov, and the vision was painful.

"The 1970s were the years of further growth of power and influence of the socialist commonwealth," he declared, looking back fondly at the era of détente. "We were able to achieve the military-strategic parity with the West. This gave us an opportunity to deal with them on an equal basis. Our dynamic policy of détente led to substantial positive shifts in international relations."

During détente, the United States had been on the retreat. "The revolutionary changes in Angola, Ethiopia, Nicaragua and other countries, which were caused by objective factors, were seen by Washington, and not without reason, as a defeat of American policy."

But those trends, and the Soviet advantage, had abruptly ended with Reagan. The American president was challenging the Soviet bloc in every sphere. "The struggle is unfolding in all directions." Reagan was restricting trade, reducing access to technology, and cranking up the arms race. Reagan's high-tech defense buildup was "especially dangerous," Andropov said, because nothing like it had ever been undertaken before. That meant there was no opportunity for retreat.

"We *cannot* allow U.S. military superiority," he grimly told the assembled leaders, "and we *will not* allow it."

To meet the challenge, the Warsaw Pact nations needed to match the Reagan buildup; they had little choice. And the race would be difficult. "The Soviet Union feels the burden of the arms race into which we are being pulled, more than anybody else does. . . . It is not a problem for Reagan to shift tens of billions of dollars of appropriations for social needs to the military industrial complex." It was as if Reagan was speaking: In a full-blown arms competition, Moscow couldn't "keep up."[12]

The CIA closely monitored the Soviet reaction to Reagan's defense buildup and knew how concerned the Kremlin was. One secret report that crossed Reagan's desk noted the hope among some in Moscow that the defense buildup would peter out. Some Kremlin leaders were counting on domestic opposition in the United

States to derail Reagan's ambitious program.[13] Another top-secret report, based on human intelligence sources in Moscow, underlined the dilemma the Kremlin was facing. Soviet leaders had actually communicated their concern about Reagan's buildup in private conversations. They were also insisting that they could match him if they needed to.[14]

★   ★   ★

R EAGAN'S FORM OF ECONOMIC WARFARE WAS PARTICULARLY EFfective. "It would not be a mistake to say that the Reagan Administration practically began an economic war against us," KGB Deputy Chairman Georgy Tsinev told operatives. By forcing Moscow into an arms race, it would severely hamstring the civilian economy. It would also weaken the Kremlin's position on the international stage, because there would be less money available to maintain the empire.[15]

Compounding the problem was the fact that Reagan seemed singularly focused on the buildup. The KGB in its 1980 assessment of Reagan had determined that for him "word and deed are the same." But there had always been the lurking hope that Reagan might turn out to be another Nixon, or at the very least another presidential cold warrior, willing to compromise on some points. But the Kremlin found him stubbornly resistant to doing any such thing.

"No matter what diplomatic tack Moscow examined or actually took," recalls Ambassador Dobrynin, "the Reagan Administration proved impervious to it. We came to realize that in contrast to most presidents who shift from their electoral rhetoric to more centrist, pragmatic positions by the middle of their presidential term, Reagan displayed an active immunity to the traditional forces, both internal and external, that normally produce a classic adjustment."[16]

In secret sessions of the Politburo, members would sit and discuss Reagan's immovable convictions. A frustrated Yuri Andropov at one point blurted out that Reagan was the "bearer of and creator of all anti-Soviet ideas, creator of all the untrue insinuations regarding our country and the other countries of the socialist community." He was not interested in simply being tough to get a better agreement, he was trying to "put together a bloc against the USSR."

"We aren't going to change Reagan's behavior," said a frustrated KGB chief.

"Reagan doesn't react to our suggestions," lamented Politburo member Tikhonov.[17]

In Stalinist North Korea, Kim Il-Sung became so incensed at what Reagan was doing that he tried to arrange for his assassination when the president visited South Korea in 1983.[18]

In Poland, where the military government was grappling with Reagan's sanctions, heightened radio broadcasts, and external support for Solidarity, officials were coming to similar conclusions. The Ministry of Internal Affairs declared that communism had never encountered a foe like Reagan. Richard Nixon had been an anti-Communist, "but his anticommunism can be considered more practical, not characterized by the traits of an 'anticommunist crusade.' " Reagan, on the other hand, was turning the struggle against communism "into an ideological creed." He believed he had a "historic mission," to eradicate communist influence around the world. "The principal goal [of the Reagan administration]," the report concluded, "is the destruction of the socialist system in all of its forms." Reagan's enemies had a clearer picture of what he was up to than the most seasoned observers in Washington.[19]

★   ★   ★

MOSCOW NOW DECIDED TO FLEX ITS MUSCLES IN AN EFFORT TO intimidate Reagan. On the bright morning of June 18, 1982, a Submarine Launched Ballistic Missile (SLBM) burst from the North Sea, flying toward the heavens on a column of fire. Moments later, two ground-based SS-11 ICBMs and an SS-20 missile were launched. It marked the beginning of the most spectacular Soviet military exercise of the Cold War.

The exercise was a simulated all-out first strike against America and Western Europe. Soviet military officials dubbed it the "seven-hour nuclear war" and considered it an opportunity to demonstrate the "might of Soviet troops to the West." Perhaps now, Reagan would be more willing to negotiate and grant concessions, just as his predecessors had been.

As the launched missiles proceeded on their trajectories, they were suddenly intercepted by Soviet ABM-X-3 anti–ballistic missile interceptors. Later in the afternoon, a Soviet rocket placed in orbit a "combat" satellite, which practiced destroying U.S. reconnaissance satellites. The mock war ended with the "devastation" of the United States and Western Europe with nuclear strikes. In all, the simulated war was a powerful display of Soviet nuclear might. Western leaders, including Reagan, anxiously watched, but it was kept secret from the general public.[20]

Later, the U.S. space shuttle *Challenger* was cruising the heavens in a tight orbit around the earth at an altitude of some 365 kilometers, conducting a variety of scientific tests and observing celestial bodies in space. Down on earth, at a massive Soviet military research facility at Sary Shagan, Soviet officials were tracking the shuttle's progress with an advanced Argun large-phased-array radar. When the shuttle came into range, they fired a thin beam of light—a megawatt laser—directly at *Challenger*. The onboard communications began to malfunction and the crew felt some physical discomfort. Later, when the shuttle returned to earth and NASA officials determined what had happened, Reagan filed a strongly worded protest to Moscow.[21]

Military operations were also launched to harass Western commercial flights going to and from West Berlin. The Soviet Navy surfaced one of its submarines underneath the USS *Kitty Hawk*. Warsaw Pact forces even fired on a U.S. Army helicopter along the German-Czech border.[22]

In 1983, more than 120 Soviet bombers congregated on Soviet air bases near the border with Afghanistan. The Kremlin had been grappling with the Afghan resistance for more than three years now, and rather than weakening, the Afghans appeared be growing in strength. With CIA covert assistance having quadrupled under Reagan, the Mujahideen were better armed, better trained, and had better intelligence than ever before. For the Kremlin the only hope seemed to be to bomb the resistance into submission.

In early March 1983, the Soviet Politburo met in secret session to discuss the events in Afghanistan. Casualties were mounting and the rebels seemed to be getting more bold.

"On the whole, the situation in Afghanistan, as you know, is difficult," reported Foreign Minister Andrei Gromyko. "Lately, certain elements of consolidation have been examined, but the process of consolidation is moving slowly. The number of gangs is not decreasing. The enemy is not laying down its weapons." The cost of fighting the war was now some 300 million rubles, and it was getting more expensive every year.

It was a difficult problem, agreed Andropov, because "we are fighting against American imperialism."[23]

The following spring, Soviet Major General Saradov, commander of the Soviet 108th Motor Rifle Division (NMRD), was watching in northern Afghanistan as dozens of Tu-16 Badger high-altitude bombers flew overhead. Moments later, he could feel the ground rumble as they dropped 500- and 1,000-pound bombs on the enemy in front of him. They were carpet-bombing the Panjsher Valley, and resistance fighters were forced to hide in the caves.

After two days of bombing, columns of Soviet tanks began pushing their way through the valley. At the same time Soviet airborne units, transported by helicopters, were dropped near the enemy. It was the beginning of the largest Soviet military operation in the history of the Afghan war. With enough firepower, said the Soviet General Staff, it was still possible to win.

The Kremlin was also determined to rise to the challenge in other outposts of the empire. In Poland, Reagan's sanctions were costing the country more than $10 billion per year. Moscow responded with a gift of $465 million and vowed to do more.[24] To allay concerns in Cuba and Nicaragua, the Kremlin approved more arms transfers.

★   ★   ★

B UT IN MEETING THE AMERICAN CHALLENGE, SOUND AND FURY would not be enough. It could also not be done on the cheap. In a speech three weeks before his death, Leonid Brezhnev declared that an increase in the military budget was necessary: "A lag in this struggle is inadmissible." When Yuri Andropov replaced him as general secretary, his first public statement was an echo of Brezhnev's words. "We know very well," he told the leadership, "that peace cannot be obtained from the imperialists by begging for it. It can be upheld only by relying on the invincible might of the Soviet armed forces."[25]

Resources were quickly diverted from the civilian economy to the military sector. In 1981, the Politburo approved a 45 percent increase in military expenditures over five years. It was a massive shift in resources that would weigh heavily on the already weak civilian economy. Two years later, the Politburo would increase military spending another 10 percent. Meanwhile, the production of civilian machinery was frozen at the 1980 level for the next five years. The military's share of Soviet GNP would rise from 22 to 27 percent during Reagan's first term, while consumption by the civilian economy would drop to less than 45 percent.

Trying to match the Reagan buildup staggered the Soviet economy. By 1982, according to former prime minister Ryzhkov, civilian consumption stopped rising for the first time since the Second World War. It was at this point, says Ryzhkov, that the Soviet economic slide began.[26]

Beyond the arms race, the Kremlin took other measures to counteract Reagan's initiatives. American efforts to cut back the flow of Western technology were beginning to bite, and more countries tightened their export policies. Yuri Andropov warned KGB leaders of the need to access these technologies. Agents in the field were ordered to do whatever they could.[27]

Accessing Western technology would be critical if the Soviet bloc were to win the Cold War. In the words of a KGB secret report, getting widespread access to science and technology "permitted the state to economize significant sums in foreign currency and ensures winning [the Cold War] in time."[28]

CHAPTER XIX

ALL IN THE
NAME OF PEACE

S CANNING THE WORLD SITUATION IN EARLY 1983, KGB CHIEF
and Soviet General Secretary Yuri Andropov looked to the
founder of the Soviet state for inspiration. Vladimir Lenin
had faced a similar situation during his earliest days in power.
Back then, the Western capitalist powers, particularly Britain and
France, had used trade sanctions and power politics to isolate the
Bolsheviks. But by the skillful use of diplomacy, Lenin had found a
way to break up the united Western front.

The weak link in the 1920s had been Germany, which was an
economic basket case and eager to sign a series of lucrative trade deals
with the Bolsheviks. Lenin used that to his advantage and was thus
able to break the "capitalist encirclement." Now Andropov was hoping to do the same. Reagan had them nervous, but they were optimistic. As Ambassador Arthur Hartman in Moscow put it, "The
Soviets apparently feel the need to demonstrate for foreign as well as
for Soviet audiences their confidence that they will be able to break
out of any new encirclement."[1]

Once again, the weak link in the Western alliance was West Germany. If this large NATO member in the heart of Europe could be
peeled off from the alliance, or the confidence of the alliance shaken,
the Cold War might still be won. A West Germany divided from the

United States would be eager to sign trade and financial deals, restart détente, and strike an arms agreement.

Exactly how to pull Germany from the NATO alliance was not a difficult matter to figure out. Public opinion surveys indicated that in 1981, 40 percent of West Germans unconditionally opposed the stationing of U.S. missiles on their soil, regardless of how many missiles the Soviet Union had targeted at them. Less than half believed that unilateral disarmament would make them vulnerable to blackmail from the east.[2] According to secret State Department cables, some German officials wanted "to find a place for the FRG somewhere between the US and the USSR."[3]

The problem was not limited to Germany. In the Netherlands, a solid majority believed that the deployment of American missiles raised serious moral questions and would increase tensions rather than keep the peace. And in Great Britain, the out-of-power Labor Party favored unilateral nuclear disarmament.

★ ★ ★

LEONID BREZHNEV HAD FIRST SEEN THE VALUE OF EXPLOITING THE peace movement back in 1976. By secretly providing money to the movement through front groups in Europe, he had been able to derail the deployment of the so-called neutron bomb. Now, facing a rejuvenated West and a stalwart Reagan, Andropov wanted to do the same. As he told the Politburo, "We have to open up a wider network to win public opinion, to mobilize public opinion of the Western countries of Europe and America against the location of the nuclear weapons in Europe and against a new arms race, that's being forced by the American administration."[4]

Many of the pieces were already in place.

The vast majority of people in the antiwar and antinuclear groups protesting throughout Western Europe were not Communists or even sympathetic to communism. Most were earnest and sincere in their desire to limit nuclear weapons. As Reagan had said during his 1982 speech in Bonn, Germany, the motive for many was summed up in a placard he had seen on the streets: "I'm afraid." Such fear was understandable, but it also created an opening for manipulation.

One earnest peace advocate whom Moscow sought to manipulate was Olaf Palme, the former prime minister of Sweden. Palme had been a longtime advocate of disarmament and had organized a seventeen-member commission to develop a plan to rid the world of nuclear arsenals. The commission included prominent world leaders, including former American secretary of state Cyrus Vance.

As the Soviet representative on the commission, Palme invited Georgi Arbatov, head of the Institute for U.S. and Canadian Studies. A regular fixture on Western television, Arbatov was touted by Western academics as a "scholar" and "serious thinker." He was also a secret agent for the KGB.

Arbatov reportedly worked hard on the commission and fought to get it to see some issues his way. Arbatov reported to the Kremlin that his involvement had been worth the effort and would help serve Soviet interests.[5]

Another sincere advocate of disarmament was Msgr. Bruce Kent, an urbane Roman Catholic priest and head of the Campaign for Nuclear Disarmament, Great Britain's largest peace organization. Kent, an advocate of unilateral nuclear disarmament, was no Communist. But the CND considered him "useful" because his advocacy was helpful to its cause. Seated near Kent at CND board meetings was Vic Allen, who was vice chairman of the CND with responsibility for the international department. Allen was a Stasi "agent of influence," and pushed the organization to take a pro-Soviet position.[6]

A frequent visitor to Western Europe was Finland's prime minister, Kalevi Sorsa, who was vice president of Socialist International, which included political leaders and heads of state from the political left throughout Europe. Sorsa was a pleasant man who seemed to speak sincerely about the need to reduce tensions. The planned INF deployment was likely to only cause tensions and not relieve them, he said. As vice president of the SI with responsibility for disarmament, Sorsa took this message to several capitals in Western Europe. While he did so, he was "confidentially collaborating" with the Soviet Union on peace issues.[7]

In Denmark, Vladimir Merkoulov from the Soviet embassy worked with the Danish Committee for Cooperation and Peace, a coalition of fifty disarmament groups, providing funds to buy newspaper ads promoting "Nordic nuclear free zones." In Portugal, two

Soviet diplomats, Yuri Babaints and Mikhail Morozov, worked with anti-NATO protesters. In the Netherlands, TASS correspondent Vadim Leonov collaborated with peace groups to direct antinuclear protesters.[8]

In West Germany, protesters led by Gert Bastain, head of Generals for Peace and a secret Stasi agent, blocked the main entrance to the U.S. Army's barracks near Neu Ulm. Members of the German Peace Union (DFU) and Committee for Peace, Disarmament and Cooperation (KFAZ), organizations funded by the Soviet bloc, joined with other peace groups to blockade American military installations in Germany.[9] Protests in the capital city of Bonn were carried out with precision. Activists would be brought to Bonn from all over Western Europe in chartered trains and buses, which according to receipts at the charter office of the Bundesbahn (Federal Railway) were paid for by front organizations of the West German Communist Party.[10]

Perhaps the most successful media event for the peace movement was the so-called Krefelder Appeal, a petition signed by 4.7 million Germans in favor of unilateral nuclear disarmament. It was hailed as evidence that large numbers of Germans were opposed to the INF deployment. But the drive had been organized by the German Peace Union (DFU), which was secretly funded by the East German Stasi to the tune of 5 million deutsche marks per year. The DFU didn't create the antinuclear sentiment in West Germany, but it nurtured and helped it reach critical mass by providing money and organization that turned sentiment into a political movement.[11]

As the antinuclear protests reached their zenith in the spring and summer of 1983, Vladimir Kryuchkov of the KGB reported at a secret conference of senior officials, "Considerable work has been done to provide support for unofficial organizations in a number of countries in their struggle against implementation of the American administration's militarist plans."

To fuel the protests, Soviet arms control negotiators made a series of proposals to gain a psychological advantage against the West. These were not serious proposals, recalls General Detinov, but they "were aimed mostly at producing a propagandistic effect and influencing the anti-missile movement."[12]

The strategy had its desired effect in Washington. Some members of Congress introduced a resolution to halt the deployment of missiles. These were "unnecessary first-strike weapons," declared Congressman Tom Downey of New York. "But we don't have a chance of stopping them and won't as long as President Reagan is in office."[13]

★   ★   ★

B Y EARLY 1983, THE PROTESTS IN WEST GERMANY HAD BECOME a backdrop to an election campaign that would be held to determine the fate of the planned missile deployment. The Social Democrats were bitterly divided over the issue. It had been Helmut Schmidt who first proposed the deployment, but since that time the left-wing faction of the party had gained influence. On January 7, 1983, the Bundestag was dissolved, and the campaign to see who would run West Germany was on. The contest was quickly dubbed the *Raketenwahlkampf* (Missile Campaign).

The Social Democrats chose Hans-Jochen Vogel to be their candidate for chancellor, and he pledged to stop the deployment. The Christian Democrats chose Helmut Kohl, who promised to honor the original NATO decision to deploy if Moscow failed to sign an agreement.

Moscow quickly tried to tilt the political campaign in Vogel's favor by playing to German fears. If the missile deployment went ahead, warned Yuri Andropov, there would be "consequences, extremely dangerous to peace in Europe." Only by not deploying the missiles would it be possible to save "Europeans from a nuclear Auschwitz."[14]

At the same time, Soviet-bloc agents inside the German government worked to advance the cause. Karl Wienand, chief whip for the SPD in the Bundestag and a close friend of Vogel's, tried to rally party members and delivered speeches against the deployment. Herbert Wehner, the SPD floor leader in parliament, did the same. Both were on the East German Stasi payroll. Wienand was receiving $5,000 per month, and Wehner (code-named KORNELIS) was a "confidential contact" for both the East Germans and the KGB.[15]

Both men played an important role in pressing the Soviet position on INF within the SPD. As a Soviet Communist Party Central Committee document later claimed, "Many arguments that had previously been presented by us to the representatives of the SPD have now been taken over by them."[16]

In early 1983, German voters went to the polls, not only to pick the next chancellor but perhaps to determine the future of the NATO alliance. Turnout was heavy, and in the end the German people voted for Kohl and the Christian Democrats. It was a strong rebuke of the SPD and Moscow; the missile deployments would go forward.

It was stunning defeat for the Kremlin, which had been hoping that the peace movement could be used to drive a wedge into the alliance. But they had "overestimated the potential of the anti-war/ anti-missile movement in Europe," admits General Detinov. To some it seemed to be a turning point of sorts. "It was one of the most intensive campaigns that the two sides ever carried over just one issue," recalls Aleksandr Bessmertynkh, who was working in the Soviet Foreign Ministry. "So the decision was definitely a great disappointment. There was a certain mood suddenly cast on Moscow that we had failed."[17]

★   ★   ★

IN THE UNITED STATES THE PEACE MOVEMENT WAS AS BROAD AND diverse as it was in Europe. Along with Reagan's daughter Patti, thousands of students, housewives, college professors, and doctors had become involved in a burgeoning antinuclear movement that was suddenly a major force in American politics. By 1982, eleven million voters in eight states and the District of Columbia had endorsed ballot measures calling for a nuclear freeze. Polls even indicated that a majority of Republicans supported a freeze.

In the Oval Office, Ronald Reagan received several top-secret intelligence reports that pointed to Soviet involvement with some American peace organizations.[18] He worried about the effect that the movement might have on his plans for a military buildup and went public with his concerns. Although most freeze supporters were sincere, he said, "one must look to see whether, well-intentioned though it may be, this movement might be carrying water that they're not aware of for another purpose."[19]

A likable and hardworking man named Romesh Chandra began appearing in Washington to attend seminars on disarmament issues and to meet with members of Congress. Congressmen Gus Savage of Illinois, Philip Burton, Ron Dellums, and Don Edwards of California, and Charles Rangel of New York participated in a two-hour briefing Chandra organized under the sponsorship of the World Peace Council. Several other members of Congress, including John Conyers and Patricia Schroeder, invited others to attend. The following day, Chandra and several other WPC activists returned to Capitol Hill for further discussions.

Based in Helsinki, Finland, the World Peace Council claimed to be an international peace organization committed to global disarmament. In reality, it was receiving $50 million a year from the Soviet Politburo and was under the direction of the International Department of the Central Committee.[20]

Generals and Admirals for Peace, another disarmament group, also made appearances on Capitol Hill. Along with the group A Citizens Organization for a SANE World (SANE), they sponsored a panel made up of former NATO officers from Germany and Italy. David Cortwright of SANE said from the podium that the panel would offer an authoritative view of the issues of disarmament. It would also end what he called "the myopia regarding the European peace movement as a creation of the Kremlin." One of the people Cortwright introduced was General Gert Bastain, who was active in Generals for Peace. Unbeknownst to Cortwright, East German intelligence was funding the organization, which it regarded as particularly helpful in spreading propaganda that would serve the Soviet cause. Bastain later traveled to other cities in the United States, declaring that the Western military buildup needed to be stopped.[21]

The KGB also tried to influence the American peace movement. In a 1986 KGB report to the Politburo, the agency took credit for "stirring up the anti-military movement in countries of the west." They could look to a number of successes, including the fact that agent Georgi Arbatov, who was subsequently revealed to be an agent, had been asked by Ted Turner to join the board of his Better World Society.[22]

But these efforts were less than successful, at least in part because of the frustration and disgust of those assigned the task. Much of the coordinating work was done by Igor V. Mikhailov of the CPSU International Department in Moscow. A veteran of the party, Mikhailov had worked for twenty years sending money to the Communist Party U.S.A. and other organizations in the United States that would promote Soviet interests. Ironically, his many years spent working on such causes had a sobering effect on him. Apparently he took a disliking to many of the fellow travelers in the West with whom he had contact. After he retired from his job in 1988, he quit the Communist Party in the Soviet Union and became a committed anti-Communist. When asked at his farewell banquet what he regretted most in his job, he snapped that it had been his inability to shut down the CPUSA.[23]

★   ★   ★

AS THE 1984 PRESIDENTIAL CAMPAIGN SEASON BEGAN, THE PRESsures on Reagan began to build. Polls indicated that his domestic policies were far more popular with the American people than his hard-line foreign policy, and that only 31 percent approved of his handling of foreign policy. It was one of the main reasons he was trailing every major Democratic candidate who was looking to run against him.[24]

The attacks on Reagan were both harsh and shrill. Averell Harriman, a former ambassador to the Soviet Union and adviser to five presidents, declared openly in the New York Times that Reagan's defense policies were so dangerous that "if permitted to continue, we could face not the risk but the reality of nuclear war." Former vice president Walter Mondale, who would challenge Reagan for the presidency in 1984, claimed that he had "ceded the moral high ground to Moscow." Senator Edward Kennedy explained that Reagan and his advisers "are talking peace in 1984 as a prelude to making war in 1985." Senator George McGovern proclaimed that he felt secure knowing that Yuri Andropov was in charge at the Kremlin, because unlike Reagan, he would prevent a war. "I think we ought to be very thankful that this man Andropov seems to be a reasonable guy and somewhat restrained. Because certainly the Reagan-Weinberger approach is one of intense confrontation. It's almost as though they were spoiling for a military showdown." Senator Ernest Hollings of South Carolina echoed that sentiment. It wasn't the Kremlin that scared him; it was Reagan.[25]

These were of course the sort of criticisms that were common in American politics. But Soviet officials were encouraged by the fact that similar opinions were being quietly whispered to them by some American leaders. Former president Jimmy Carter dropped by Soviet ambassador Dobrynin's residence on a day in late January 1984 to discuss the state of the world. Carter was concerned about Reagan's defense buildup, Dobrynin recalled. The former president went on to explain that Moscow and the world would be better off with someone else in the White House. Otherwise, "there would not be a single agreement on arms control, especially on nuclear arms, as long as Reagan remained in power."

At an official dinner later in the year, Dobrynin ran into Speaker of the House Thomas P. "Tip" O'Neill. The witty O'Neill, who often swapped jokes with Reagan, was less hospitable when talking to the Soviet ambassador. No effort should be spared to prevent "that demagogue Reagan" from being reelected, O'Neill told him. "If that happens, Reagan will give vent to his primitive instincts and give us a lot of trouble, probably put us on the verge of a major armed conflict. He is a dangerous man."

Ironically, while these efforts were intended to undermine Reagan, they probably helped him by increasing Soviet fear of him.

While other American leaders were less harsh, they were nonetheless out to limit Reagan's defense buildup. Senator Charles Percy, a Republican from Illinois, came to Dobrynin to offer advice on how to deal with Reagan's arms control proposals. He advised Moscow to apply a gentle touch. "You are just playing into Reagan's hands" if you take a hard-line position, he coached.[26]

The common refrain seemed to be that the poor state of superpower relations was a result of Reagan's unreasonable position. The irony is that as these criticisms were being lodged against Reagan, in the halls of the Kremlin some were of a decidedly different opinion. Viacheslav Dashichev, a senior adviser to General Secretary Yuri Andropov, advised his boss that when it came to Reagan's strong policy, the Kremlin had no one to blame but themselves. Reagan was

simply reacting to the aggressive policies Moscow had been pursuing in the 1970s.[27]

But the political threat to Reagan was real. Former president
Gerald Ford had joined Richard Nixon in suggesting that the arms
buildup needed to be slowed down. The American Business Conference, typically part of the GOP political base, came out in favor
of military cutbacks. GOP governors declared that his defense plans
were "screwball" because they cost so much. On Capitol Hill, even
stalwart Republicans like Senator John Warner of Virginia were
floating ideas like reducing the size of the armed forces by 5–7 percent to save money.

Even within his own administration Reagan had his critics.
Chief of Staff James Baker, presidential assistant Richard Darman,
and OMB Director David Stockman quietly made it known that
Reagan's defense budget requests were excessive. But as the pressures
built, Reagan remained firm. He would not curtail his planned military buildup. "I'm sticking with what I said," he told aides. And he
made it abundantly clear that he would not let the election influence
his strategy toward the Soviet Union. "The president would have
willingly lost the second election if it came down to changing his Soviet policy," recalls Robert McFarlane.[28]

★   ★   ★

WHAT THE KREMLIN SAW IN THESE PUBLIC AND PRIVATE WORDS
of criticism directed at Reagan was *fear*; many were afraid
that the superpower confrontation could spin out of control and
into war.

Like Nikita Khrushchev in the 1950s, Soviet-bloc intelligence
officials thought that fear could be a powerful tool. In this case, they
wanted to use it to apply pressure to Reagan in hopes of putting a
brake on his policies. They even identified particular leaders who
would be prone to this approach. As one top-secret intelligence report explained:

"We must offer a sensible alternative in contrast to those of the
leading powers of American Imperialism, and look for other politicians, such as Democrats [Paul] Warnke, [Cyrus] Vance, [Harold]
Brown, [Robert] McNamara, [Tip] O'Neill, [Gary] Hart, as well as

Republicans [William] Proxmire, [Charles] Matthias, [Charles] Percy and in its broadest meaning also [Richard] Nixon and [Henry] Kissinger. They must be counted on to give a sensible alternative to give up the Reagan politik, and gradually approach them about the fear of a direct confrontation between USA and USSR. The starting point is to target those politicians in very separate ways so that their motive is sufficient fear that the United States is making a decision based on limited knowledge and insight, and that peaceful coexistence is necessary for capitalism to survive. . . . The opinion of these politicians could have significant influence over the [Reagan] Administration in their strategic decisions."[29]

Despite these initiatives, the Kremlin failed to derail Reagan.

On a cold December in 1983, Soviet ambassador Oleg Grinevsky paid a visit to Yuri Andropov, who was lying sick in a hospital bed. As he entered the room, Grinevsky noticed that Andropov's countenance was different. In part it was a result of his illness; in part it was a reflection of his growing pessimism.

"The international situation is very tense," he told Grinevsky. "For the first time since the Caribbean Crisis [Cuban Missile Crisis] the United States and the Soviet Union are going at it head-on. The United States wants to change the existing strategic situation and they want to have the opportunity of striking the first strategic strike. And we . . ." He fell silent. "Our economy is in a pitiful condition. It must be greatly accelerated, but our hands are tied by the Afghan war. Americans do everything in order not to let us out of Afghanistan. We were unable to stop them from placing their medium-range missiles in Europe. Frankly, we lost that battle. Americans will be performing the song 'Everything Is Fine, Beautiful Lady.' They will make you sing along, you will be made to sing the chorus to them. Therefore, don't give up. Otherwise, it will look like defeat. There is one thing left to us, just like the 19th century after the Crimean war. We must have the slogan: 'Russia, concentrate, gather your strength.' If we are strong, we will be respected and nobody will think of or remember human rights. If we are weak, all will fall apart. The main thing is strength, but strength is dependent on economic development."

One month later, he died.[30]

CHAPTER XX

REAGAN MAKES GORBACHEV POSSIBLE

I N THE FALL OF 1983, TWO VERY SENSITIVE PIECES OF INTELLI-gence crossed Ronald Reagan's desk in the Oval Office.

The first was a memo concerning British intelligence and was being passed on at the suggestion of Margaret Thatcher. A KGB colonel named Oleg Gordievsky, who was secretly working with British intelligence, had passed along some alarming news. Some in the KGB, he reported, had come to the radical conclusion that Reagan might be preparing to launch a first strike and were running drills to prepare for such an attack. The other was a memo from the CIA's National Intelligence Council. Herb Meyer, the Council's vice chairman, was an economist who had written about the Soviet economy for years. He had now produced a stunning memo that declared the Soviet Union was entering a "terminal phase" and that the prospects for war were real. Events seemed to confirm what Meyer was saying. Only weeks earlier, the Soviet Union had blown a Korean civilian airliner out of the sky, killing 269 people.

"I believe the current outbreak of violence is more than coincidence," Meyer wrote. "More precisely, I believe it signals the beginning of a new stage in the global struggle between the Free World and the Soviet Union." The Soviet Union was in its "terminal phase," Meyer declared boldly. "If present trends continue, we're going to win the Cold War."

Reagan's strategy was working. "The flow of wealth from West to East is less than the Soviets had anticipated it would be by now." The successful invasion of Grenada had been a "shocking setback" for the Soviets, and the deployment of missiles in Europe "is about to change the balance of power in Europe back in our favor.

"The Soviet economy is heading toward calamity. Something fairly drastic has to give, and fairly soon. It's a matter of simple arithmetic."

The Kremlin was on the horns of a dilemma. They needed to either "slash the defense budget" or enact "massive economic reforms. Either remedy would threaten the Communist Party's grip on power."

But before the death rattle of communism could be heard, Meyer worried, there might be fireworks. The Kremlin could simply accept the fate of its pending demise, or it could pursue a grim alternative and "decide to go for it," strike first and hope to win a war. The possibility was real, and the United States needed to "design, articulate, and implement a strategy for dealing with the Soviet Union that will avoid war. The thrust of this strategy, simply put, should be to deny the Soviets an external solution to their problem."[1]

Several members of the cabinet had been arguing for some time that Reagan needed to soften his policy toward Moscow. Secretary of State George Shultz, for one, believed that it was time to engage the Kremlin in a dialogue and arms control. Shultz had proposed a summit meeting back in 1982, but Reagan had balked at the idea. Reagan's wife, Nancy, was also passionate about her husband taking a more moderate course. She was less concerned with the geopolitics of the question, and the image of her husband as a warmonger deeply bothered her. She wanted him to be remembered as a peacemaker.

Reagan had been surprisingly immune to these pressures early in his administration. But now, armed as he was with this intelligence information, the tenor of his policy began to change.

Weeks later he delivered an address to the nation. It was a major address about relations with the Soviet Union. Abandoning talk of crusades and a struggle against evil, he instead spoke about the differences between the two superpowers and the need to find "common interests."

"Neither we nor the Soviet Union can wish away differences between our two societies and our two philosophies," he said. "But we should always remember that we do have common interests. . . .

"Just suppose for a moment that an Ivan and Anya could find themselves, say, in a waiting room or sharing a shelter from the rain or a storm with a Jim and Sally, and there was no language barrier to keep them from getting acquainted. Would they then deliberate the differences between their respective governments? Or would they find themselves comparing notes about their children and what each other did for a living? Before they parted company they would probably have touched on ambitions and hobbies and what they wanted for their children and the problems of making ends meet. And as they went their separate ways, maybe Anya would say to Ivan, 'Wasn't she nice, she also teaches music.' Maybe Jim would be telling Sally what Ivan did or didn't like about his boss. They might even have decided that they were all going to get together for dinner some evening soon.

"We must establish a better working relationship," Reagan concluded, "one marked by greater cooperation and understanding." But he added a word of caution. "Cooperation and understanding are built on deeds, not words."

Many dismissed the speech as simplistic, or as an attempt by Reagan to change his image for the 1984 election. But the new tone continued. Secretary of State Shultz made several speeches stressing "the American commitment to reduce the vast stockpiles of arms in the world." He also offered a proposal for the "complete and verifiable elimination of chemical weapons on a global basis." And he talked about the prospects of a summit meeting between Reagan and Konstantin Chernenko, the new Soviet general secretary.[2]

★   ★   ★

BUT WHILE THE DIPLOMATIC TONE WAS CHANGING, THE UNDERLYing strategy against Moscow was intensifying.

As Reagan spoke of the need for further cooperation, he was

dramatically escalating the war in Afghanistan. A covert aid program that had been relatively small in 1981 had grown to some $300 million per year and had become the most expensive covert operation in American history. By 1986, Reagan would send an incredible $470 million to the Afghanistan resistance. The Afghans were getting more advanced arms, better intelligence, and superior equipment.

Meanwhile, the Kremlin was sending out feelers for American help in leaving Afghanistan. In April 1983, Moscow had proposed in Geneva that it would withdraw if Pakistan would cease its support for the Afghan resistance. UN officials became involved and tried to broker an agreement.

Pakistani Foreign Minister Yaqub Khan flew to Washington to pitch the idea to the Reagan administration. But Reagan did not want to give the Soviets a graceful way out. How Moscow left Afghanistan was as important as when. At the National Security Council, an influential paper was being circulated under an "eyes only" cover sheet written by Richard Pipes, who had left the NSC in January to return to Harvard. Titled "The Soviet Union in Crisis," Pipes's paper argued that Moscow's failure to secure an honorable retreat from Afghanistan would cause enormous credibility problems for the Kremlin. "Any humiliation of its forces at the hands of foreign powers could raise doubts in the minds of Soviet citizens whether it is as omnipotent as it claims to be." Reagan didn't want to give Moscow the chance to exit Afghanistan and claim that it had achieved some sort of victory.[3]

At the same time, the war in Afghanistan was beginning a dangerous new phase. Back in early 1983, CIA Director Bill Casey and National Security Adviser William Clark had come to the Oval Office with a new proposal. Soviet Central Asia, said Casey, was the soft underbelly of the Soviet Union. It was populated with people who had much more in common with the Afghans than with their masters in Moscow. Casey was proposing that Reagan take the war into the Soviet Union itself, by training, equipping, and supporting members of the Afghan resistance to cross the border and hit military targets on Soviet soil.

Nothing like it had ever been suggested, but Reagan agreed and signed off on the proposal.[4]

Casey then returned to Pakistan to discuss the plan with members of the Pakistani ISI, who were managing the war. One of those present at the meetings was Brig. Mohammad Yousaf, who was handling the Afghan war for the ISI.

Casey suggested to the ISI that the operation could start with the smuggling of written propaganda material across the border. Eventually it could be followed by armed uprisings. "He was convinced that stirring up trouble in this region would be certain to give the Russian bear a bellyache," Yousaf recalls.[5]

The CIA paid for tens of thousands of copies of the Holy Koran to be translated into Soviet Uzbek and the production of several books describing Soviet atrocities against Muslims. Soon they were finding their way across the border into the Soviet Union, carried by Afghan resistance fighters who rowed the Amu River in small rubber boats.

Resistance fighters also began crossing the border to collect intelligence. "I was impressed by the number of reports of people who wanted to assist," Yousaf recalls. "Some wanted weapons, some wanted to join the mujahideen in Afghanistan, and others wanted to participate in operations inside the Soviet Union."[6]

In early 1985, after being trained and equipped by the CIA, Afghan resistance fighters began conducting sustained military operations inside the Soviet Union. On one occasion, thirty fighters attacked two hydroelectric power stations in Tajikistan. In another instance, there was a rocket attack on a Soviet military airfield. In all, there were dozens of ambushes.

As these attacks continued, they clearly touched a nerve in Moscow. The newspaper *Izvestiya,* which scarcely carried information on the Afghan war on its pages, ran a stern article denouncing "the violation of our country's scared border."[7]

The American Consulate in Peshawar, Pakistan, closely monitored the Kremlin's reaction, noting in one cable that the Mujahideen "have the military capabilities to carry out larger attacks inside the enemy territory."[8]

As the war raged in Afghanistan (and inside the Soviet Union itself), Reagan looked for other opportunities to support anti-Communist insurgents. In Africa, anti-Communist guerrillas were fighting in Angola to overthrow the Marxist government. Back in

1975, when Marxist guerrillas backed by Cuban soldiers had taken over Angola, Reagan had called for American aid to their opponents. By the summer of 1985, he got the chance to do just that. Five million dollars was also allocated for Cambodians fighting the communist government of Vietnam.

Reagan was bold and open about the battle he was waging in the developing world. "Let us . . . offer the world a politics of hope, a forward strategy of freedom," he told the Irish Parliament in Dublin. "Those old verities, those truths of the heart—human freedom under God—are on the march everywhere in the world. All across the world today—in the shipyards of Gdansk, the hills of Nicaragua, the rice paddies of Kampuchea, the mountains of Afghanistan—the cry again is liberty."

The tide was turning in the developing world, and Reagan wanted to win. But he also knew that it was a drain on Moscow. The CIA calculated that while the United States was spending less than a billion dollars per year to support these insurgents, it was costing the Kremlin $8 billion to finance the counterinsurgency operations.[9]

The Kremlin watched the tides of war shifting with great frustration. "The USA skillfully exploits the fact that in 'low-intensity conflicts' it is much cheaper to support guerrillas than the government," wrote Alexei Izyunov and Andrei Kortunov.[10]

In Poland Reagan was also hanging tough. Ordinary Poles were listening to his speeches on Radio Free Europe and Voice of America. They read about his expressed belief that the Soviet Union was an "evil empire." And they understood that his hard line on sanctions, which was making their life and that of the communist government much more difficult, was designed to keep Solidarity alive. Alone among Western leaders (with the exception of Margaret Thatcher), anti-Communist activists looked to him to bring freedom to their country.

"Ronald Reagan was considered a god by some in my country," recalls Colonel Henryk Piecuch, a top official in the Interior Ministry at the time. "This pertains especially to the lower ranks of Solidarity."[11]

In May 1983 the magazine *Paris Match* conducted a secret poll of six hundred Poles who were traveling to the West and found that sense of faith in Reagan. When asked who was the "last hope" for Poland, Reagan came in third, behind only the Pope and the Virgin Mary. (Solidarity leader Lech Walesa came in fourth.)[12]

Reagan was providing material support to the Solidarity Underground. But as he won victories in Grenada, proceeded with the missile deployment in Europe, and sustained his military buildup, it lifted the veil of invincibility that many associated with the Communists. "The assistance from American government for 'Solidarity' was essential because toward the end of the 1980s it was clearly felt that the United States was winning the competition with the USSR, not only economic and military, but also political and ideological," says former interior minister General Kiszczak. "For decades people supporting the Polish People's Republic had a sense that they were on the side of the strong. In the second half of the 1980s, the West was becoming the 'strong one.' Thus, both Solidarity and the Polish United Workers' Party [Communist Party] people were slowly gaining the consciousness of who was winning and losing in the historical sense. This was more important than the concrete assistance and support extended to the opposition by the United States."[13]

★   ★   ★

WITH A SOFTER DIPLOMATIC TONE BUT A COMMITMENT TO roll back Soviet power around the world, Reagan could look back in 1984 and see what he had accomplished. He had overseen the swelling of the military—3,000 new combat aircraft, 3,700 strategic missiles, and 10,000 new tanks. They were being produced at twice the rate of the 1970s. And the SDI program, still in its embryonic stage, was growing. International agreements signed with Japan, West Germany, Great Britain, Italy, and Israel brought these countries into the research program.

At the same time, the noose tightened further on exports to the Soviet bloc. Sweden and Austria, two neutral countries that had for decades served as transshipment points for technologies going to the Soviet bloc, agreed to limit high-tech exports. Dozens of items were added to the restricted list of what could be shipped. The Kremlin became so frustrated, it even went so far as to register a formal complaint with the General Agreement on Tariffs and Trade (GATT) in Geneva, claiming that Reagan was unfairly restricting the free flow of trade. If Reagan had his way on technology, the Kremlin claimed, "the wheel would still be on the [restricted] list today."[14]

★ ★ ★

PERHAPS THE MOST STUNNING ECONOMIC WEAPON REAGAN sought to wield against Moscow came not from Washington but from Saudi Arabia.

Early in his first term, Reagan had been determined to win over the Saudis and have them join him in his war against communism. "The Saudis were one of the most important components of the Reagan strategy," Alan Fiers, the former CIA station chief in Saudi Arabia, told me.[15] King Fahd and the Royal Family were concerned about the threat posed by Moscow's allies in the region. There were 1,500 Soviet military advisers in South Yemen, 500 in North Yemen, 2,500 in Syria, 1,000 in Ethiopia, and 1,000 in Iraq. In short, the Saudi Kingdom was almost completely surrounded by Soviet military advisers. And with 10,000 troops in Afghanistan, the prospect that the Kremlin might be willing to use force was real.

Reagan had been determined to show that he was a reliable ally. In 1981, he secured the passage of AWACS and fighter aircraft to Saudi Arabia, despite determined opposition from the Israeli lobby. Later, he announced the formation of a U.S. Central Command (USCENTCOM), with responsibility for the Persian Gulf region. Through USCENTCOM, Reagan was pledging to deploy nearly three hundred thousand troops to protect the Saudis. By early 1985, the U.S. Air Force was breaking ground on a project called Peace Shield, a technologically advanced integrated air defense system around Saudi Arabia. It was a computerized command, control, and communications system that would link Saudi AWACS planes with five underground command centers and seventeen long-range radar stations. Four hundred Americans would staff the facility and maintain constant contact with the USS *La Salle*, the command post for USCENTCOM.

What Saudi Arabia offered Reagan was the ability to alter world oil prices. The Saudis were a swing producer, and depending on whether they produced 2 million barrels a day (mbd) or 9, the price of oil would rise or fall.

In Reagan's administration, there was no question what the preference would be. In 1983, economists at the U.S. Treasury Department had concluded that lower international oil prices would be a boost for the U.S. economy. A $5 drop in the price of a barrel of oil would increase the U.S. gross national product by about 1.4 percent, reduce inflation, and increase disposable income. Lower oil prices would also directly reduce the U.S. trade deficit.[16]

But if lower prices were a boon to the United States, they were a bust to the Kremlin. CIA analysts had concluded that for every one-dollar drop in the price of a barrel of oil, Moscow would lose between $500 million and $1 billion per year in critical hard currency.[17]

★ ★ ★

ONE OF THE FIRST FOREIGN HEADS OF STATE TO VISIT REAGAN at the start of his second term was King Fahd of Saudi Arabia. Reagan and Fahd sat in the Oval Office for a private, off-the-record meeting. Meanwhile, Sheik Yamani, the Saudi oil minister, met privately with Secretary of State George Shultz and Energy Secretary John Harrington. A secret briefing memorandum prepared for Shultz on February 9, 1985, outlined the issues and positions of the United States. Implicit was the assumption that world oil prices were too high and that the United States would benefit from a reduction. The key objectives of the meeting were discussing the world oil price situation and allegations that the United States was manipulating oil markets. "OPEC ministers including Yamani have accused the U.S. of engineering a plot to drive down oil prices to some preconceived level."

The administration had no preconceived level. But there had been an extensive lobbying effort to see prices fall.

"We wanted lower international oil prices, largely for the benefit of the American economy," recalls Ed Meese, the White House counselor at the time. "The fact that it meant trouble for Moscow was icing on the cake."[18]

"It was to our advantage all around," recalls Admiral John Poindexter, Reagan's national security adviser. "It was in our interest to drive down the price of oil as low as we could. We saw it as a very important objective to keep the price of oil down."[19]

Much of the lobbying was done by CIA Director Bill Casey, who had regular secret meetings with Fahd concerning the Soviet threat and his insurgent wars against the Soviet empire. He also talked to Fahd about oil prices.

"Bill Casey was keeping an eye on oil prices almost daily, and so were we," recalls Roger Robinson, who headed the International Economics section of the National Security Council. "It was the centerpiece of the Soviet hard currency earnings structure and principal funding source of its military industrial complex."[20]

Casey told others about his efforts. He informed Glenn Campbell, the chairman of the President's Intelligence Oversight Board, that he was talking to the Saudis about it. "He was going to approach the Saudis about reducing prices," Campbell told me. "He didn't offer too many details. He just mumbled after that."[21]

Defense Secretary Caspar Weinberger was another administration official who spoke to the Saudis. Weinberger had a long history with the Saudis; he had dealt with them in private life when he was with the Bechtel Corporation. Now, as secretary of defense, he had great pull because of the critical security and military commitments that had been made. "I raised the issue in general discussions with Saudi officials—the defense minister, Prince Bandar, and King Fahd," recalls Weinberger. "They knew we wanted as low an oil price as possible. Among the benefits were our domestic economic and political situation, and a lot less money going to the Soviets. It was a win-win situation." There were no quid pro quos, Weinberger told me. "But one of the reasons we were selling the Saudis all those arms was to get lower prices."[22]

★ ★ ★

IN THE LATE SUMMER OF 1985, FIVE MONTHS AFTER FAHD'S MEETing with Reagan, Saudi officials quietly alerted Washington that they should expect a dramatic increase in oil production and a big drop in world oil prices. "They told us in advance that we could expect a sizable jump in production," recalls Secretary Weinberger.[23]

Then, in August 1985, the Saudis opened the oil spigots. In the first few weeks, daily production jumped from less than 2 million barrels to almost 6 million. By the late fall of 1985, crude production had climbed to almost 9 million barrels a day. As a result, oil prices plummeted. In November, crude oil sold at $30 a barrel; barely five months later, it stood at $12.

As prices plunged, the Kremlin began losing billions in desperately needed hard currency.

★   ★   ★

AS REAGAN PRESSED AHEAD, A DEBATE RAGED IN THE KREMLIN. The Soviet economy continued in the tailspin that had started in 1982. Inefficiency had always been a problem. But now, under the weight of more military spending and meeting the Reagan challenge, the economy was in actual decline for the first time since the Second World War. Having failed to split the NATO alliance, it was clear that the Soviets would only fall further behind a rejuvenated America in the arms competition.

Ever since the death of Stalin, the Kremlin had quietly been divided into two camps, with competing visions about which direction the Soviet Union should go. Hard-liners wanted to stay the course and forge ahead with a policy of confrontation and repression. Reformers believed that this old model would not work. The economy would end in ruins, and failure to change would mean eventual defeat in the cold war.[24]

For the past twenty years the hard-liners had been ascendant. And it was easy to see why. Their approach had worked brilliantly. A massive military buildup and an aggressive posture in the world had brought them superpower status; Soviet prestige was enormous, and only the United States could match the might of the Soviet Union. The tide of history seemed to be moving in the Soviet direction. The economic problems that plagued their system were covered up, thanks to the infusion of trade, technology, and cash from the West.

But after four years of Ronald Reagan, it seemed to be a different world. There were no longer revolutionary gains in the developing world, only defeats. On every continent, Soviet allies were under siege by American-backed insurgents.

Reagan seemed to be reversing the currents of history. As Central Committee member Karen Brutents lamented, Reagan had somehow changed the game. Unlike President Carter, who was "more flexible," Reagan "wholly rejects the recognition of any kind of independence and self-determination of the national liberation movement and passes it off as a result of 'the subversive activity' of the Soviet Union." Reagan's "universal anti-Soviet strategy" meant America was willing to use force against "unwelcome regimes." As a result, "there is no guaranteed 'automatic' revolutionary potential there [in the developing world.]."[25]

Among the Soviet military brass, the mood was equally bleak. No longer riding high with the belief that they had achieved superiority, they instead looked apprehensively at the future. The Strategic Defense Initiative (SDI) was a major concern. Whatever critics were saying about it in the West, Soviet military and intelligence officials were frightened.

SDI "played a powerful psychological role," recalls KGB general Nikolai Leonov. "And of course it underlined still more our technological backwardness. It underlined the need for an immediate review of our place in world technological progress."

Another KGB general, Sergei Kondrashey, recalls that SDI "influenced the situation in the country to such an extent that it made the necessity of seeking an understanding with the West very acute." Beyond fear, SDI created a sense of helplessness. Alas, there was nothing they could do to match Reagan's military program. General Makhmud Gareev, Deputy Chief of the Soviet General Staff, recalls many officers believing it "was beyond our power" to compete against Reagan.[26]

Over at Soviet military intelligence (GRU), General Chervov commissioned an extensive study to determine whether the Soviet empire could compete with a rejuvenated America. When he released it to the Politburo late in 1984, it contained glum news: The gap between America and the Soviet Union would widen and not narrow.[27]

Gyula Horn, Hungary's foreign minister, attended a party with Soviet marshals and generals in Moscow, and observed a profound sense of defeat.

As the vodka began to flow, "the respected officers had a glass too many and opened up," he recalls. "One of them began to hold forth loudly about the need to press the nuclear button as soon as possible, before the imperialists could gain superiority over us in every field. The others shouted down my protests and received their comrade's insane words with great ovation."[28]

The great debate between hard-liners and reformers came to a head when General Secretary Konstantin Chernenko died in early March 1985. Chernenko was the last of the old generation of Kremlin leaders who had experienced firsthand the ravages of the Second World War and rose to power during the Stalinist era. Now a new generation would be taking over, and it was clear that whoever succeeded him would dramatically shape the entire destiny of the Soviet empire.

For Foreign Minister Gromyko, it was a critical if difficult choice to make. Nicknamed "Grim Grom" because of his inflexible and rigid manner, Gromyko had become Ambassador to the United States way back in 1943. Ever since, as he climbed his way up the diplomatic establishment, he had been a hard-liner. Now, because of his seniority, he had extraordinary power. More than any individual, he would determine who would rule the Soviet empire.[29]

Gromyko had all the markings of a hard-liner. And yet he had seen enough over the past four years to know that something needed to change.

He had become obsessive about what Reagan was doing. In September 1984, when he visited the United States, he met with former senator George McGovern to discuss the state of superpower relations. He was very concerned about Reagan. Reagan and his advisers "want to cause trouble," he said. "They want to weaken the Soviet system. *They want to bring it down.*"[30]

Days later when Gromyko visited the White House, he pulled no punches with Reagan himself. After denouncing the defense buildup, he declared: "Behind all this lies the clear calculation that the USSR will exhaust its material resources before the USA and therefore be forced to surrender."[31]

Perhaps Gromyko's greatest anxiety was over SDI. In early January 1985 he traveled to Geneva, Switzerland, for a meeting with Secretary of State George Shultz. The two men sat down in the U.S. Mission on January 7, and according to the classified transcript of the private meeting, Gromyko was horrified.

"If the U.S. did have such a defensive system in place," he declared, "it would have the capability to inflict a first nuclear strike against the USSR with impunity. One needs no special gift of perspicacity to understand this; it is clear almost to the point of being primitive. If the Secretary were to view this situation from atop the tower, he would reach the same conclusion.

"The U.S. wants to gain advantage over the Soviet Union, and the defensive system if developed would be used to bring pressure on the Soviet Union. Let us not mince words, even if they are harsh ones: the system would be used to blackmail the USSR."[32]

Two months later, General Secretary Chernenko died, and the battle lines were quickly drawn between the hard-liners and the reformers. Hard-liners came mostly from the ranks of the planning bureaucracy and favored Grigori Romanov, a member of the Central Committee and former Leningrad party chief. On the other side were the reformers, who championed a young man named Mikhail Gorbachev. The reformers were led by the Foreign Ministry, the KGB, and the military.

As the Kremlin leadership gathered to discuss the choice, it was Gromyko who took center stage. As he abandoned his own hard-line instincts, his anxieties about Reagan's challenge got the best of him. He threw his support to Gorbachev, describing him as a brilliant man with a keen intellect, clear principles, and firm convictions.

"Comrades," he said in now-memorable words, "this man has a nice smile, but he has teeth of iron."

In his nominating speech, Gromyko made special mention of the external challenges that the Soviet Union was facing. "Perhaps because of my official responsibilities, it is rather clearer to me than to other comrades that he can grasp very well and very quickly the essence of those developments that are building up outside our country in the international arena."

Perhaps more than any other Kremlin leader, Gorbachev was an advocate of radical reform. Like Gromyko, he was keenly aware of the challenge posed by Reagan to the Soviet system. The Soviet Union would have to change in order to compete. As he put it in 1984, "Only an intensive, fast developing economy can ensure the strengthening of the country's position in the international arena, enabling it to enter the new millennium appropriately, as a great and prosperous power."[33]

★ ★ ★

I N A VERY REAL SENSE, GORBACHEV OWED HIS SELECTION TO THE pressures Reagan was exerting on the Soviet system. Those who believe that only internal political factors inside the Soviet Union brought Gorbachev to power fail to appreciate the stress that Reagan was placing on the Kremlin. Gorbachev's selection as general secretary, says Georgy Shakhnazarov, one of his foreign policy advisers, was the result of "internal domestic pressures and Reagan's rigid position and that of his administration." The fact was, says Shakhnazarov, that the Soviet Union was "falling behind" the United States and reform offered the opportunity to catch up.[34]

The vote for general secretary would be a close one. Three key Soviet institutions—the Foreign Ministry, the military, and the KGB—forged a coalition that helped to bring Gorbachev to power. Not coincidentally, all three were primarily concerned with the Soviet Union's international standing and were also concerned about their eroding position around the world. Foreign Minister Gromyko wanted to ensure victory for Gorbachev, so he secretly ordered Ambassador Dobrynin in Washington to prevent Politburo member Vladimir V. Shcherbitsky, who was in the United States at the time, from coming back to vote. Shcherbitsky was a solid vote against Gorbachev. He was told by Dobrynin that there were no connecting flights back to Moscow; he arrived a day too late to vote.[35]

On his first day in office, Gorbachev walked through the halls of the Kremlin and arrived for a meeting with the Central Committee. In a brief speech, he laid out his strategy for handling the domestic challenges he faced and for dealing with Reagan. "We will firmly follow the Leninist course of peace and peaceful coexistence. . . . We value the successes of detente in international tensions achieved in the 1970s, and are ready to participate in the continuation of the process of starting peaceful, mutually beneficial cooperation between states on the bases of equal rights, mutual respect and non-interference in internal affairs."[36]

Gorbachev quietly sent out feelers to Reagan, seeking some kind of accommodation. He was hoping that Reagan might take the bait and be willing to strike a bargain.

"The USSR needs an arms control agreement for economic reasons," reported a secret cable from the American embassy in Moscow after meetings with Soviet officials. "The economy is virtually on a 'war footing,' and economists calculate that only half the increase in production sought by the leadership can be achieved without a substantial diversion of resources away from the military. The military leadership has not pressured Gorbachev not to offer 'deep cuts' in the nuclear arsenals and would accept whatever agreement the leadership reached with the U.S."[37]

Reagan was now where he had hoped to be. He had been advising American presidents since 1963 that if they engaged in a military buildup, Moscow would never be able to match them. Gorbachev was interested in a summit meeting with Reagan at the earliest possible moment. The President was glad to oblige him.

CHAPTER XXI

THE AGING LION
VS. THE YOUNG TIGER

RONALD REAGAN STOOD BY THE WINDOW OF THE ELEGANT Swiss chateau at Fleur d'Eau waiting for the arrival of Mikhail Gorbachev. The world was watching, and hundreds of reporters had gathered outside to record this first encounter between the two men. Reagan looked out onto the circular driveway and flashed the reporters a thumbs-up.

There were high expectations for the summit. Would they come to terms on nuclear weapons? Would they agree on a Soviet withdrawal from Afghanistan? Would they agree on strategic defense?

But along with the high expectations there was also concern. Some openly wondered whether Reagan was up to the task. Gorbachev was quick-witted and shrewd, the young reformer whose appearance Richard Pipes had predicted back in 1982 when Reagan's secret strategy was being put together. Unlike Soviet leaders from the recent past, he was also youthful, dynamic, and charismatic. He had already impressed Western leaders such as Margaret Thatcher and François Mitterand with his mastery of statesmanship.

Weeks before the summit meeting, advisers had given Reagan a mountain of briefing papers to read; everything from the ABM treaty to the history of the czars was covered. But he was seventy-four now. His aides saw that he could fatigue more quickly and his mind seemed less focused than it was when he was younger.

Reagan read the briefing books. But he never claimed to be a depository of technical detail. There was a multitude of issues that were going to be discussed—human rights, Afghanistan, arms control, and strategic defense. But Reagan was an intuitive thinker and believed that core issues mattered more than the individual topics, which were symptoms, not the problem itself. The root cause of the Cold War, he had said back in 1967, was the nature of the Soviet system itself. Powerful totalitarian governments made war; democracies did not. So whenever he met with Soviet leaders, he was interested in core issues more than symptoms of the Cold War divide.

It had been that way in the spring of 1984 when Politburo member Vladimir Shcherbitsky, a proud Ukrainian who had been an old friend of Brezhnev's, visited the White House. He and Reagan sat down for what Shcherbitsky assumed would be a discussion about arms control. But Reagan instead spent most of the time complaining about the lack of freedom in the Soviet bloc and the inherent flaws of communism. Shcherbitsky left frustrated and more than a little angry. When Andrei Gromyko came to the White House later in the year, expectations were high that there might be a diplomatic breakthrough. Richard Nixon advised Reagan to be "as businesslike as possible" and to avoid preaching to Gromyko. Reagan, of course, totally ignored this advice and instead lectured the foreign minister on the horrors of communism.[1]

No American president had ever spoken to Kremlin leaders this way. But for Reagan, this was a calling. He had written Nixon back in 1959 congratulating him for standing up to Khrushchev in the so-called Kitchen Debate. "They needed to hear that," he had written. Believing that his life had been spared in 1981 for the purpose of defeating communism, he felt he had a larger mission than simply trying to secure a better arms control agreement. As he had written in his top-secret directive on national strategy, his goal was not to coexist with the Soviet Union but to "transform" it. He was already squeezing the Soviet economy and was in the midst of a political and geopolitical offensive against the Kremlin. Now he wanted to harness the corrosive power of freedom.

One month before he left for Geneva, he was aboard *Marine Corps One,* the presidential helicopter, flying over Manchester, New Hampshire, with that state's Governor John Sununu. As they looked out over the houses, Reagan told him, "What I'd really like to do with Mikhail Gorbachev is to pick any house down there" and introduce him to the "working people" of America. "I'd like to ask him to compare our way of life with that of the Soviet Union."[2]

★   ★   ★

W HEN REAGAN HEARD THE WAILING HORNS OF THE SOVIET motorcade in the distance, he stepped out of the Swiss villa and into the icy cold air that was blowing strongly off nearby Lake Geneva. Outside, the assembled media were bundled up in overcoats and parkas to fight off the biting wind. But Reagan emerged in his blue suit—no coat, no hat, no scarf—and waited as the black Zil limousine, with a Soviet flag flying from the right fender, pulled into the driveway.

Reagan, the aging lion, was about to meet Gorbachev, the young tiger.[3]

Gorbachev stepped out of the limo dressed in a charcoal-gray hat and a matching scarf, wrapped up in a heavy overcoat. As Reagan descended the steps of the villa, coatless and standing upright, greeting him confidently, an unexpected portrait emerged.

The aging lion, twenty years older, was substantially taller and towered over the young tiger, who was bundled up and looking less confident in the cold wind. Sergei Tarasenko, a Gorbachev aide, remembers watching the spectacle unfold.

"We came to the porch and I saw President Reagan coming out to greet Gorbachev in a well-tailored suit, looking young with a good haircut, you know. Maybe he was made up a little bit, but skillfully. He projected an image of a young, dynamic leader. And Gorbachev came out of this tank-like limo, black limo, in a standard Politburo hat, in a scarf, in an autumn overcoat, a heavy overcoat, looking like an old guy."[4]

A surprised Gorbachev shook Reagan's hand. "Where is your coat?"

"It's inside," Reagan said before leading the young tiger by the elbow into the villa.

★   ★   ★

BEFORE THE SUMMIT, GORBACHEV HAD PROPOSED AN ARMS CONtrol agreement reducing the strategic nuclear arsenals of both sides by 50 percent. It was a strong proposal, and there were high hopes among many in the West that a breakthrough might be around the corner. Moscow had never been so bold in an arms control proposal.

But as the two men sat down in comfortable chairs, the aging lion said nothing about the proposal. Indeed, he said nothing about any of the issues at all. Instead, he told the young tiger a joke.

An American and a Russian meet. "My country is the best," the American says, "because I can walk to the White House and tell the President he is doing a lousy job."

"Big deal," responds the Russian. "My country is just as good. I can go to the Kremlin and tell Gorbachev the same thing: 'Reagan is doing a lousy job.'"

Gorbachev chuckled.

Reagan grinned. He was breaking the ice. But he was also doing more. As always, his stories had a point or a purpose behind them; it had been that way ever since he started using illustrations in his public speeches thirty years earlier. Reagan was telling a funny joke about communism. But just below the surface, there was a sharp edge of truth that revealed the absurdity of the Soviet system.

Every time the two would meet, Reagan would have a couple of jokes ready in his arsenal, gently zinging the Soviet leader about the absurdities of his system.

Another Reagan joke: An American took a trip to the Soviet Union. On the way to Kennedy Airport, he rode in a cab driven by a college student.

"What are you going to do after graduation?"

"I haven't decided yet."

When he arrived in Moscow he jumped into another cab, which was also driven by a university student.

"What do you want to do when you finish college?" he asked.

"I don't know," the student responded. "I haven't been told yet."

Gorbachev sat grim-faced when he heard that one.

And another:

Two guys were standing in line at the vodka store. Gorbachev had just placed restrictions on the sale of vodka. They were there for a half hour, then an hour, then an hour and a half.

"I'm sick of this," one finally said. "I'm going over to the Kremlin to shoot Gorbachev."

The man left and returned about an hour later.

"Well, did you shoot him?"

"Hell, no," he responded. "The line up there is a lot longer than this one."

Gorbachev could only offer an uneasy smile.[5]

★   ★   ★

WITH THE ATMOSPHERE RELAXED A BIT, REAGAN STARTED BY talking in unusually blunt and direct language. "Let me tell you, Mr. General Secretary, why we fear you and why we *despise* your system." Then he went on to reel off Soviet crimes: human rights violations and the occupation of Eastern Europe, the invasion of Afghanistan, support for revolutionaries around the world. None of the briefing books in the mountain Reagan had read through had suggested this as his opening gambit; it was pure Reagan.

Gorbachev sat and listened testily. This was not what he had been expecting; Nixon, Ford, and Carter had never talked to Brezhnev this way.

"He lectured me as though I was a suspect or maybe a student, and I cut him short," Gorbachev later recalled. "I said, 'Mr. President, you are not a prosecutor. I am not the accused. You are not a teacher. I am not a student.' "

Reagan smiled, confident that he had established the high ground. Then the two men began talking about the issues at hand. They discussed regional conflicts—Afghanistan, Nicaragua, Africa— and then broke for lunch. Reagan huddled with his advisers, and Gorbachev went back to the Soviet embassy and had lunch with some American peace activists. The two men returned to the villa later in the afternoon.

As Gorbachev arrived, the negotiators from both sides were arrayed in front of each other, ready to go into verbal combat over throw weights, ICBMs, and international law as it applied to Afghanistan. Reagan suggested, however, that the two men meet alone with only their interpreters present. Gorbachev was surprised but readily agreed. They took a long walk behind the villa, along the gentle Lake Leman.

They talked about Reagan's movie career, and Gorbachev explained that he had seen his performance in *King's Row*. When they arrived at the boathouse along the shore, they went inside, where a fire was roaring in the fireplace.

Before he left for Geneva, Reagan had read some intelligence reports amid the mountain of briefing papers. As always, he readily consumed these reports, which described the Soviet Union's desperate economic situation. "Gorbachev faces an economy that cannot simultaneously maintain rapid growth in defense spending, satisfy demand for greater quantity and variety of consumer goods and services, invest the amounts required for economic modernization and expansion and continue to support client-state economies. Gorbachev, in our view has a clear understanding of these limitations; he is obviously extremely impatient that they be addressed now."[6]

The men sat in chairs that faced the crackling fire. After rambling through several topics, Reagan looked into Gorbachev's eyes and, in a voice he later described as his "most plaintive, wistful tone," told him:

"I do hope for the sake of our children that we can find some way to avert this terrible, escalating arms race . . ." Then he paused. Gorbachev, thinking that Reagan was finished, smiled and opened his mouth to speak. But before the words could come out, Reagan continued. ". . . because if we can't, America will not lose it, I assure you."

Reagan continued staring into Gorbachev's eyes while the Russian interpreter translated his words. After Gorbachev heard the words, he nodded. Reagan put a friendly hand on Gorbachev's shoulder and said, "Well, I've really enjoyed our conversation, but now I guess we had better get ready for dinner."[7]

As the summit entered its second day, it became clear that Gorbachev was zeroing in on Reagan's Strategic Defense Initiative (SDI). He was making bold offers to radically cut the Soviet nuclear arsenal. But it all hinged on Reagan's willingness to abandon SDI. Unlike many in the West who questioned whether it would actually work, it provoked passions of fear in Gorbachev. He was, recalls aide Anatoly Chernyaev, "excited and even inflamed" whenever the subject came up.[8]

The Soviet offer to cut nuclear weapons was historic. But if SDI stood in the way, the entire summit would be for naught. Some Reagan advisers worried about dashed expectations. "We may end up with only an agreement to meet again," Secretary of State Shultz lamented as the summit was nearing an end. "The Soviets are wary of a final agreement. They are afraid Reagan will bang 'em on SDI and human rights. If there is no agreement on statements, it could fall apart, except an agreement to meet."

Many outside the administration agreed, suggesting that SDI was a nice tool to get a better agreement, nothing more. Before the summit, Richard Nixon had called SDI the "ultimate bargaining chip" and advised Reagan to use it to get the best strategic arms treaty possible.[9]

But Reagan's faith in the system was real; he didn't want to bargain it away. Not only did he think it could prevent a nuclear war, he believed it was the ultimate weapon to use against the Kremlin. For three decades now, Reagan had spoken out about how Moscow used "fear of the bomb" to bully its way on the world stage. If, as Reagan believed, SDI could make nuclear missiles obsolete, the Kremlin would lose its most powerful asset. So Reagan hung tough and ignored the advice; there would be no agreement limiting SDI.

★ ★ ★

AFTER THE TWO MEN LEFT GENEVA, THE AGING LION FLEW BACK to Washington having gained much while giving up nothing. Gorbachev had made key concessions on strategic nuclear weapons and intermediate-range weapons. But he also flew home with an appreciation for the Young Tiger. Gorbachev was different from previous Soviet leaders; he was more candid and willing to admit to some Soviet failures. And there was something curious, he found, in their discussions. "The president mentioned to me that he was struck by how much Gorbachev talked about God," recalls author Suzanne Massie, who advised Reagan about the Soviet Union.[10]

But Reagan was keenly aware that he was in the driver's seat. He wrote in a private memo just after he returned: "If he really wants an arms control agreement, it will only be because he wants to reduce the burden of defense spending that is stagnating the Soviet economy. This could contribute to his opposition to SDI. He doesn't want to face the cost of competing with us."[11]

For his part, the Young Tiger left Geneva with a strange new respect for the Aging Lion, who still apparently had plenty of fight left in him. "Gorbachev immediately started to like Reagan, and that was a very surprising thing," recalls Aleksandr Bessmertynkh. "I think Reagan had something which was so dear to Gorbachev and that was sincerity."[12]

★   ★   ★

MIKHAIL GORBACHEV WAS DETERMINED TO SAVE THE SOVIET system. But he needed Reagan's help. There were two issues that were particularly troublesome. "The first was disarmament and the second was Afghanistan," recalls Anatoly Chernyaev. Gorbachev needed disarmament to revive the economy, and he needed a way out of Afghanistan that would save face and maintain Soviet credibility.

After six years of combat in Afghanistan, the Kremlin had failed to defeat the enemy. And young men were coming home in caskets in ever-greater numbers. Back in 1983, there had already been wide discussions in the Kremlin about the need to withdraw. The war was having "a catastrophic effect upon the position of the Soviet Union," recalls Ambassador Oleg Grinevsky.

The trouble was, Reagan wasn't about to let them leave in any way that would allow them to hold on to their honor. A simple retreat on Reagan's terms was unacceptable, because it would destroy Soviet credibility. "Without a ghost of justification," recalls Sergei Tarasenko, they simply could not leave. "We needed something to save face."[13]

Soviet international prestige was on the line. Throughout the Cold War, the Soviets had never been forced to retreat from the battlefield. If they did so now, they would risk losing everything.

"We hear from India, and from Africa, that if we leave, it would be a blow to the authority of the Soviet Union and in the national-liberation movement; the imperialism would start an offensive in the developing countries if we leave Afghanistan," Gorbachev grumbled in a secret session of the Politburo. "A million of our soldiers went through Afghanistan. And we will not be able to explain to our people why we did not complete it. We suffered such heavy losses! And what for? We undermined the prestige of our country, brought bitterness. For what did we lose so many people?"[14]

Trapped by Reagan, but believing that he could not simply withdraw, Gorbachev examined his options and decided to escalate the war and try to win. He recruited General Mikhail Zaitsev, one of the golden boys of the Soviet Army, to take over command in Afghanistan. Daring and courageous, Zaitsev had been given the prestigious command of Soviet forces in Germany at a young age. If anyone could win in Afghanistan, Zaitsev could.

Gorbachev offered the commander a free hand. Special weapons could be used, including camouflaged mines and liquid gas explosives; the special forces (Spetsnaz) were at his disposal. He could have all the airpower he needed to pound the enemy.

Back in Washington, the White House took notice of Gorbachev's move. What had begun as a modest covert operation to support the Afghan resistance under Carter had blossomed under Reagan into the largest covert operation in U.S. history. But news of Zaitsev's plans raised serious concerns. To be more effective on the battlefield, the Afghan resistance needed better air defenses. Throughout the war, the Soviets had been able to pound away with heavy bombers comforted by the knowledge that the resistance lacked effective surface-to-air missiles. Now CIA Director Bill Casey and National Security Adviser Robert McFarlane approached Reagan about giving advanced SAMs to the resistance. They explained the urgency of the situation, about Gorbachev's new attempt to win. Reagan didn't need to hear any of it.

"Everyone wanted to move fast," recalls Robert McFarlane. "But he wanted to move even faster."

"Do whatever you have to do to help the mujahedin not only to survive, but to *win*," Reagan told them.[15]

Robert McFarlane and several members of the NSC staff were put to work developing a new strategy for the covert war in Afghanistan. After they were finished, Reagan signed it. The top-secret directive (NSDD-166) declared that the new goal in Afghanistan was to defeat the Soviets on the battlefield. And to make the strategy workable, the arms spigot was opened even further. In 1985, the CIA delivered 10,000 rocket-propelled grenades and 200,000 rockets, more than had been delivered in the entire five previous years combined. And a new exotic weapon made an appearance.

★ ★ ★

ON A SMALL HILL ONLY A SHORT DISTANCE FROM THE JALALABAD airfield in Afghanistan, resistance commander Ghaffar and his men huddled in the brush waiting for the enemy. At three in the afternoon, a group of eight Soviet HIND gunships approached the airfield and prepared to land. The HIND helicopters were particularly despised by Ghaffar and his men; they had inflicted heavy casualties on resistance fighters and civilians alike.

As the HINDs hovered about six hundred feet above the airstrip, Ghaffar gave an order. Three of his men stood up holding Stinger missile launchers, and with cries of "Allah o akbar" pulled the trigger, sending missiles screaming into the air. The first missile malfunctioned and fell harmlessly. But the other two slammed into their targets, and two massive HIND helicopters crashed to the ground. The fighters screamed with excitement before firing off two more missiles, which slammed into two more targets. The remaining gunships, flown by now-panicking pilots, hastened away.

It was the first taste of Reagan's next phase of the war. Over the next year, the resistance would fire off two hundred Stinger missiles; 75 percent would hit their targets.

Suddenly, Soviet pilots flying over Afghanistan began refusing to fly missions below 15,000 feet, the effective range of the Stinger. Bombing, which had been so effective, was no longer practical, as pilots refused to fly low enough. And Kremlin nerves were clearly jarred by the new weapon. Sergei Tarasenko, the principal foreign policy assistant to the Soviet foreign minister, recalls, "I went with Shevardnadze to Afghanistan six times . . . and when we were coming into Kabul airport, believe me, we were mindful of Stinger missiles. That's an unpleasant feeling. You were happy when you were crossing the border and the loudspeaker would say, 'We are now in Soviet territory. Oh, my God. We made it!' "

Weeks after Ghaffar's men fired off the first Stinger, a videotape and a box arrived in the Oval Office. Reagan sat in a chair and someone popped the tape into the VCR. For the next several minutes, he watched the blurry images of Stinger missiles knocking Soviet helicopters from the sky. The tape came with a note of apology to the President: The tape was shaky because the Afghan cameraman had been so excited about the new weapon.

After the tape was finished, Reagan was handed the box. He opened it up and inside found a memento of gratitude from the Afghan resistance: a used tube from the first Stinger fired in Afghanistan.[16]

★   ★   ★

I N GENEVA, GORBACHEV HAD FAILED IN HIS EFFORT TO DERAIL SDI. Reagan was stubbornly going ahead, and he was doing it with gusto. The SDI budget was going to double in 1986, and European nations like Germany, France, Italy, and Great Britain, along with Israel and Japan, were being recruited to join the research program. Gorbachev was concerned.

Some were advising him that SDI would not work, that it should be of little concern. But Gorbachev was obsessed with it. As he told the Central Committee, Reagan was betting on the fact that the Soviet Union was afraid of the system, that was part of the strategy. But the fact was that, given American technological prowess, nothing was impossible for the Americans.[17]

The key for Gorbachev was not falling behind; it was essential to keep pace. "There is no other way," he told the party faithful. "The competition that has grown more acute under the impact of scientific and technological progress is affecting those who have dropped behind ever more mercilessly."[18]

Shortly after his return from Geneva, Gorbachev authorized another dramatic jump in military spending, just as Brezhnev and Andropov had done several years earlier in their bid to keep up with Reagan. Over the next five years, military spending would go up 8 percent per year, and it would prove painful. National income was stagnant, and to pay for the increase, Gorbachev was forced to cut imports of consumer goods from the West by 20 percent.[19] Compounding the problem was that plunging world oil prices, brought about by Saudi Arabia's boost in production, would cost him $7 billion in critical hard currency.[20]

It was a particularly difficult time to do it, because Gorbachev was trying to redirect the Soviet economy. "We have to combine both guns and butter," he glumly told the Politburo. "It is very, very hard."[21]

"We are stealing everything from the people," an anguished Gorbachev told the Central Committee. "And turning the country into a military camp. And the West clearly wants to pull us into a second scenario of the arms race. They are counting on our military exhaustion. And then they will portray us as militarists. And they are trying to pull us in on the SDI."[22]

★   ★   ★

FORTY MILES SOUTH OF EAST BERLIN STOOD A TOP-SECRET MILITARY installation known simply as Objekt 74. Off-limits to even most members of the East German military, the facility was a training base, but not for the armed forces.

Every so often a small group of civilians would arrive with a special intelligence unit dubbed "XXII-8." The civilians were not from East Germany, but were instead members of various left-wing terrorist groups operating in the West. With the help of Stasi specialists, they would learn how to use small arms and grenade launchers, and become skilled in the art of planting bombs.[23]

Erich Mielke, a four-star general and head of the Ministry of State Security, had set up the operation in the 1970s. Broad-shouldered and stocky, with black hair combed straight back, Mielke believed that terror had its uses. He himself had been involved in the brutal murder of two Berlin policemen as a young communist street fighter before the Second World War. West Germany's Red Army Faction (RAF) had accumulated a record beginning in the 1960s of targeting prominent Germans with assassination. Mielke thought they could be useful, so he set up a series of safe houses the group could use in East Berlin to elude their captors in the West.

Several members of the RAF became agents for the Stasi. And at Objekt 74, the East Germans trained RAF members to attack Americans living in Germany. In early 1981, RAF terrorists visited the facility to train for an attack on the moving car. A Mercedes sedan outfitted with mannequins made of cloth and stuffed with sawdust was blown up using a rocket-propelled grenade (RPG). Several months later, the same RAF members fired an RPG at a car with U.S. general Frederick Kroeesen and his wife Rowene seated in the back seat. The two survived, thanks to the vehicle's armor plating. The same terrorists were also trained to plant bombs, and they later detonated one at U.S. Air Force headquarters in Ramstein. Twenty people were injured.

East German leader Erich Honecker embraced the RAF, convinced they were freedom fighters. He asked East German party ideologists to produce a detailed study explaining how the RAF was using terror as a legitimate form of "self defense against the repressive policies of the capitalist west."[24]

Honecker had a "kind of fanatical love for the RAF," recalls a former member of the East German Politburo.[25]

Like Gorbachev, Mielke and Honecker were anxious about Reagan's vision of a strategic defense system, paranoid that he would establish "technical and economic superiority for decades to come," as one intelligence report warned. And as European countries negotiated participating in the program, they became targets of the RAF.[26]

On July 6, Karl-Heinz Beckhurts, director of research at the Siemens Company, an SDI contractor, and an adviser to the West German government on SDI talks, was driving outside of Munich. A remote-controlled bomb detonated nearby and killed him instantly. The RAF left a note at the scene declaring that he had been killed because of his involvement with "secret negotiations" with Washington over SDI.

Weeks later, in October, Gerlad von Braunmuhl was shot dead by a masked gunman while leaving a taxi outside his home in Bonn. Von Braunmuhl had been a principal adviser to the German foreign minister during SDI talks with Washington. The RAF claimed responsibility for this attack, too, declaring that "today we have, through the Ingrid Schubert Commando, shot dead the secret diplomat von Braunmuhl."

Five months later, Italian general Licio Giogeri was gunned down by assassins in Rome. Director General of the Department of Space and Armaments Procurement at the Defense Ministry, Giogeri was the principal negotiator in SDI cooperation talks with the Reagan administration. The Union of Fighting Communists claimed responsibility for the attack, and in a rambling fourteen-page communiqué declared Giogeri had been "struck down exclusively for his responsibility exercised following the Italian adhesion to the Star Wars project." The letter closed with the words "No to Star Wars."

★   ★   ★

SINCE THE DECLARATION OF MARTIAL LAW IN POLAND, REAGAN had hung tough on his plans regarding sanctions. He never budged; only the release of political prisoners and the granting of the right of Solidarity to organize would lead him to end punitive sanctions. In the meantime, he continued to beam thousands of hours of radio programming into the country, encouraging the underground and letting them know that the world was watching. Reagan was, as Lech Walesa put it, giving "strength and sustenance" to the underground movement.

For five years, martial law authorities had been quietly hunting down leaders of the Solidarity Underground. Many had managed to elude authorities by shifting locations and using disguises—hair, makeup, fake mustaches, hats—stolen from university theater departments by sympathetic students. But by 1986, they had much of the leadership under lock and key. The trouble for martial-law authorities was that they had won the battle but were losing the war.

With the opposition leadership in jail, the fate of the Polish underground looked bleak. But for the military government, the economic situation was disastrous. Reagan's sanctions were taking a big bite: In 1980, trade between the West and Poland was $7.5 billion. By 1986, it was barely $1 billion. Unable to export to the West, Poland saw its foreign credits dry up, too. Before 1980, Warsaw had been borrowing up to $8 billion per year. By 1985, that figure had plummeted to a mere $300 million.

With the economy in desperate straits, ending Reagan's sanctions became the top priority. In July 1986, General Jaruzelski declared a general amnesty and all political prisoners were freed. The enemies of the regime returned to the streets, free to rejoin the underground. The gambit to crush Solidarity had failed.

Back in Washington, Reagan received the news with cautious enthusiasm. A critical precondition to the ending of sanctions had been the right of Solidarity to organize. Jaruzelski was not promising that, so Reagan's instincts were to keep the sanctions in place. But a voice came from Poland: Lech Walesa and nine other prominent Solidarity leaders issued a statement asking Reagan to alter his stance because the sinking economy "threatened the rulers and the ruled, and future generations."

Reagan agreed and lifted sanctions. But he offered Jaruzelski a stern warning: Another crackdown and sanctions would be reinstated. Backed by the full weight of Reagan's threat, Walesa and other opposition leaders declared that they would defy Jaruzelski and began organizing again. "We do not want to act clandestinely," Walesa announced.

Jaruzelski, facing a Hobson's choice of seeing the economy tank or the opposition organize, was forced to relent. Another crackdown never came.

CHAPTER XXII

THE TRAP

IT WAS EARLY OCTOBER 1986, AND RONALD REAGAN WAS SITTING in the Oval Office preparing for his next conference with Mikhail Gorbachev. The plans for the meeting had been made quickly; the two men would meet in the town of Reykjavík, Iceland, for what was described as an informal discussion. Usually such meetings were planned weeks in advance, but Reagan had less than ten days to prepare.

Seated across the desk from him was Lyn Nofziger, a longtime friend and political adviser. A former newspaperman with an affinity for Mickey Mouse ties, Nofziger had hooked up with Reagan when Reagan was governor. Now he was dropping by to see his old friend; he was worried.

Friends knew that Reagan had a weakness that could cost him dearly in his dealings with Gorbachev. Always able to charm his opponents, Reagan seemed to believe that if they liked him, they liked his views. Nofziger and others were worried that Gorbachev might be able to charm Reagan into a bad deal.

"Mr. President, a lot of us are fearful of what is going to go on in Iceland. We think there is talk about making a deal, and I want you to know that there are a lot of people out there who support you because of your strong stand against the USSR."

Reagan grinned at his old friend. "Lynwood, I don't want you to ever worry. I still have the scars on my back from the fights with the communists in Hollywood. I am not going to give away *anything*."[1]

Reagan was still actively reading the intelligence reports that were being passed to him. They painted a picture of a Soviet economy in desperate straits and a Gorbachev in need of a deal. It was critical for Gorbachev to achieve détente with the West in order to reform his country. "Gorbachev probably hopes to encourage downward pressure on US defense spending and greater access to Western technology and trade credits," wrote the CIA. "To the extent he is successful, his ability to maintain the momentum of the industrial modernization program will be enhanced."[2]

As Reagan boarded *Air Force One* for the flight to Iceland, he tried to dampen hopes. There were no ceremonies or dinners planned; no detailed negotiations were expected. Instead, the two leaders would spend Saturday and early Sunday morning together before flying home Sunday afternoon.

On the flight over, Reagan read a bit and slept. When *Air Force One* touched down on the cold and rainy tarmac in Iceland, he was greeted by Iceland's president before his motorcade proceeded to Hofdi House, a plain two-story villa where the leaders would meet. Along the way, small clusters of people had gathered carrying candles. Hofdi House was several miles out of town. Unlike Geneva, where the media had been ever present, in Reykjavík they would be kept at a distance. The leaders would go head-to-head, alone.

The two men met and shook hands before sitting down across from each other at a small dining room table. Gorbachev this time came armed with even more proposals than he had offered in Geneva. Instead of a 50-percent cut in strategic nuclear missiles, he was offering their complete elimination. And on intermediate-range nuclear forces (INFs), he was willing to accept Reagan's terms for their complete elimination from Europe. They were tantalizing offers. Reagan listened, then began talking about core issues again.

"I am convinced that historical facts are on our side. Long ago Karl Marx said—"

"Well, earlier the President referred to Lenin," snapped Gorbachev, "and now he's moved on to Marx."

"Everything that Marx said, Lenin said it too. Marx was the first, and Lenin was his follower. And they both said that for the success of socialism it must be victorious throughout the world. They both said that the only morality is that which is in keeping with socialism. And I must say that all the leaders of your country—except you, you still have not said such a thing—more than once stated publicly, usually at party congresses, their support for the proposition that socialism must become worldwide, encompass the whole world, and become a unified world communist state. Maybe you have not managed to express your views on this yet, or you do not believe it. But so far you have not said it. But all the others said it!"

Reagan then went on to outline the history of the Cold War.

"And how can we overcome our mistrust of you if even during World War II when we were fighting together, you did not want to allow Allied bombers flying from England to land in your country before making the return flight?

"And what happened after the war's end? Beginning in 1946 we made 19 proposals at various international conferences to eliminate nuclear weapons. At that time we were the only country in the world with nuclear weapons. But you did not want to participate in the realization of our proposals. A little later the USSR deployed missiles on Cuba, 90 miles from our shores.

"I could continue, give other examples of similar steps in a policy which illustrates your conviction of the world mission of socialism. Naturally, this cannot help but arouse our suspicions that you have hostile intentions in relation to us. You, however, have no facts that indicate that we, our people, are yearning for war. There could not be anything more untrue."

Gorbachev didn't offer a defense of Marx or Lenin. But he pressed Reagan on his strategy for dealing with communism.

"I was very surprised when I heard that just before our meeting in Reykjavík you stated in your speeches that you remained loyal to the principles set forth by you in your speech at Westminster Palace. And in that speech you said that the Soviet Union is the Evil Empire, and called for a crusade against socialism in order to drive socialism onto the scrap heap of history. I will tell you, that is quite a terrifying philosophy. What does it mean politically, make war against us?"

"No," Reagan responded coolly. "The difference between us has

always been and still is that we in the United States have a Communist Party whose representatives can vote in elections and even hold
certain elected positions and propagate their philosophy, while you
do not have anything like that. Instead of trying to convince people
that your ideas are right, you impose these ideas and therefore
groups of people in the third world now and then seize power and
the communist party gets a monopoly on power. . . . That is the difference. We think that only the people themselves can determine
what kind of government they would like to have."

Again, Gorbachev offered no real defense, but instead said that
philosophical differences should not preclude "purely human relations between us."

"Unquestionably," Reagan responded. "Although I would like to
try to convince you to join the Republican Party."

Gorbachev chuckled. They moved to the subject of Gorbachev's
proposals. Reagan lectured the Soviet leader about the troubles with
the Soviet economy. Gorbachev fumed.

"The money with which the Russians could have bought grain
ended up in the United States and Saudi Arabia because of the sharp
drop in oil prices. So the United States already has this money. . . .
We know who began this process of cutting oil prices, and whose interests it is in."

But Gorbachev returned to his proposals. He was offering Reagan almost everything the President could want. It would give the
United States a clear advantage: A greater portion of America's nuclear arsenal was on bombers, which would not be covered by eliminating ballistic missiles. But it was contingent on one thing: Reagan
needed to abandon SDI.

Reagan looked squarely across the table at Gorbachev. "I am
convinced that I cannot retreat from the policy I have declared in the
field of space and defensive weapons. I simply cannot do it."

Gorbachev grew frustrated. "I am increasingly convinced of
something I knew previously only secondhand. The President of the
United States does not like to retreat."[3]

The two men took a break. Reagan met with his advisers.

"He's brought a whole lot of proposals, but I'm afraid he's going
after SDI," he grumbled.[4]

The two men then went back to work and continued battling throughout the day and into the night. Gorbachev kept pressing, but Reagan stood firm, refusing to take the bait. The Aging Lion, it appeared, was more than a match for the Young Tiger.

Soviet officials watched with anticipation and grew to have a grudging respect for the man they were grappling with. With no advisers speaking into his ear, he was a formidable foe. As Sergei Tarasenko recalls:

"We saw President Reagan was a human being—not a politician, but a human being, dedicated, and believing strongly in certain ideas. You could not argue with him; you could not productively argue with him on his so-called pet projects. He believed in these things, he really believed them, and you felt it."[5]

Finally, as the talks continued through the second day, Reagan closed his notebook and stood up.

"The meeting is over," he said, then looked at Secretary of State George Shultz. "George, we're leaving."

As they stood in the hallway putting on their coats, Gorbachev tried one last time. "Can't we do something about this?" Gorbachev asked as Reagan put on his coat.

"It's too late."[6]

★   ★   ★

AT SEVEN O'CLOCK IN THE EVENING, REAGAN AND GORBACHEV emerged from Hofdi House. Reagan got in his limousine and headed straight for *Air Force One,* defiant and angry. Secretary Shultz stayed behind for a press briefing, disappointed at the outcome. He stood before the world's media with a tear in his eye.

For Gorbachev, Reykjavík was a bitter experience. He had arrived with the hope of springing a trap and convinced that he could get Reagan to abandon SDI, but he himself had been outmaneuvered. Reagan, far from giving in, had proved to be a tough adversary. Instead of obtaining an agreement to end SDI, Gorbachev had granted concession after concession. Reagan had pocketed them and would hold Gorbachev to all of them during future talks. Gorbachev's gambit had failed. And it was now apparent that Reagan was not interested in doing anything that would help Gorbachev save the Soviet system.

"The fate of the country is on the line, and we are really at a historical turning point," Gorbachev told the Politburo shortly after Reykjavík. "They look at us in the West and wait for us to drown."[7]

Andrei Gromyko, the grim diplomat, was furious at having been outmaneuvered. "The Americans saw our weakness," he snapped, "and now they are applying pressure along that line, tearing out new concessions from us."[8]

Reagan took the lessons of Reykjavík to heart. Recognizing that Gorbachev wanted to get him to abandon SDI, he soon signed a top-secret directive declaring that he would never change his position on SDI. In short, there would be no deals on SDI with the Soviets.[9]

★   ★   ★

SHORTLY AFTER REAGAN RETURNED TO WASHINGTON, AN OB-scure Lebanese newspaper, *Al-Shiraa,* published a story exposing what it called an arms-for-hostages deal between the United States and Iran. When the story was repeated in the Western media, a firestorm erupted. Further disclosures would quickly follow, threatening the future of the Reagan presidency.

During his first term in office, Reagan had become increasingly concerned about the plight of American hostages being held in the Middle East. He had met with hostage families and was moved by their fear and anxiety over the fate of their loved ones. The President had particular empathy for William Buckley, the CIA station chief in Beirut. Reagan had been personally briefed by Buckley early on in his administration, and shortly after Buckley had been kidnapped, Reagan had watched a videotape of him put out by his captors. It was clear that Buckley had been tortured; Reagan was horrified.

There was talk in the White House of a rescue mission, but as administration officials explored the military options, they came to a dead end. They simply didn't know where the hostages were being held.

At about the same time Reagan struggled with the hostage problem, there was discussion in the White House about a strategic opening to Iran. There were said to be moderates in Tehran who would welcome warmer relations with the United States. On the advice of aides, Reagan came to believe that if there was an opening, perhaps Tehran could influence the captives and help secure their release.

After contact was made with the Iranians, it quickly became clear that the currency for any relationship would be arms. Tehran was engaged in a life-and-death struggle with Iraq, and desperately needed military equipment if Iran was to hold its own on the battle-field. Reagan's top advisers, including Secretary of State Shultz and Defense Secretary Weinberger, adamantly opposed arms sales to Tehran on the grounds that Iran was a sponsor of terrorism. Reagan wrestled with the question for several days.

For the war against communism, Reagan at several critical mo-ments rejected the counsel of his advisers to carry out daring and ul-timately successful courses of action. It was a testament to Reagan's courage. But this time ignoring the advice of top aides would lead him to disaster.

The fallout from the disclosure mounted. An investigation re-vealed weeks later that not only had the administration sold arms to Iran, but that someone in the administration had diverted profits from those sales and given the money to the contras fighting in Nicaragua. It was a stunning revelation; Reagan's approval ratings plummeted. Suddenly Washington was abuzz with talk of criminal indictments, a presidential resignation, perhaps even impeachment.

In Moscow, the KGB watched with particular glee as the scandal enveloped Reagan. Not only was it weakening Reagan's personal popularity, but it was threatening to undermine his "mili-tarist" policies.[10]

CHAPTER XXIII

FREEDOM TOUR

REAGAN DISLIKED TRAVELING, AND AT AGE SEVENTY-SEVEN, IT was taking a tremendous toll on his tired body. His health had been in decline—a colon operation, a prostate operation, and skin cancer. But when the opportunity arose in the early spring of 1988 to go to Moscow for a final summit meeting with Gorbachev, he embraced it eagerly. It was a chance to get out of Washington and away from the mounting investigation of the Iran-Contra affair. Reagan seemed to be tired and weak; during the Tower Commission hearings convened to investigate the matter, Reagan had failed to remember various events and then mistakenly had read a private memo from his staff out loud.[1]

There would be no new agreements signed in Moscow. In 1987, Reagan and Gorbachev had inked the Intermediate Nuclear Force (INF) Treaty, in which Moscow had given in to Reagan's demands for a zero option in Europe. And after the Iran-Contra matter broke, there had been speculation that Reagan would be eager to cut further deals with Gorbachev in an effort to boost his image. The Kremlin still had an attractive arms control offer on the table, and many were pushing Reagan to sign commercial agreements with the Kremlin.

But for Reagan the trip to Moscow seemed to be less about securing a diplomatic agreement than pushing just once more against the Soviet edifice. He knew that this would be perhaps his last chance to go out on the ramparts in the battle he had been fighting for more than forty years.

Less than a year earlier, he had taken the opportunity to go for a third time to West Berlin. After an economic summit in Venice, *Air Force One* had flown him to the tiny enclave in the heart of the Soviet bloc; he had found the whole experience exhilarating.

When he had first announced his intention to make the trip, West Berlin officials had suggested that he speak before a small crowd in front of the old Reichstag, a proud building that stood blocks away from the wall that had divided the city for more than two decades. But Reagan insisted on speaking at the Brandenberg Gate, the two-hundred-year-old arch in the center of Berlin, only a few yards from the brick and mortar of the Berlin Wall. German officials expressed concerns that a major speech in such a location might be provocative. But Reagan was firm; besides, he wanted to be provocative.[2]

There had been other hurdles. As White House speechwriter Peter Robinson began circulating the draft of the speech he had prepared, State Department and even some White House officials balked at the language. It might prove too incendiary to Soviet-bloc leaders; it might be—there was that word again—"provocative." But Reagan read the draft and then made a few edits of his own.

When Stasi chief Erich Mielke heard in East Berlin that Reagan was going to deliver a major speech at the foot of the wall, he went into a near panic. "We must count on provocative and slanderous abuse of the DDR," he wrote in a secret directive. He ordered a general alert to the secret police; "the highest amount of vigilance" was called for in light of what Reagan would probably say.[3]

Before the speech at the Brandenberg Gate, Reagan was taken on a tour of this outpost in the heart of East Germany. As he stood near the Reichstag, he noticed words crudely spray-painted on the wall. "This wall will fall," it read. "Beliefs become reality." Reagan took note of the simple yet powerful words and mentioned it to the news media people traveling with him. "Yes, across Europe, this wall will fall. For it cannot withstand faith. It cannot withstand truth. The wall cannot withstand freedom. . . ."

At the gate itself, Reagan stood before tens of thousands who were waving flags in anticipation of what he would say. Bracing himself against a brisk yet gentle wind, he spoke about freedom and the need for real change behind the Iron Curtain. "Mr. Gorbachev," he said, "tear down this wall." The crowd erupted; nothing so clear and absolute had ever been said at the wall before. For Reagan, it was not a new idea; he had first suggested it back in 1967. But now he was saying it in the heart of Europe, at the center of the Cold War divide. And the world was watching.[4]

★   ★   ★

N OW, IN THE LATE SPRING OF 1988, HE WAS GOING TO DELIVER the same clarion call in Moscow.

Air Force One descended slowly at Moscow's Vnukovo Airport. Reagan was arriving in the capital of a global empire that was troubled. The economy was continuing its descent. People of different nationalities around the country were restless. Mikhail Gorbachev was desperately trying to correct a ship that was listing badly. The economy was in such bad shape that the Soviet General Staff had concluded that unilateral cuts were necessary to stave off collapse.

Gorbachev badly needed a deal from Reagan to make his reform program—called *perestroika*—work.

"Gorbachev immediately understood that the *perestroika* he planned to implement in his own country was impossible in the Cold War situation," recalls Aleksandr Bessmertynkh. "Gorbachev placed the task of ending the Cold War and stopping the arms race at the very top of his priority list." The General Secretary hoped that Reagan, troubled by Iran-Contra, would now be willing to cut a deal in an effort to boost his reputation.[5]

But Reagan resisted the temptation; he had no interest in rescuing the Soviet economy. Back in 1963 he had advised against relieving "the strain on the shaky Russian economy." It would only give the Kremlin hope that "their system will through evolution catch up and pass ours." Reagan was going to stick to his agenda and use every opportunity to advance the frontiers of freedom. As for his own reputation, Reagan would follow a course that he had laid out back in Hollywood: He was going to do what he believed was right and leave the rest to history.

Fourteen years had passed since an American president had visited Moscow. Back then, it had been Richard Nixon, who had arrived to discuss détente, arms control, and the prospects for trade. Gorbachev was now hoping for a dialogue on the same topics. He even wanted a joint statement that "peaceful coexistence" would be the basis of superpower relations. But Reagan had a different idea. As he put it shortly after he arrived, this summit meeting was about the struggle "for peace and . . . liberty."[6]

From the airport Reagan was taken to an arrival ceremony in the Kremlin's majestic St. George's Hall. There he greeted Mikhail Gorbachev warmly and said, "Thank you and God bless you." As the words left his mouth and were translated into Russian, many of the Kremlin leaders who were present visibly blanched. As one Russian diplomat recalls, "The heretofore impregnable edifice of Communist atheism was being assaulted before their very eyes by a man who had made his name as a hard-line anti-communist."[7]

Reagan had a genuine admiration for Gorbachev, who he knew was trying to take communism where it had never been before. But he had no doubts that Gorbachev's goal was to save the system and not to destroy it. The two men chatted amiably for several minutes and then Reagan echoed politely the words he had uttered in Berlin: Why not dismantle the wall? Gorbachev looked awkwardly at the President and then changed the subject.

It was an all-too-familiar exchange by now. As Gorbachev's translator, Igor Korchilov, remembers these sessions, Reagan was smooth and calm and spoke "as if he were a parent trying to reason with a child who had said something terribly wrong." Gorbachev, on the other hand, would often get flustered and angry. "It appeared that Reagan's logic and reasoning were a hard act for him to follow," recalls Korchilov.[8]

That afternoon Ronald and Nancy Reagan strolled casually along the Arbat, an old street that had been converted into a pedestrian mall. Hundreds of merchants and artists were selling goods, and there was music in the air from several violinists who were playing for spare change. The Secret Service had been opposed to the outing on security grounds, but Reagan had overruled them (something he rarely did). As the Reagans walked and greeted people, a crowd gathered. Reagan was now smiling and exchanging greetings with several hundred Muscovites cheering "Reagan! Reagan!" But as the crowd continued to grow and to surge forward in the hope of shaking his hand, plainclothes KGB officers suddenly took control. In an instant, there was kicking and punching as the officers tried to clear the crowd. Reagan watched the melee in anger, just as he had watched an innocent East Berliner being harassed by the police during his 1978 visit to East Germany. The Secret Service hustled him off because of security concerns, but the experience served as a vivid reminder. "I've never seen such brutal manhandling as they did on their own people who were in no way getting out of hand," he wrote in his diary. "Some things haven't changed."

The following day, Reagan rose early for more meetings with Gorbachev. The Kremlin had hoped that Reagan might weaken, that the sort of indecision they had seen in his testimony before the Tower Commission on the Iran-Contra affair might now reappear so they could take advantage of it. But as the two leaders discussed human rights in animated conversations, Gorbachev became increasingly frustrated with his lack of progress with Reagan. After the morning session, Reagan took a drive to the outskirts of Moscow and his limousine pulled up in front of an old stone building. The old thirteenth-century Danilov Monastery had been used as a factory to make umbrellas and, later, refrigerators. Now, with some liberalizing under Gorbachev, it was being reopened as a monastery. Reagan had written a friend privately in 1981, declaring that religion was "the Achilles' heel" of the Soviet empire. Now he wanted to have a firsthand look. He quietly toured the place and met with several bearded clerics. Before he left, he offered a silent prayer.

That evening, the President's limousine pulled up to a prerevolutionary mansion called Spaso House. There was extraordinary security, and Ron and Nancy Reagan stepped out of the car dressed for a night of entertaining. Escorted by the American ambassador, they ambled into an 820-foot long ballroom where there were a dozen tables surrounded by guests, each assigned a seat marked with White House cards embossed with the presidential seal. As the Reagans entered the room, the crowd erupted with cheers and stood up from the tables, which were weighed down with fine china and delicate silverware, to offer an ovation.

This was no state dinner for dignitaries; there were precious few diplomats in the ballroom. Soviet officials were nowhere in sight. Instead, the roughly one hundred people crowded into the ballroom were considered little more than chattel by the Kremlin; but Reagan was about to give a grand party in their honor.

These were Jewish refusniks, Pentecostals imprisoned for their faith, human rights activists, and freedom advocates. Reagan had never met any of the people in the room, but they certainly knew him.

In 1979, Reagan had advised that "a little less détente with the Politburo and more encouragement to the dissenters might be worth a lot of armored divisions" in the Cold War. Now here he was to meet the armored division face-to-face.

Reagan's clear moral denunciation of communism over the course of his presidency was by now legendary. When he had given his "evil empire" speech in 1983, political prisoners had tapped on walls and talked through toilets to share what he had said with fellow inmates. It had energized and emboldened them, and given them hope. Now he wanted to bolster them face-to-face.[9]

He walked through the crowd, shaking hands and even embracing men and women whom he had applauded years before for their moral courage. As he spoke, he was cautiously optimistic about the reform process Gorbachev had begun. "We hope that one freedom will lead to another and another," he explained.

As he spoke before the group, there was a slight quiver in his voice. "I came here hoping to do what I could to give you strength. Yet I already know it is you who have strengthened me, you who have given me a message to carry back. Coming here, being with you, looking into your faces, I have to believe the history of this troubled century will indeed be redeemed in the eyes of God and man, and that freedom will truly come for all. For what injustice can withstand your strength? And what can conquer your prayers?"

Afterward, a dissident Russian Orthodox priest who had been

recently released from a labor camp sat teary-eyed. Reagan had secured his release and that of many others in the room. Boris Perchatkin, another dissident in the room, explained how the meeting emboldened him. "His words gave us the feeling that our fight is not something trivial but something important, which we should redouble our efforts to continue."[10]

The following day, after another session with Gorbachev, Reagan bounded up some steps and stood before hundreds of eager young students. Moscow State University was Gorbachev's alma mater and the most prestigious institution of higher learning in the Soviet bloc. These were the children of the Soviet elite, and they were eager to hear what Reagan might have to say.

With an enormous bust of Vladimir Lenin peering down from behind and a large banner with the hammer and sickle strung up behind him, Reagan began to calmly stake a claim for freedom and faith. It was a new speech, but in many respects it was a recycled version of the words he had uttered hundreds of times before to audiences in the 1950s. To his young audience, unaccustomed to hearing about freedom, it was pure thunder.

"Freedom is the right to question and change the established way of doing things. It is the continuing revolution of the marketplace. It is the understanding that allows us to recognize shortcomings and seek solutions. It is the right to put forth an idea, scoffed at by the experts, and watch it catch fire among the people."[11]

As the words came from his mouth, you could almost see the bust of Lenin wince.

Believing that his life had been spared in 1981 for this purpose, Reagan spoke about how freedom ultimately came from God and faith. "Even as we explore the most advanced reaches of science, we are returning to the age-old wisdom of our culture, a wisdom contained in the Book of Genesis in the Bible. In the beginning was the spirit, and it was from this spirit that the material abundance of creation issued forth. But progress is not foreordained. The key is freedom—freedom of thought, freedom of information, freedom of communication."

It was as if he was fulfilling a promise he had made to Providence. Change was coming to the communist system, he said, but change needed to spring forth from "the eternal things, from the source of all life, which is faith."

When he finished, Reagan was greeted with wild applause. He took a few questions from students, and as he left the podium, he was given a standing ovation.[12] "It was not the Reagan that we expected," a political science major from the audience told the *Washington Post*. "There was nothing old-fashioned or stale about him. He seemed to be so lively, active and thinking. This was a pleasant surprise."[13]

Gorbachev, of course, had expected the worst from Reagan, so although the audience heard his speech it was not broadcast in the Soviet Union; indeed, the newspapers and television stations barely mentioned it.

It was a whirlwind four days that Reagan spent in the Soviet Union. Little was accomplished in terms of diplomacy. There were no breakthroughs on arms control. But Reagan had come to the Soviet Union with a purpose—namely, to take the gospel of freedom into the heart of the Soviet empire. Now he could look back and say that he had accomplished his mission.

But as he stood next to Gorbachev in front of the world media, it was clear that his vigor was gone. He stumbled over a few questions and seemed disoriented; the Aging Lion was tired now. Gorbachev, standing only feet away, noticed, and the Young Tiger, out of deference, gently raised his hand and called the press conference to an end.

CHAPTER XXIV

GOODBYE

S IX MONTHS AFTER HE LEFT MOSCOW, RONALD REAGAN WAS aboard *Air Force One,* westbound for California. Gone was the nuclear football that had been nearby for eight years. He was now ex-President Reagan, and as the plane descended on southern California, the staff, press, and Secret Service on board gathered around for a last round of handshakes. "Mission accomplished, Mr. President," someone yelled. "Mission accomplished."

Days after Reagan left Washington, a group of men gathered around a table in Warsaw, Poland. General Kiszczak, the hard-line interior minister, was shaking hands with former political prisoners. It was the first meeting of fifty-seven delegates to discuss the future of Poland. Mikhail Gorbachev, strapped for cash and no longer able to support the empire, had announced that he was cutting free the countries of Eastern Europe. The communist leaders would now have to handle internal matters themselves; they could no longer count on the military support of the Soviet Army. The talks were awkward to say the least, but progress was made. In May, relatively free elections were held; Solidarity won ninety-two out of one hundred uncontested seats in the Senate and all but one of the seats in the lower house of the Polish parliament. Lech Walesa was eventually elected president, and the Solidarity movement later announced plans to rename Constitution Square, in the heart of Warsaw, Ronald Reagan Square. Said Marian Krzaklewski, chairman of Solidarity: "Reagan was the main author of the victory of the free world over the 'evil empire.'"

★   ★   ★

ON FEBRUARY 15, 1989, THE LAST SOVIET SOLDIER LEFT AFGHANI-stan. It was the first complete military defeat in Soviet history. According to Sergei Tarasenko, it made crystal clear that Moscow could not use force to hold its crumbling empire together. While free from Soviet domination, Afghanistan quickly descended into civil war. The country would later be largely neglected by the outside world, and an extreme Islamist group known as the Taliban would take power.

In May 1989, Mikhail Gorbachev let the Sandinista government in Nicaragua know that the Soviet Union could no longer afford to provide aid. The following year, the Sandinistas were voted out of power in free elections.

In early June, two hundred thousand people gathered for a ceremony in Budapest's Heroes Square. Five coffins were lying in front of the crowd, each bearing the name of a man who had been sentenced to death as a traitor after the 1956 revolution. The ceremony gave rise to more protests, and a few months later the Communist Party voted itself out of existence.

In Prague, seven thousand students from Charles University gathered at a cemetery to commemorate the death of a young man killed during an uprising against the Nazis. After the ceremony, they marched on Wenceslas Square. The police gathered and attacked with clubs, batons, and their fists, beating the students mercilessly. News of the violence spread quickly and opposition forces gathered. Weeks later, the communist government all but collapsed. Later, student leaders would explain that their heroes were Ronald Reagan and Margaret Thatcher.[1]

In mid-October, the East German city of Leipzig was illuminated by the light of thousands of candles as people gathered and sang

"Dona Nobis Pacem." The peaceful protest spread, and two days later, Erich Honecker resigned. Weeks later, the entire Politburo quit. On November 9, the Berlin Wall was breached and thousands of East Germans surged through the Wall's crossing points and were greeted by West Berliners carrying champagne. "The Wall is gone! The Wall is gone!"

The collapse of the Soviet empire came at a dizzying pace. Reagan had always said that fear was communism's most important weapon. Now around the world, in outposts and in the heart of the empire, ordinary people were acting fearlessly. Ronald Reagan watched from California, pleased with what was taking place while characteristically not taking any of the credit. By early 1990, invitations were being extended for him to return to Europe in what some in the media dubbed his "victory lap."

In early September 1990 Reagan arrived in Berlin, greeted by a city newspaper that had printed the words to a new love song written in honor of him, "The Man Who Made Those Pussyfooters and Weaklings Feel Ashamed." He made his final pilgrimage to the Wall and was given a hammer and chisel. He was seventy-nine now, but he took a few pieces out of the large gray edifice. Then he walked along the death strip where East German border guards had once operated with orders to shoot anyone trying to escape. He shook hands with ordinary Germans. "Thank you, Mr. President," one resident shouted. "Well," he said in response, "we can't be happy until the whole world knows freedom the way we do."

From Germany he traveled to Gdansk, Poland, the birthplace of the Solidarity movement. He was greeted by torrential rain and hail, but seven thousand people had shown up for a public ceremony in his honor, chanting, "Thank you, thank you!" while singing "Sto Lat," a song in honor of Polish heroes. As the crowd watched, Lech Walesa's former parish priest presented Reagan with a sword.

"I am giving you the saber for helping us to chop off the head of communism," he said.[2]

A POSTMORTEM

W HEN RONALD REAGAN WAS SIXTEEN YEARS OLD, HE wrote a story about two boys who thwart an act of terrorism. Two men are planning to put poison gas into the Treasury Building in Washington, D.C., to kill everyone inside. Then, donning gas masks, they expect to loot the building of all its money. But two young men overhear them plotting and get hold of a map that spells out the grisly scheme. Risking certain death if they are caught, they follow the terrorists to their hideout and then go to the police.

Written in the first person, the story clearly shows that young Ronald Reagan admired the raw courage of the boys, who risk not only life and limb but also ridicule from a skeptical police who may not believe them. But the two heroes persevere, and the terrorists are caught.

Those virtues that Reagan so admired—courage and character— are what the nearly half-century battle against communism required most of him. Beginning in Hollywood and throughout his presidency, Reagan was always willing to speak the truth about communism. Sometimes his strong views brought physical threats against his life and family. More often, they would prompt ridicule or denunciation of him as a dangerous ignoramus. In either case, Reagan un-flinchingly pressed on, opposed by old friends, cabinet officers, and sometimes even members of his own family.

A public life by definition depends in large part on public opinion. For politicians, failure to pay attention to public opinion means professional death. Over the course of U.S. history, Ameri-can presidents have certainly demonstrated a willingness to chal-lenge public opinion and proceed down a difficult path they view as necessary. One thinks of Lincoln on the eve of the American Civil War. But in the twentieth century, few American presidents have proven to be as immune to public criticism as Reagan was. Some, like Eisenhower, were cautious in the face of the critics and conservative by temperament. Others, like FDR, were reluctant to step ahead of public opinion. Even Richard Nixon, who claimed loudly to shun the opinions of the establishment, was still captive to it, concerned about how he was viewed or would be remem-bered.

But throughout the course of his public life, Reagan was strangely impervious to public opinion. While recognizing and ap-preciating the realities of electoral politics, Reagan was steadfast in his execution of the war against communism. In the face of poll numbers that showed widespread disapproval of his defense and for-eign policies, criticism from elder statesmen, ridicule from the media, and withering attacks from his political opponents, Reagan didn't seem bothered. He embodied the sense of rugged individual-ism that we so often associate with cowboys of the Old West; Rea-gan was truly his own man.

Of course, Reagan was a master politician. He understood the value of symbols and images in winning votes. But he was about more than his personal ambitions or vacant symbolism. He believed in ideas much larger than himself, and his ideas did not shift over the course of his public life, nor did he ever attempt to camouflage them. When they seemed unpopular, he clung to them stubbornly. When established opinion called them simpleminded, he smiled and pressed ahead. Reagan cared deeply about these ideas; he would not jettison them simply to collect more votes. As Tom Wicker of the *New York Times* said of Reagan in the 1960s, his "greatest asset is that he is not trying to fool anybody; he is simply saying what he thinks."[1]

When Reagan thought about the world, he did not do it in the abstract way of most academics. If ideas did have consequences, Reagan believed that embracing and advocating the right ideas was the best way to be a leader of consequence. He had not only his views about policies, but a worldview, and he had a strong sense of his place and America's in the currents of history. When he spoke about the Cold War, his words were charged with a sense of personal conviction unlike that of any other Cold War president. Some no doubt will challenge or disagree with his view of the world, but few if any would question his sincerity.

In retrospect, it is clear that Reagan was largely correct about communism and his critics were wrong. Soviet communism was the threat that he claimed it was, and was vulnerable in the way he said it would be. He was on the correct side of the great battles of his forty-year struggle against communism. Moscow and its supporters did try to gain a level of control in Hollywood; the peace movement in the 1970s and 1980s was being influenced by the Soviet Union; and Moscow and Havana did have plans to subvert Central America. Archives in the former Soviet bloc settle these debates.

He also predicted that the Soviet Union would "end up on the ash heap of history" half a dozen years before others saw it. How did a C student in economics from Eureka College envision all of this?

It is difficult to say with complete certainty. There were external influences over the course of the Cold War that directed and focused his thinking, as well as concepts and ideas that he developed on his own. But far from being a simple conduit for presidential aides and others who believed only they knew the proper course of action, Reagan embraced many of these ideas before he was president. He was himself once asked how he figured all of this out, and he gave an interesting answer. Rather than claiming superior intellect, he simply pointed out that everyone knew the Soviet Union was evil, expansionist, and in trouble; but no one wanted to say it. Courage, it seems, made all the difference, an important lesson in an age when supreme importance seems to be placed on the intelligence of our leaders rather than their courage.

If there were few leaders during the Cold War willing to consistently speak out openly about the evils of the communist system, there were fewer still who were willing to battle it directly. No American throughout the history of the Cold War up until Reagan had been willing to make rolling back and defeating communism a primary goal. Even anti-Communists like Richard Nixon subscribed to the seductive idea that stability was most important and that a healthy Soviet Union was important for long-term peace. But Reagan understood that communism by its nature was a danger to peace because it relied on fear and external enemies to maintain its legitimacy. Only by its defeat would the Cold War end, so he chose to force tensions to a decisive conclusion rather than hide them.

Many of Reagan's most critical initiatives were launched alone. He approved massive defense increases in 1981, even though a majority of his cabinet was opposed and former presidents Nixon and Ford were advising him to cut spending. He launched the Strategic Defense Initiative (SDI) almost entirely by himself, informing his secretary of state and most other advisers only hours before he announced his plans to the public. When he took a hard line over the declaration of martial law in Poland in an effort to keep Solidarity alive, he did so with scant support from any major ally save Great Britain's Margaret Thatcher. All the while, he was ridiculed for failing to grasp the intricacies of the global situation.

Even when the opportunity arose to secure his place in history by striking a diplomatic bargain with Gorbachev at Reykjavík, Reagan resisted the temptation, much to the consternation of many who were watching. He would not change course, even in pursuit of personal political glory.

This approach of going it alone gave Reagan his most spectacular successes, but it also spawned his greatest failure. In the Iran-Contra affair, he went against the advice of many of his most trusted advisers, believing that a daring covert initiative that contradicted his publicly stated policy would succeed in freeing the hostages and bringing Iran into the Western fold.

★ ★ ★

HOW DID REAGAN CONTRIBUTE TO THE DEMISE OF THE SOVIET empire? You can draw up a scorecard and count the economic costs that Reagan's policies placed on a struggling Soviet economy, using Moscow's numbers:

> The second strand of the European natural gas pipeline
>   Reagan stopped: lost revenue, $7–8 billion per year
> The cost of counterinsurgency operations against Reagan-
>   backed guerrillas: $8 billion a year
> Extra arms shipped to Cuba to soothe anxieties over Grenada:
> $3 billion
> Military spending increases announced to match Reagan:
> $15–20 billion per year
> Lost revenue due to restrictions on technology imports: $1–2
>   billion per year
> Lost revenue from a sudden drop in oil prices: $5–6 billion
>   per year
> Extra aid delivered to Poland after Reagan's sanctions: $1 billion

THIS AMOUNTS TO A HEFTY PRICE TAG FOR A SUPERPOWER THAT had total hard-currency earnings of approximately $32 billion at the time.

Or you can look at the body blows that the Soviet empire suffered. Military defeat in Afghanistan demoralized the Kremlin and the military as they suffered their first defeat of the Cold War. At the same time, the survival and eventual triumph of Solidarity in Poland burned a hole in the heart of the empire that could never be filled. In both of these cases, Reagan proved decisive in victory.

Since the end of the Cold War, a debate has raged about how it ended. One person who never got wrapped up in this debate was Ronald Reagan. One of the last items to be removed from his Oval Office desk in January 1989 was a small sign that read: "It's surprising what you can accomplish when no one is concerned about who gets the credit."

Today we live in a world very different from the one only a quarter century ago. There is no longer talk of a large-scale war in Europe, no fear of a massive nuclear strike. Understanding Reagan's struggle and final triumph over communism involves more than debating the past or deciding who gets the credit. It provides us with wisdom and hope for the struggles of today and tomorrow. Reagan's hope that we be guided not by fear but by courage and moral clarity is as apt today as it was during the height of the Cold War.

NOTES

INTRODUCTION

1. See Frances Fitzgerald, *Way Out There in the Blue* (New York: Simon and Schuster, 2000) and Edmund Morris, *Dutch: A Memoir of Ronald Reagan* (New York: Random House, 1999); Jane Mayer and Doyle McManus, *Landslide: The Unmaking of the President, 1984–1988* (Boston: Houghton Mifflin, 1988); Michael Paul Rogin, *Ronald Reagan, the Movie, and Other Episodes in Political Demonology* (Berkeley: University of California Press, 1987).

2. Henry Kissinger is quoted in Peggy Noonan, *When Character Was King: A Story of Ronald Reagan* (New York: Viking, 2001), p. 249; Robert Dallek, *Ronald Reagan: The Politics of Symbolism* (Cambridge: Harvard, 1999), p. 193; Stanley Hoffman, "The New Orthodoxy," *New York Review of Books*, April 16, 1981; *Los Angeles Times*, October 3, 1982, p. 5; *Time*, December 13, 1982, p. 12.

3. Fred Greenstein, "Ronald Reagan: Another Hidden-Hand Ike?" *PS: Political Science and Politics* 23 (1990), pp. 7, 13.

4. Frances Fitzgerald, op cit., pp. 22–23, 25, 38, 209.

5. Isaiah Berlin, *The Hedgehog and the Fox: An Essay on Tolstoy's View of History* (New York: Simon and Schuster, 1986), p. 1.

6. Quoted in Lawrence F. Kaplan, "We're All Cold Warriors Now," *Wall Street Journal*, January 18, 2000 and Dallek, op cit., p. xviii.

7. For more on the constant crisis in the Soviet economy see Gordon M. Hahn, "An Autopsy of the Soviet Economy: Soviet Documents Now in the Hoover Archives Reveal Seventy Years of Economic Bungling," *Hoover Digest*, no. 4, 1998, pp. 174–77.

8. Dallek, op cit., p. x.

CHAPTER 1: ONE-MAN BATTALION

1. See *Variety*, February 9, 1949; Anne Edwards, *Early Reagan: The Rise to Power* (Morrow, 1987), p. 307; and Stephen Vaughn, *Ronald Reagan in Hollywood: Movies and Politics* (Cambridge University Press, 1994), p. 37.

2. See Kenneth Lloyd Billingsley, *Hollywood Party: How Communism Seduced the American Film Industry in the 1930s and 1940s* (Prima, 1998) and David J. Saposs, *Communism in American Unions* (New York: McGraw-Hill, 1959), pp. 44, 47.

3. For Communist Party activities in Hollywood see FBI secret memo, Subject: Communist Infiltration-Motion Picture Industry, File Number 100-138754, Serial 1003, Parts 8–15 (FOIA). See also Billingsley, op cit., pp. 51–52; Ella Winter, *And Not to Yield* (New York: Harcourt, 1963), p. 227.

4. Philip Dunne, *Take Two: A Life in Movies and Politics* (Limelight Editions, 1992), p. 128.

5. Quoted in Neil Gabler, *An Empire of Their Own: How the Jews Invented Hollywood* (Crown, 1988), p. 334.

6. Stephen Vaughn, op cit., pp. 121–32.

7. See the VENONA intercepts relating to Toledano, Ref. # 3/nbf/7573, National Security Agency (FOIA).

8. *Jurisdictional Disputes in the Motion Picture Industry*, Committee on Education and Labor, House of Representatives, 1948, pp. 1681–82.

9. Kirk Douglas, *The Ragman's Son* (Simon and Schuster, 1988), p. 136.

10. Bill McGoogan, "How the Commies Were Licked in Hollywood," *St. Louis Globe-Democrat*, clipping in Schary Papers, State Historical Society of Wisconsin.

11. Ronald Reagan, *Where's the Rest of Me?* (New York: Dell, 1965).

12. Quoted in Christopher Anderson, *An Affair to Remember: The Remarkable Love Story of Katharine Hepburn and Spencer Tracy* (Morrow, 1997), p. 190.

13. Reagan's sworn testimony in Jeffers v. Screen Extras Guild, July 1, 1955, 3396, SCCA–SAD.

14. See Stephen Vaughn, op cit., and Edwards, op cit.

15. Ronald Reagan, *Where's the Rest of Me?*, p. 179.

16. Hedda Hopper, "Mr. Reagan Airs His Views," *Chicago Sunday Tribune*, May 18, 1947, p. 7, and Roy Brewer "The Full Story of Our Stand on the Coast," *IATSE Official Bulletin*, May 1947, p. 6.

17. See Sterling Hayden's Testimony, April 10, 1951, House Un-American Affairs Committee Hearings, 1951, part 1, pp. 142–43; also Hayden is quoted in the *Los Angeles Express and Herald Examiner*, December 9, 1953.

18. His statement is noted in FBI secret memo, op cit.

19. FBI secret memo, op cit.

20. Edwards, op cit.

21. Ronald Reagan-Jane Wyman divorce records, Los Angeles County Court House Archives, Case # D360058.

22. Ronald Reagan testimony, *House Un-American Activities Committee*, 1947, pp. 118–26.

23. Quentin Reynolds, "Movie Probers Let Down by Stars But Customers Love the Show," clipping in Ronald Reagan FBI File (100-138754-A), FOIA.

CHAPTER II: "YOU TOO CAN BE FREE AGAIN"

1. Lloyd Billingsley, op cit., pp. 204–207.

2. Ronald Reagan, "How Do You Fight Communism?" *Fortnight*, January 22, 1951, and McGoogan, "How the Commies Were Licked," op cit.

3. See transcript of Reagan's interview in 1980 in Robert Scheer, *With Enough Shovels* (Random House, 1982), p. 255.

4. Quoted in James Bassett, "Communism in Hollywood," *New York Mirror*, May 28, 1951, from Ronald Reagan FBI File, op cit.

5. Hearings Regarding the Communist Infiltration of the Motion Picture Industry, House Committee on Un-American Activities, House of Representatives, 1952, p. 2417.

6. Lloyd Billingsley, op cit.

7. Stephen Vaughn, *Ronald Reagan in Hollywood* (New York: Cambridge University Press, 1994), pp. 197–202.

8. Ronald Reagan, "Motion Pictures and Your Community," *Kiwanis Magazine*, #36 (August 1951), p. 25.

9. *New York Times*, October 29, 1947.

10. *Daily Worker*, July 30, 1952, p. 7.

11. Ronald Reagan letter to Sam Harwood, Jr., December 1952, quoted in Edmund Morris, *Dutch: A Memoir of Ronald Reagan* (New York: Random House, 1999), p. 292.

CHAPTER III: PILES OF CARDS IN RUBBER BANDS

1. Memorandum of Conversation, Department of State, Washington, October 3, 1955, Foreign Relations of the United States, vol. XIV, p. 545.

2. Dwight Eisenhower, "Chance for Peace," speech on April 16, 1953.

3. January 3, 1958, cabinet meeting notes, Eisenhower Papers, Whitman File: DDE Diary, Box 18, Dwight Eisenhower Presidential Library.

4. NSC 162/2, October 30, 1953, National Archives; John Lewis Gaddis, *Strategies of Containment* (Oxford University Press, 1982), p. 155.

5. Transcript of a Central Committee CPSU Plenum, June 28, 1957, *Instoricheskii arkhiv*, 3–6, 1993.

6. "Minutes of Discussion Between Delegation of the PRL [People's Republic of Poland] and the Government of the USSR," October 25–November 10, 1958, AAN, KC PZPR, p. 113, t. 27, translated by Douglas Selvage.

7. Antonin Ben, Jaromir Navratil, and Jan Paulik, eds., *Vojenske otazky eskoslavenske reformy, 1967–1970: Vojenska varianta Ie Oeni* (Brno: Dopln, 1996), translated by Vojtech Mastney.

8. Ronald Reagan letter to Mrs. And Mrs. Elwood Wagner, Wagner Collection at the Reagan Ranch, Young America's Foundation.

9. Edwards, op cit., p. 457.

10. Quoted in Deborah Hart Strober and Gerald S. Strober, *Reagan: The Oral History of An Era* (Houghton Mifflin, 1998), p. 3.

11. Ronald Reagan, Veteran's Day Address, North Albany Junior High School, Oregon, reprinted in Ronald Reagan, *The Creative Society: Some Comments on Problems Facing America* (Devin-Adair, 1968), p. 51.

12. From his speech, "Business, Ballots, and Bureaus," May 1959, reprinted in Davis W. Houck, ed. *Actor, Ideologue, Politician: The Public Speeches of Ronald Reagan* (Greenwood Press, 1993), p. 25.

13. Ronald Reagan to Richard Nixon, September 7, 1959, Vice Presidential Papers, Richard Nixon Presidential Library. Nixon quoted Richard Nixon, *The Memoirs of Richard Nixon* (New York: Grosset and Dunlap, 1978), p. 214.

14. "Warns of Red Menace: Film Star Ronald Reagan to Speak," *Bakersfield Californian*, September 16, 1961, pp. 19–20, and Ronald Reagan, "Encroaching Control," *Vital Speeches of the Day*, September 1961.

15. Ronald Reagan speech before the Merchants and Manufacturers Association in Los Angeles, reprinted in Reagan, *The Creative Society*, p. 15.

16. Excerpts from Reagan's speech, "Are Liberals Really Liberal?" Ronald Reagan Subject Collection, Box 1, Speeches and Writings Pre-1966, Hoover Institution Archives, Stanford University.

17. Kennedy Profile in TsKhSD, F. 5, Op. 30, D. 335, Ll. 92–108.

18. TsKhSD, F. 5, Op. 30, D. 335, Ll. 92–108.

19. SED Archives, IfGA, ZPA, Internal Party Archive, J IV 2/202/130.

20. Quoted in Michael R. Beschloss, *The Crisis Years: Kennedy and Khruschev 1960–1963* (HarperCollins, 1991), p. 225.

21. Philip Benjamin, "Robert Frost Returns with Word of Khrushchev," *New York Times*, September 10, 1962.

22. Dobrynin's secret cable appears in Richard Ned Lebow and Janice Gross Stein, *We All Lost the Cold War* (Princeton University Press, 1994), pp. 523–26.

23. Sorensen's admission of this appears in Bruce J. Allyn, James G. Blight, and David A. Welch, eds., *Back to the Brink: Proceedings of the Moscow Conference on the Cuban Missile Crisis, January 27–28, 1989* (University Press of America, 1992), pp. 92–93.

24. Edwards, op cit.

25. Kurrt Schuparra, *Triumph of the Right: The Rise of the California Conservative Movement, 1945–1966* (M.E. Sharpe, 1998), p. 113.

CHAPTER IV: A BULLET WITH HIS NAME ON IT

1. LBJ Address to the American Alumni Council, July 12, 1966, in *Public Papers of the Presidents of the United States, Lyndon B. Johnson, 1966*, Vol. 11 (U.S. Government Printing Office, 1967), p. 720.

2. Bundy to Johnson, May 22, 1964, Johnson Papers, NSF–NSC Staff File, Box 1, "Memos for the President, Vol. 1," Lyndon Baines Johnson Presidential Library.

3. Top Secret memorandum of the Southeast Asia Department, USSR Foreign Ministry, "Soviet Moral and Political Support of and Material Aid to the South Vietnam Patriots," March 24, 1966, SCCD, fond. 5, opis 50, delo. 777, listy 58–59.

4. Summary, Power briefing, April 28, 1964, Johnson Papers, NSF Agency File, Box 11–12, Defense Dept. Vol.1, LBJ Presidential Library.

5. See, for example, his speech "What Price Peace?" in Ronald Reagan, *The Creative Society* (New York: Devin-Adair, 1968), pp. 49–59.

6. "Johnson Telegram Provoked GOP Governors to Refuse Endorsement of War Policies," *New York Times*, October 19, 1967.

7. Ronald Reagan, *The Creative Society: Some Comments on Problems Facing America* (Devin-Adair, 1968), pp. 52–55. The book is a collection of Reagan's speeches, which the introduction notes are "almost entirely self-written." See also "Summary of Views on Vietnam War by Leading Presidential Candidates," *New York Times*, August 2, 1968.

8. "Summary of Views on Vietnam War by Leading Presidential Candidates," *New York Times*, August 2, 1968.

9. "Reagan in New Role: Yale Lecturer on History," *New York Times*, December 5, 1967, and "Reagan Keeps Smiling at Yale Despite Sneers and Hostile Air," *New York Times*, December 7, 1967.

10. "Town Meeting of the World: The Image of America and the Youth of the World, May 15, 1967," National Archives, RFK Collection, File Unit TRAN-RFKTELAPP, Item 7G.

11. "Reagan Guard Routs Two Firebombers," *New York Times*, July 11, 1968, and "Reagan Shrugs Off Plot Report, But His Protection Is Increased," *New York Times*, July 22, 1968.

12. The account comes from Winthrop Griffith, "People's Park—270' x 450' of Confrontation," *New York Times Magazine*, June 29, 1969.

13. William P. Clark, interview with the author.

14. Kirkpatrick Sale, *SDS* (New York: Random House, 1973), p. 627.

15. All information on Weathermen intelligence contacts is from FBI Report classified "Top Secret" *Foreign Influence—Weather Underground Organization*, Volume II, August 25, 1976 (FOIA).

16. Daryl Lembke, "Cuban Spy Link to Ford, Reagan Death Plot Probed," *Los Angeles Times*, March 19, 1976, and Ronald Koziol, "Informant Says Cuban Spy Aided Terrorists in Murder Plot," *The Miami Herald*, March 19, 1976.

CHAPTER V: THE DEAL

1. Memorandum of Conversation of the Ambassador of the USSR to the USA, A.F. Dobrynin with Kissinger, Aide to President Nixon, July 12, 1969, SCCD, f. 5, op. 61, D 558, LI. 92–105. See also Jim Hershberg, "New Evidence on the Cold War in the Third World and the Collapse of Détente in the 1970s," *Cold War History Bulletin*, no. 8–9.

2. Dobrynin memorandum, op cit.

3. The Committee for State Security (KGB), April 19, 1971, no. 983–A, TsKhSD, f.5, op. 63, D. 193, Ll. 33–38.

4. This document is quoted in Jim Hershberg, "New Evidence on the Cold War in the Third World and the Collapse of Détente in the 1970s," *Cold War International History Project Bulletin*, no. 8–9.

5. "The U.S. in the International Environment: An Overview," attached to Osgood memorandum to NSC staff, July 7, 1969 pp. 1, 6–8, Richard Nixon Papers, Box 1, EX FO, WHCF, National Archives and Records Administration (NARA).

6. See Joan Hoff, *Nixon Reconsidered* (New York: Basic Books, 1993), pp. 158–60.

7. *Time* magazine, January 3, 1972 p. 15. Emphasis added.

8. Nixon to Kissinger, June 16, 1969, Box 1, PPF, WHSF, NPM, NARA.

9. Henry Kissinger, Press Conference of July 3, 1974, reprinted in *Survival*, xvi: 5 (September/October 1974) and Senate Foreign Relations Committee, Strategic Arms Limitation Talks (Washington, D.C., U.S. Government Printing Office, 1972), pp. 394–5.

10. "Defense Budget-Cutting," *The New York Times*, June 6, 1972.

11. General Danilevich, interview in *Soviet Intentions, 1965–1985, Soviet Post–Cold War Testimonial Evidence* (BDM Corporation, McLean, Virginia, September 22, 1995). Report was prepared for the Department of Defense Office of Net Assessment.

12. General Danilevich, op cit.

13. Aleksandr Savel'yev and Nikolay Detinov, *The Big Five: Arms Control Decision-making in the Soviet Union* (Westport, Ct.: Praeger, 1995), p. 2.

14. Andrei Kolesnikov, "In the Second Circle," *Moscow News*, no. 32, 1992; *Komsomolskaya Pravda*, June 20, 1991.

15. "The Plague War," transcript, *Frontline,* PBS, October 13, 1998, pp. 10–13.

16. See David F. Winkler, *Cold War at Sea: High-Seas Confrontation Between the United States and the Soviet* (Naval Institute Press, 2000), and *Understanding Soviet Naval Developments* (U.S. Department of the Navy, 1978), 3rd Edition, pp. 21–22.

17. Malcolm Muir, Jr., *Black Shoes and Blue Water: Surface Warfare in the United States Navy, 1945–1975* (Washington, D.C.: Naval Historical Center, 1996), p. 202.

18. Undated study conducted in early 1972, U.S.-U.S.S.R. Incidents at Sea, Operational Archives, Naval Historical Center; Memorandum of conversation between Bubnov, Okun and Shinn, August 27, 1970, U.S. Department of State (FOIA).

19. See David F. Winkler, *Cold War at Sea*, op cit., pp. 126–27.

20. Savel'yev and Detinov, op cit., p. 4, and see interview with Vitalli Leonidovich Kataev, Chairman of the Central Committee Defense Industry Department in *Soviet Intentions*, op cit., pp. 97–98.

21. Savel'yev and Detinov, op cit., pp. 25, 28.

22. Dobrynin, *In Confidence*, p. 475.

CHAPTER VI: FIRE AND HEAT MAKE STEEL

1. "Students on Coast Set a Bank Afire; Guard Call Likely," *New York Times*, February 26, 1970, and "Youths Battle Police on Coast," *New York Times*, February 27, 1970. Inauguration information from *Sacramento Union*, January 5, 1971, and *Los Angeles Times*, January 5, 1971.

2. Barry Goldwater, *Goldwater* (New York: Doubleday, 1988), p. 256.

3. "Hatfield Says There May Be No Nixon Slate in 1972," *New York Times*, June 28, 1970, and Tom Wicker, "In the Nation: The Specter of Ronald Reagan," *New York Times*, June 30, 1970.

4. *Sincerely, Ronald Reagan* (Ottawa, IL: Green Hill, 1976), p. 75.

5. Chiang Asks People Not to Lose Heart," *New York Times*, October 10, 1971.

6. "Reagan Meets Thieu in Saigon And Defends One-Man Race," *New York Times*, October 16, 1971.

7. "Reagan Calls on Park," *New York Times*, October 16, 1971, and "Notes on People," *New York Times*, October 19, 1971.

8. Conversation is from the Richard Nixon Tapes, National Archives and Records Administration, October 22, 1971.

9. *Sincerely, Ronald Reagan*, pp. 21–22.

10. *Sincerely, Ronald Reagan*, pp. 123–24.

11. *Sincerely, Ronald Reagan*, p. 123.

CHAPTER VII: MOVING FORWARD

1. "Text of the 'Basic Principles of Relations Between the United States of America and the Union of Soviet Socialist Republics,' May 29, 1972," *Weekly Compilation of Presidential Documents*, vol. 8 (June 5, 1972), pp. 943–44.

2. U.S. State Department Memorandum of Conversation, Leonid Brezhnev, et al., Henry Kissinger, et al., April 22, 1972, p. 12 (FOIA).

3. Savel'yev and Detinov, op cit., p. 25.

4. A.S. Kalashnikov, interview in *Soviet Intentions, 1965–1985: Soviet Post–Cold War Testimonial Evidence*, op cit.

5. Oleg Grinevsky's comments at *Understanding the End of the Cold War, 1980–1987: An Oral History Conference*, Brown University, May 7–10, 1998, translated and transcribed by Jeffrey W. Dillon, edited by Nina Tannenwald, Provisional Transcript, May 1999, p. 82.

6. General Yuri Yashin, "Information Confidentiality a Government Concern," *Military News Bulletin*, no. 9, September 1994.

7. William J. Broad, "Russian Says Soviet Atom Arsenal Was Larger Than West Estimated," *New York Times*, September 26, 1993.

8. National Security Decision Memorandum 247, March 14, 1974 (FOIA).

9. Special National Intelligence Estimate, *The Soviet Gas Pipeline in Perspective*, Director of Central Intelligence, SNIE 3–11/2–82, 21 September 1982, pp. 6–7, 9 (FOIA).

10. *The Soviet Bloc Financial Problem as a Source of Western Influence* (National

Intelligence Council Memorandum, Central Intelligence Agency), NIC M 82–10004, April 1982, p. 1 (FOIA).

11. See the reporting on the 61ˢᵗ Meeting of the National Defense Council of the GDR, June 23, 1980, MZP, VA–01/3955.

12. See MZP, Va-Strausberg/29371, pt. 1, MZP, VA–01/39528, MZP, VA–01/39524.

13. David Winkler, *Cold War at Sea*, op cit.

14. Elmo R. Zumwalt, *On Watch: A Memoir* (New York: Quadrangle/New York Times Books, 1976), pp. 446–47.

15. Aleksandr Yakovlev, "The Unknown War: Soldiers in Distant Jungles," *Komsomolskaya Pravda*, February 2, 1990, and Aleksandr Oliynik, "Bratstvo Rezohdennoe v Boyakh," *Krasnaya Zvezda*, December 25, 1997.

16. KGB to MO, May 6, 1970, TsKhSD, f. 5, op. 62, d. 535, il. 32–35, 36.

17. TsKhSD, f. 5, op. 62, d. 535, il. 71–90, 80.

18. V. N. Bezukladnikov, to MO and attached letter from Neto to CPSU Central Committee, July 14, 1970, TsKhSD, f. 5, op. 62, d. 536, il. 195–220.

19. Vladislav Yanelis, "The World Around Us: the Angolan Knot, the Balance in Our Budget's African Item," *Literatura Gazeta*, June 6, 1990, and Al'bert Pavlov, "Russkie osy v Afrike," *Soldat Odachi*, September 1995.

20. Transcript of Honecker-Castro meeting, April 3, 1977, Stiftung "Archiv der Parteien und Massenorganisationen der ehemaligen DDR im Bundesarchiv (Berlin)," DY30 JIV 2/201/1292.

21. See Karen N. Brutents, former first deputy head of the CPSU Central Committee's International Department comments in Odd Arne Westad, ed., *Workshop on US-Soviet Relations and Soviet Foreign Policy Toward the Middle East and Africa in the 1970s*, Oral history transcript, Lysebu, October 1–4, 1994 (Oslo: Norwegian Nobel Institute, 1994), pp. 76–77.

CHAPTER VIII: ATHENS OR SPARTA?

1. Harold Agnew, interview with the author.

2. Reagan's visit is discussed in Edward Teller, *Memoirs: A Twentieth-Century Journey in Science and Politics* (Cambridge, MA: Perseus, 2001), p. 509.

3. Edwin Meese, interview with the author.

4. See "Reagan Wants GOP Governors to Endorse Missile Defense," *New York Times*, May 2, 1969, and "GOP Governors Ask Nixon to Consult," *New York Times*, May 3, 1969.

5. For more on Maxwell Hunter see his obituary, "Maxwell Hunter: Brilliant Scientist at the Heart of US Space and Missile Plans," *The Guardian,* November 26, 2001. Details of the Hunter-Reagan relationship are from Chris Lay, interview with the author.

6. Laurence W. Beilenson, *Power Through Subversion* (Washington, D.C.: Public Affairs Press, 1972), p. 241.

7. See Reagan's radio address on treaties, October 18, 1977, reprinted in Kiron Skinner, Annelise Anderson, and Martin Anderson, eds. *Reagan, in His Own Hand* (New York: Free Press, 2001), p. 52.

8. See letter to Dr. McDowell, reprinted in *Reagan, in His Own Hand*, op cit., p. 455.

9. "2 GOP Leaders Score Ford Policy," *New York Times*, June 2, 1975.

10. Comments at the Conservative Political Action Conference, January 25, 1974, Hoover Institution Archives, Stanford University.

11. See Reagan's radio address on History, August 7, 1978, reprinted in Kiron Skinner, Annelise Anderson, and Martin Anderson, eds., *Stories in His Own Hand* (New York: Free Press, 2001), p. 53.

12. "Town Meeting of the World: The Image of America and the Youth of the World, May 15, 1967," National Archives, RFK Collection, File Unit TRAN-RFKTELAPP, Item 7G.

13. See letter to Dr. McDowell, reprinted in *Reagan, in His Own Hand*, op cit., p. 455.

14. See Reagan's nationwide campaign speech, March 31, 1976, Hoover Institution Archives, Stanford University.

15. Christopher Andrew and Vasili Mitrokhin, *The Sword and the Shield: The Mitrokhin Archive and the Secret History of the KGB* (New York: Basic Books, 1999), p. 242.

16. Michael Reagan interview, Deborah Hart Strober and Gerald S. Strober, eds., *Reagan, The Man and His Presidency: The Oral History of An Era* (Boston: Houghton Mifflin, 1998), p. 9.

17. Ibid., pp. 9–10.

CHAPTER IX: NOT ENOUGH STATURE

1. David Binder, "A Modified Bloc Is Around as U.S. Policy," *New York Times*, April 6, 1976, pp. 1, 14.

2. Georgii Markovich Kornienko, *Khocodnaia voina: svidetel'stvo ee uchastnika* (Moscow: International Relations, 1995).

3. Christopher Andrew and Vasili Mitrokhin, *The Sword and the Shield*, op cit., pp. 211–13.

4. TsKhSD, f. 5, op. 77, d. 642, 1. 18–21.

5. Stiftung Archiv der Parteien und Massorganisationen der ehemaligen DDR im Bundesarchiv (Berlin), DY 30 J IV 2/201/1365.

6. Donald S. Spencer, *The Carter Implosion: Jimmy Carter and the Amateur Style of Diplomacy* (New York: Praeger, 1988), pp. 30–31, 86–89.

7. Record of Conversation between Soviet Foreign Minister Gromyko and President Carter, September 23, 1977, Archive of Foreign Policy, Russian Federation (AVP RF), Moscow.

8. Memorandum of Conversation, The White House, December 30, 1977, (FOIA).

9. *U.S. Human Rights Policy: A 20-Year Assessment*, United States Institute of Peace Special Report, June 1999, p. 7.

10. NIE 11–4–77, "Soviet Strategic Objectives," Central Intelligence Agency, pp. vii, ix.

11. 1978 U.S. Position Paper; COMSIXTHFLT, 220711Z, January 1977, to CINCUSNAVEUR London U.K., Subject: U.S.–U.S.S.R. Incidents at Sea (INCSEA) Agreement, Folder 1977, INCSEA Planning and Review, Operational Archives, NHC.

12. "Soviet Allocation of Defense Resources to Selected Geographic Areas and Roles," November 2, 1978 (CIA). Declassified and available at the Jimmy Carter Presidential Library.

13. Richard L. Kugler, *Commitment to Purpose: How Alliance Partnership Won the Cold War* (Santa Monica, California: RAND Corporation, 1993), p. 325.

14. John Lehman, *Command of the Seas* (New York: Scribner's, 1988), p. 163, and David Winkler, *Cold War at Sea*, op cit.

15. Memorandum of Conversation between East German Paul Markovski and

CPSU CC International Department head Boris Ponomarev in Moscow, February 10, 1978, SAPMO–Barch, DY 30 IV 2/2.035/127.

16. Memorandum of Conversation between Soviet Ambassador in Ethiopia A.P. Ratanov and Cuban Ambassador in Ethiopia Jose Peres Novoa, February 10, 1977, TsKhSD, f.5, op. 73, d. 1637, l. 85.

17. Notes of Conference with Advisor for Political Issues of USA Embassy in Ethiopia Herbert Malin, 2 February 1977, TsKhSD, f. 5, op. 73, d. 1638, il. 28–33.

18. Memorandum of Conversation between East German Paul Markovski and CPSU CC International Department head Boris Ponomarev in Moscow, February 10, 1978, SAPMO–Barch, DY30 IV 2/2.035/127.

19. Soviet Foreign Ministry and CPSU Central Committee International Department, Background Report on the Somali–Ethiopian Conflict, April 3, 1978, TsKhSD, f. 5, op. 75, d. 1175, il. 12–23.

20. Quotes are from Thomas L. Hughes, "Carter and the Management of Contradictions," *Foreign Policy*, Summer 1978, pp. 34–55; Simon Serafy, "Brzezinski: Play It Again, Zbig," *Foreign Policy*, Autumn 1978, pp. 3–21; and Elizabeth Drew, "Brzezinski," *New Yorker*, May 1, 1978.

21. Information on the early connection between the KGB and the Sandinistas comes from the KGB files brought to the West by former KGB employee Vasili Mitrokhin, specifically volume 6, chapter 5, part 5 of his massive collection. See Christopher Andrew and Vasili Mitrokhin, *The Sword and the Shield*, op cit., p. 363.

22. "Request by the International Department of the CC CPSU," December 27, 1976 and "Secretariat of the CPSU request by the International Department of the CC CPSU," August 18, 1976. These documents were obtained by Vladimir Bukovsky.

23. All of these quotations are taken from Informational Letter on Contemporary Cuban-American Relations, 26 April 1979, Embassy of the USSR to the Republic of Cuba, TsKhSD, f. 5, op. 76, d.828, ll. 1–13.

24. Soviet Ambassador to Cuba V. I. Vortnikov, Memorandum of Conversation with Fidel Castro, 25 June, 1979, TsKhSD, f.5, op. 76, d. 833, ll. 40–42.

25. Richard Allen, "Ronald Reagan: An Extraordinary Man in Extraordinary Times," Peter Schweizer, ed., *The Fall of the Berlin Wall: Reassessing the Causes and Consequences of the End of the Cold War* (Hoover Institution Press, Stanford

University, 2000), p. 51. Additional details came from an interview with the author.

26. See Reagan's radio broadcasts on SALT II in *Reagan in His Own Hand*, op cit., pp. 82–86.

27. Radio broadcasts "Chile," July 27, 1979, for critique of Carter's human rights policy, and on the Soviet Union, "Bukovsky," June 29, 1979, "Soviet Workers," May 25, 1977, *Reagan in His Own Hand*, op cit.

28. Richard Allen, op cit.

29. A copy of the dossier was obtained by John Koehler and made available to the author. It is now part of the John O. Koehler Collection, Hoover Institution Archives, Stanford University.

CHAPTER X: EXPLOSIONS

1. *New York Times*, June 28, 1979, and *Washington Post*, June 28, 1979.

2. Christopher's comments were made in December 1979 and reprinted in *Department of State Bulletin*, March 1980, p. 69.

3. "On the signing of a plan of ties between the CPSU and the Sandinista Front of National Liberation of Nicaragua," signed by K. Brutents and P. Smolsky, March 14, 1980. Document obtained by Vladimir Bukovsky.

4. These Stasi reports are part of the John O. Koehler Collection at the Hoover Institution Archives and have been examined by the author.

5. Quoted in Herbert Romerstein, "Some Insights Derived from the Grenada Documents," in Dennis L. Bark, ed., *The Red Orchestra,* vol. II: *The Case of Africa* (Stanford, California: Hoover Institution Press, 1988).

6. "Eastern Caribbean: Rising Cuban Influence," 20 July 1979, Central Intelligence Agency (FOIA).

7. Transcript of Conversation between Cuban Premier Fidel Castro and East German leader Erich Honecker, May 25, 1980, Stiftung Archiv der Parteien und Massorganisationen der ehemaligen DDR im Bundesarchiv (Berlin), DY 30, J IV 2/201/1365.

8. TsKhSD, f. 5, op. 77, d. 642, ll. 18–21; translation by Svetlana Savranskaya.

9. All quotations taken from Transcript of Conversation between Cuban Premier Fidel Castro and East German leader Erich Honecker, Havana, 25 May,

1980, Stiftung Archiv der Parteien und Massorganisationen der ehemaligen DDR im Bundesarchiv (Berlin), DY 30, J IV 2/201/1365.

10. "Reagan Announces, Urges Strength at Home, Abroad," *Washington Post*, November 14, 1979.

11. Reagan speech before the Chicago Council on Foreign Relations, March 17, 1980. Transcript in Citizens for Reagan, Box 7, Hoover Institution Archives, Stanford University.

12. Christopher Andrew and Oleg Gordievksy, *KGB: The Inside Story* (New York: HarperCollins, 1990), p. 575.

13. White House transcript, memorandum of conversation, December 11, 1979 (FOIA).

14. Department of State cable #13083, May 24, 1979 (FOIA).

15. Memo for the President from Zbigniew Brzezinski, December 29, 1979 (FOIA).

16. Memo to the President from Zbigniew Brzezinski, December 26, 1979 (FOIA).

17. Department of State Report, *Afghanistan and Pakistan*, January 1, 1980 (FOIA).

18. Francis Fukuyama, *The Future of the Soviet Role in Afghanistan: A Trip Report, September 1980*, A Rand Note, N–1579–RC (Rand Corporation, Santa Monica), pp. 12–14.

19. See Soviet Defense Minister Dimitri Ustinov's secret report to the Central Committee on "Foreign Interference" in Afghanistan, October 2, 1980, APRF, f. 3, op. 82, d. 177, il. 84–86.

20. Central Committee Politburo Transcript, February 7, 1980, APRF, f. 3, op. 120, d. 44, il. 73, 77–80.

21. See James O. Goldsborough, "Europe Cashes in on Carter's Cold War," *New York Times Magazine*, April 27, 1980, and James Reston, "The Allies' Doubting Assent," *New York Times*, January 18, 1980.

22. Central Committee CPSU Politburo transcript, January 17, 1980, APRF, f. 3, op. 120, d. 44, il. 31, 42–44.

23. Ronald Reagan to Lorraine Wagner, February 15, 1979; Lorraine Wagner Collection, Alice and George Atkinson Conference Room, Young America's Foundation, Santa Barbara, California.

CHAPTER XI: WORD AND DEED

1. Edward Walsh, "Carter to Return to 'Peace or War' Issue," *Washington Post*, September 28, 1980.

2. Tom Shales, "The Harassment of Ronald Reagan," *Washington Post*, October 31, 1980.

3. Robert Scheer, transcript of interview in *With Enough Shovels*, op cit., p. 237.

4. Full exchange is reprinted in Robert Scheer, *With Enough Shovels*, op cit., p. 140.

5. Scheer, op cit., p. 259.

6. Lou Cannon, *President Reagan: Role of a Lifetime* (New York: Simon and Schuster, 1991), p. 297.

7. Quoted in Lou Cannon, *President Reagan: Role of a Lifetime*, op cit., p. 93.

8. Memo from Advisory Group, Main Administration for Reconnaissance (Foreign Espionage), HVA translation from Russian, report 1156/90, SU 717/80, July 18, 1980. This is a German copy of the report.

9. See "Boris Yuzhin," *U.S. News & World Report*, October 18, 1999.

10. For more on Hammer and his Soviet connections, see Edward J. Epstein, *Dossier: The Secret History of Armand Hammer* (New York: Random House, 1996).

11. Dobrynin, *In Confidence*, pp. 459–60.

12. Ronald Reagan, *An American Life*, pp. 221–22.

13. Memo from Deputy Chief Grossman, Main Administration for Reconnaissance (Foreign Espionage), HVA translation from Russian, SU 1018/80, November 18, 1980.

14. A. S. Kalashnikov, op cit.

15. Comments in Understanding the End of the Cold War, 1980–1987: An Oral History Conference, Brown University, May 7–10, 1998; translated and transcribed by Jeffrey W. Dillion; edited by Nina Tannewald, Provisional Transcript, May 1999, p. 83.

16. This account is taken from Richard Kerr and Peter Dixon Davis, "Mornings in Pacific Palisades: Ronald Reagan and the President's Daily Brief," *Studies in Intelligence*, vol. 42, no. 2 (Center for the Study of Intelligence, Central Intelligence Agency).

CHAPTER XII: THE HAND OF GOD

1. See Robert D. McFadden, Joseph Tredster, and Maurice Carroll, *No Hiding Place: The New York Times Inside Report on the Hostage Crisis* (New York: Times Books, 1981), p. 213.

2. William P. Clark, interview with the author; Tom Reed, interview with the author.

3. Quote is from Reagan's speech for Barry Goldwater given in 1964.

4. Interview with the President, March 3, 1981, *Presidential Documents*, vol. 17, (March 19, 1981), pp. 231–32.

5. General Jack Chain, interview with the author.

6. LCDR J. S. Nielson, Position Paper, Subject: USS Lockwood Alleged INCSEA Violations, 19 May 1982; Chief of Naval Operations message to USDAO Moscow, 081717Z, May 1982, Subject: Soviet Navy Response to Message on INCESEA Agreement, Folder 10 Review Planning and Review; Op–616 memorandum to OP–06, Subject: Incidents at Sea Review in Moscow, 26 July 1984, Folder, 12th Annual Review, Operational Archives, NHC.

7. Dobrynin, op cit., p. 523.

8. Edmund Morris, op cit., pp. 431–32.

9. Parr recounts this story in Peggy Noonan, *When Character Was King: A Story of Ronald Reagan* (Viking, 2001), p. 195.

10. Ronald Reagan, comments to the Conservative Political Action Conference, January 25, 1974.

11. The meeting with Cardinal Cooke is recounted in "A Year Later, Subtle Imprint Left by Attack on President," *Washington Post*, March 30, 1982, and Tom Freiling, *Reagan's God and Country* (Vine Books, 2000), p. 9; Wirthlin comment is from Freiling, op cit., p. 9; Bill Clark comments are from interview with the author.

12. "President Pays Visit to the Bedside of Cardinal Cooke," *Washington Post*, September 26, 1983.

13. Extensive excerpts from this interview appear in the appendix of Robert Scheer, *With Enough Shovels*, op cit., pp. 254–55.

14. Ronald Reagan, speech before the Conservative Political Action Committee, March 20, 1981.

15. Ronald Reagan, speech before the Conservative Political Action Conference, January 25, 1974.

16. *New York Times*, May 28, 1981, IV, 20.

CHAPTER XIII: THEY CAN'T KEEP UP

1. Dobrynin, op cit., p. 483.

2. Story and quotes taken from Caspar Weinberger, interview with the author; Edwin Meese, interview with the author; Ambassador Edward Rowny, comments in *Understanding the End of the Cold War, 1980–1987: An Oral History Conference*, Brown University, May 7–10, 1998, p. 31. See also the comments of Robert McFarlane, op cit., p. 32.

3. Ronald Brownstein and Nina Easton, *Reagan's Ruling Class: Portraits of the President's Top 100 Officials* (Washington, D.C.: Presidential Accountability Group, 1982), pp. 433–38, and *Time*, April 27, 1981 p. 28.

4. Dobrynin, op cit., p. 479.

5. George C. Wilson, "Weinberger, in His First Message, Says Mission Is to 'Rearm America,'" *Washington Post*, January 23, 1981, p. A3; Richard Halloran, "Plan for Military Spending Is Major Shift for Peacetime," *New York Times*, February 19, 1981, p. B5.

6. "Interview with the President," October 16, 1981, *Presidential Documents*, vol. 17 (October 26, 1981), pp. 1160–61. Emphasis added.

7. Dobrynin, op cit., p. 486.

8. Defense Guidance, FY 1984–1988 (Top Secret), p. 7.

9. Defense Guidance, op cit., pp. 3–4, 6, 8, 10.

10. Defense Guidance, p. 25.

11. Information from William P. Clark, Assistant to the President for National Security Affairs, speech on "National Security Strategy" before the Center for Strategic and International Studies, Georgetown University, May 21, 1982. Text provided to the author by Mr. Clark.

12. David Wigg, interview with the author.

13. William P. Clark, interview with the author.

14. "Warsaw Pact Forces Opposite NATO," NIE 11–14–81, National Intelli-

gence Estimate, 7 July 1981 (Director of Central Intelligence: Central Intelligence Agency), p. 4 (FOIA).

15. "Soviet Potential to Respond to US Strategic Force Improvements, and Foreign Reactions," SNIE 11–4/2–81, Special National Intelligence Estimate (Directorate of Intelligence, 6 October 1981), pp. 8, 26 (FOIA).

16. Robert McFarlane, interview with the author.

17. Thomas R. Rochon, *Coalitions and Political Movements: The Lessons of the Nuclear Freeze* (Boulder: Lynne Riemer, 1997), p. 1, and William J. Palmer, *The Films of the Eighties: A Social History* (Carbondale: Southern Illinois University Press, 1993), p. 182.

18. Tom Minga, "Panel Hears Children Tell of Nuclear War Fears," *Education Week*, September 28, 1983, and "Cyanide Debates Are a Copout," *Philadelphia Inquirer*, November 17, 1984.

19. "Nuclear War—Bad for Health," *Philadelphia Daily News*, March 27, 1984.

20. "Freeze Debated Informally," *Washington Post*, August 21, 1984.

21. See "Preparations for the Soviet-American Conference 'Medics Against Nuclear War,' " Secretariat of the Communist Party of the Soviet Union, January 13, 1981, no. 245/14.

22. Ronald Reagan, *An American Life* (New York: Simon and Schuster, 199), p. 566; William Clark, interview with the author; Patti Davis quoted in Adriana Bosch, *Reagan: An American Story* (New York: TV Books, 1998), p. 209.

23. Robert McFarlane, interview with the author.

24. John Poindexter, interview with the author.

25. George Shultz, interview with the author.

26. Robert McFarlane draft memo to William P. Clark, March 22, 1983. Obtained from William P. Clark.

27. *Congressional Quarterly*, March 26, 1983.

28. "Eliminating the Threat from Ballistic Missiles," NSDD–85 (signed March 25, 1983), p. 1.

29. Comments in William Wohlforth, ed., *Witnesses to the End of the Cold War* (Baltimore: Johns Hopkins University Press, 1986), p. 33.

30. "Andropov Says U.S. Is Spurring a Race for Nuclear Arms," *New York*

Times, March 27, 1983, and *Star Wars: Delusions and Dangers* (Moscow: Military Publishing House, 1985), p. 17.

31. "Soviet Directed Energy Weapons—Perspectives on Strategic Defense," March 1985, CIA Working Paper, p. 15 (FOIA).

32. Comments by Generals Detinov and Slipchenko are from "Understanding the End of the Cold War, 1980–1987: An Oral History Conference," Brown University, May 7–10, 1998, Provisional Transcript, May 1999, pp. 37–40, 50–51.

33. "Possible Soviet Responses to the US Strategic Defense Initiative," CIA Interagency Intelligence Assessment, NIC M 83–10017 (September 12, 1983), pp. 5–12.

CHAPTER XIV: A PLAN

1. Ronald Reagan, *The Creative Society*, op cit., pp. 49–50.

2. "U.S. National Security Strategy," National Security Study Directive (NSSD) 1–82, pp. 1–2 (FOIA).

3. William P. Clark, interview with the author.

4. "U.S. National Security Strategy," National Security Decision Directive Number 32 (NSDD–32), May 20, 1982 (FOIA).

5. Richard Pipes, "Détente and Reciprocity," in G.R. Urban, ed. *Détente* (New York: Universe Books, 1976), p. 185.

6. "The Man Not Worried by the Bomb," *Washington Post*, April 11, 1982.

7. "Response to NSSD 11–82: U.S. Relations with the USSR," National Security Council classified "secret," December 6, 1982, pp. 1–43 (FOIA).

8. "U.S. Relations with the USSR," NSDD–75, pp. 1–9 (FOIA).

CHAPTER XV: THE CHANCE OF A LIFETIME

1. See CPSU politburo session, August 25, 1980, *Novaia i Noveishaia Istoriaa*, no. 1, 1994, p. 84.

2. See Wojciech Jaruzelski, *Mein Leben fur Polen: Erinnerungen* (Munich: Piper, 1993).

3. Minutes of CPSU Politburo session, September 10, 1981.

4. Letter from Hungarian Socialist Workers' Party Central Committee to PUWP CC, September 17, 1981, Hungarian National Archives, Department

of documents on Hungarian Workers' Party and Hungarian Socialist Workers' Party, 288., f. 11/4400, p. 121.

5. Memorandum of Conversation between Bulgarian Foreign Minister P. Mladenov and Polish Ambassador VI. Naperaj, October 6, 1981, DA MVNR, Opis. 38, A.E. 2192, I. 180–84.

6. Memorandum regarding the Meeting between Comrade Leonid Ilyich Brezhnev, Erich Honecker, and Gustav Husak in the Kremlin, May 16, 1981 SAMPO-BArch ZPA, vorl.SED 41559.

7. "Report on the Work of the Committee on State Security of the USSR for 1981," April 13, 1982, APRF, f. 81, op. 3, d. 2556, no. 289–op.

8. "Spravka o faktakh i prichinakh politicheski vrednykh proyavlenii so storony otdel'nykh voennosluzhashchikh, prizvannykh voenkomatami Litovskoi SSR," Dispatch No. 17–286s LVOA, f. 1771, Apy. 260, B. 182, La. 87–95.

9. Report regarding a confidential discussion with the Supreme Commander of the Combined Military Forces of the Warsaw Pact Countries on April 7, 1981, in Legnica following the evaluation meeting of the Joint Operative-Strategic Command Staff Exercise 'Soyuz–81,' reprinted in *Cold War International History Project Bulletin 11*, pp. 120–21.

10. "Bericht uber ein vertrauliches Gesprach mit dem Oberkommandierenden der Vereinten Streitkrafte der Teilnehmerstaaten des Warschauer Vertrages am 07.04.1981 in LEGNICA," bl. 54.

11. State Department Telegram From: American Embassy Moscow, To: Secretary of State, Subject: Prophylactic Measures Taken in Lithuania Against Polish Contagion, August 5, 1981 (FOIA).

12. From: American Embassy Moscow, To: Secretary of State Washington (Priority), Subject: Polish Diplomat Comments on Soviet-Polish Relations, September 30, 1981, p. 2 (FOIA).

13. Comments on November 18, 1986, *Presidential Documents*, vol. 22 (November 22, 1986), p. 1581.

14. Mark Kramer, "Colonel Kuklinski and the Polish Crisis, 1980–1981," *Cold War International History Project*, Bulletin no. 11, pp. 54–55.

15. CIA Memorandum, From: Robert M. Gates, For: Director of Central Intelligence William Casey, Subject: Assistance to Poland: Tuesday's NSC Meeting, December 4, 1981, pp. 1–2 (FOIA).

16. See DCI Memo titled, "Poland—Muddled through year 1981," December 10, 1981, p. 1 (FOIA).

17. Richard Pipes, interview with the author.

18. CIA Memo, "Response to DCI Queries," December 17, 1981, pp. 1–4 (FOIA).

19. President Ronald Reagan note on Poland, December 1981, EXSEC Collection, HOS Series, National Archives and Records Administration.

20. From American Embassy Bonn, To: SecState WashDC, December 18, 1981 U.S. Department of State Telegram, pp. 1–2 (FOIA).

21. State Department Telegram From: Secretary of State to: XUSNMR SHAPE, Subject: U.S. Statement on Poland, February 4, 1982, p. 2 (FOIA).

22. Report to the Politburo by the Department of International Relations of the Central Committee of the Hungarian Socialist Workers' Party, December 8, 1980, Hungarian National Archives (Budapest), Department of Documents on the Hungarian Workers' Party and the Hungarian Socialist Workers' Party, 288, f. 5/815, p. 19.

23. General Czeslaw Kiszczak, correspondence with the author.

24. Quoted by Erich Honecker during his meeting with Jaruzelski, March 29, 1982, J IV/2/201/1422 Bd 20, Zentralarchiv der SED, Stiftung Archiv der Parteien und Massenorganisationen der DDR im Bundesarchiv, Berlin. See also State Department Telegram, From: American Embassy Bonn To: Secretary of State, Subject: Chancellor Schmidt's January 14 Bundestag Speech, p. 2 (FOIA).

25. State Department Telegram, From: American Embassy Bonn, To: Secretary of State, Subject: Rakowski Meeting December 30 with German Industrialist Wolff Von Amerongen, January 4, 1982 (FOIA).

26. Department of State Memorandum of Conversation, Subject: Secretary Haig's Breakfast Meeting with FRG Chancellor Schmidt, January 6, 1982, pp. 2–8 (FOIA).

27. "Poland: Summary of Country Positions/Actions," Department of State Briefing Paper, classified "Secret," pp. 1–4 (FOIA).

28. "Post-NAC Press Statement," U.S. Department of State, January 11, 1982. Emphasis in original.

29. Quoted in Walter Hixson, *George F. Kennan: Cold War Iconoclast* (New York: Columbia University Press, 1989), pp. 275–76.

30. State Department Telegram, From: American Embassy Moscow, To: USICA, Subject: Poland Solidarity Day Attacked in Press, January 29, 1982, p. 2 (FOIA).

31. Glowny Zarzad Polityczny WP, Zarzad Propagandy I agitacji, "Stanowisko Panstw NATO I Propagandy Zachodniej Wobec Stanu Wojennego w Polsce," Informacja nr. 30/82, pp. 6–7.

32. CPSU CC Politburo transcript, January 14, 1982.

33. Office of Technology Assessment, *Technology and Soviet Energy Availability* (Washington, D.C.: 1981), pp. 5, 14, 63.

34. Quoted in "Inefficiencies Hamper Soviet Energy Plans," *Baltimore Sun,* August 13, 1983.

35. State Department Telegram, From: Secretary of State, To: American Embassy Bonn, Subject: Secretary's Meeting with FRG Economics Minister Ambsdorff—February 23, 1982: Discussion of Poland and Alliance Relations, Secretary's Office, p. 7 (FOIA).

36. "O'Neill Talks to Shultz, Recalls Bill to Lift Pipeline Sanctions," *Washington Post*, September 29, 1982.

37. Roger Robinson, interview with the author.

38. "East-West Economic Relations and Poland-Related Sanctions," National Security Decision Directive Number 66, November 29, 1982, pp. 1–2, and the "Summary of conclusions" attached to the directive, pp. 1–2 (FOIA).

39. Data from "Economic Data Chart—USSR," in U.S. Department of State Scope Paper, the Secretary's Meeting With Soviet Foreign Minister Shevardnadze in Helsinki, July 31, 1985, p. 34 (FOIA).

40. CIA Memo classified "Secret," "Poland: More Reports of Unrest," February 9, 1982, pp. 1–2 (FOIA).

41. Ronald Reagan to John O. Koehler, dated July 9, 1981. Copy given to the author by Mr. Koehler.

42. Jeff Stein, "Mystery Man of American Diplomacy," *Boston Globe Magazine,* August 29, 1982, p. 12.

43. See *Washington Post*, December 16, 1985.

44. General Vernon Walters, interview with the author. There is no transcript available of the meeting with the Pope. However, Walters kept notes and has a detailed diary.

45. Confidential State Department cable, For: The Ambassadors of NATO countries, From: Lawrence S. Eagleburger, Subject: Poland, January 9, 1982 (FOIA).

46. Biuletyn Informacyjny, nr. 4 (Warsaw: Zarzad Polityczno-Wychowawczy MSW, Wydzial Szkolenia i Propagandy, 1986).

47. For an interesting and well-researched history of the activities of the International Rescue Committee, see Eric Thomas Chester, *Covert Network: Progressives, the International Rescue Committee, and the CIA* (London: M.E. Sharpe, 1995).

48. IRC, Minutes of the Executive Committee, May 4, 1960, box 4, Buttinger Papers, Harvard–Yenching Library.

49. John McDonough to Allen Dulles, April 16, 1942, entry 160, box 10, RG 226, papers of the OSS, National Archives; International Rescue Committee, *That Freedom May Not Perish* (New York: IRC, 1957).

50. Leo Cherne, "Thirty Days That Shook the World," *Saturday Review*, December 22, 1956, p. 22, Harold H. Martin, "The Man Who Wanted to Help Hungary," *Saturday Evening Post*, December 29, 1956, pp. 53–54.

51. See Leon Cherne to J. M. Kaplan, January 14, 1965, box 24; Garrett Ackerson Jr. to William vanden Heuvel, May 27, 1963, box 24; Garrett Ackerson Jr. to Egon Bahr, October 14, 1964, box 24; Cherne to Kaplan, January 14, 1965, box 24, Cherne, notes from Bahr Discussion, 1964; Leo Cherne to William Fitelson, November 9, 1964, box 24, all from the Leo Cherne Papers, Boston University. For a public account of the shooting incident at the wall, see *New York Times*, October 6, 1964, and *New York Times*, October 8, 1964.

52. See Frank R. Barnett, "Afterword—Twelve Steps to Reviving American PSYOP," in Carnes Lord and Frank R. Barnett, *Political Warfare and Psychological Operations* (Washington, D.C.: National Defense University Press, 1989), p. 212. Note: Barnett worked for the American Friends of Russian Freedom as well.

53. Marek Zielinski, "Struktury Emigracyjne b. Nszz 'Solidarnosc' (1981–1984)," Ministerstwo Obrony Narodowej, Szefostwo Wojskowej Sluzby wewnetrznej (Warsaw: 1985), pp. 23–24, 29–30.

54. General Kiszczak, correspondence with the author.

55. "Analiza stanu zagrozenia" (Warsaw: January 1986), p. 30.

CHAPTER XVI: THE CRUSADE

1. On the French visit, see "Imagery High on Reagan Summit Agenda," *Washington Post*, May 30, 1982, and "Fears and Fetes in France," *Washington Post*, June 5, 1982.

2. "Pope Asks Reagan to Seek Peace, Aid Poor," *Washington Post*, June 8, 1982.

3. Information on the protests, including the key role played by the PCI, is from "Italian Left Unconvinced by Reagan's Pilgrimage of Peace," *Washington Post*, June 8, 1982. Information on Kremlin's financial support of the PCI comes from Christopher Andrew and Vasili Mitrokhin, *The Sword and the Shield: The Mitrokhin Archive and the Secret History of the KGB* (New York: Basic Books, 1999), pp. 276–78, 294–301.

4. "About Soviet campaign for disarmament," Soviet Secretariat of the Politburo, Communist Party of the Soviet Union, no. 9/4, May 21, 1976; "Financial Aid to World-wide Peace Committee," Secretariat of the Politburo, no. 126/8, September 26, 1978; "Plans of anti-NATO Activities," Secretariat of the Politburo, no. 206/15, April 15, 1980. Documents obtained by Vladimir Bukovsky.

5. See Milton S. Katz, *Ban the Bomb: A History of SANE, the Committee for a SANE Nuclear Policy* (New York: Praeger, 1987), p. 147.

6. It was Niemöller who uttered the powerful statement: "First they came for the Communists, but I was not a Communist so I did not speak out. Then they came for the Socialists and the Trade Unionists, but I was neither, so I did not speak out. Then they came for the Jews, but I was not a Jew so I did not speak out. And when they came for me, there was no one left to speak out for me."

7. From the German archives see "Zusammengerechnet erhielt die DFU damit jahrlich 4 836 000 DM aus der DDR," SAPMO–BA DY 30 IV B 2/2.208/5 BI. 34. See also Hubertus Knabe, "Der lange Arm der SED," *Aus Politik und Zeitgeschichte*, September 1999.

8. Sergei Grigoriev, "The International Department of the CPSU Central Committee; It's Functions and Roles in Soviet Foreign Policymaking and its Rise and Fall Following the Major Reorganization of the Central Party Apparatus Under Gorbachev," Strengthening Democratic Institutions Project, Harvard University John F. Kennedy School of Government, December 1995, p. 48.

9. John O. Koehler, *Stasi: The Untold Story of the East German Secret Police* (Boulder, Colorado: Westview Press, 1999), pp. 189–90.

10. Wehner's statement is from Richard C. Thornton, *The Carter Years: Toward A New Global Order* (New York: Paragon House, 1991), p. 73. Information on his Stasi comes from David Childs and Richard Popplewell, *The Stasi: The East German Intelligence and Security Service* (New York: New York University Press, 1996).

11. Edmund Morris, *Dutch: A Memoir of Ronald Reagan* (New York: Random House, 1999), p. 461.

12. "President Calls for 'Crusade,' " *Washington Post*, June 9, 1982.

13. Joel Brinkley, *New York Times*, February 15, 1987.

14. History of the NED is from Joel M. Woldman, "The National Endowment for Democracy," *Issue Brief: Congressional Research Service*, September 3, 1985, pp. 1–19, and U.S. General Accounting Office, "Events Leading to the Establishment of National Endowment for Democracy," GAO/NSIAD–84–121, July 6, 1984.

15. David Ignatius, "Innocence Abroad: The New World of Spyless Coups," *Washington Post*, September 22, 1991.

16. "Poland's Prospects Over the Next 12 to 18 Months," Special National Intelligence Estimate, SNIE 12.6–82, September 1, 1982, p. 1.

17. Jan Nowak to Carl Gershman, July 25, 1984; National Security Archives. See also *National Endowment for Democracy Annual Report 1985*, p. 19.

18. NED summary, "Committee for Independent Culture, Poland," Summary and Program Description, National Endowment for Democracy, undated; National Security Archive.

19. Letter from Jan Nowak to Carl Gershman, op cit.

20. Independent Polish Agency, National Endowment for Democracy Paper, not dated; National Security Archive.

21. "Proposal for Receiving a Support Grant for Publishing of the Book by George Orwell, *Animal Farm,*" Problems of Eastern Europe, August 7, 1986, National Security Archive.

22. See *National Endowment for Democracy Annual Report, 1988* and Robert Pear, "U.S. Helping Polish Underground with Money and Communications," *New York Times*, July 10, 1988, pp. 1, 14, and Rowland Evans and Robert Novak, "Solidarity Rides the Airwaves," *Washington Post*, April 24, 1985, p. A25.

23. *National Endowment for Democracy Annual Report, 1987*, pp. 34–44.

24. Letter from William P. Kiehl, Counselor of Embassy in Prague to Mr. Yale Richmond, National Endowment for Democracy, April 2, 1986, National Security Archive.

25. NSDD–54, "United States Policy Toward Eastern Europe," September 2, 1982 (FOIA).

26. See John Whitehead and Georgy Shakhnazarov, "Understanding the End of the Cold War, 1980–1987: An Oral History Conference, Brown University," May 7–10, 1998, pp. 226–28.

27. Reagan and Koehler maintained an active correspondence. This quote is from Koehler's letter of June 11, 1981. Obtained from Mr. Koehler.

28. "Reagan Lashes Communism," *Washington Post*, June 15, 1985.

29. Natan Sharansky, "Afraid of the Truth," *Washington Post*, October 12, 2000.

30. "United States International Broadcasting," National Security Decision Directive (NSDD–45), July 15, 1982, pp. 1–4 (FOIA).

31. Artyom Panfilov and Yuri Karchevsky, *Subversion by Radio* (Moscow: Novosti Press Agency Publishing House, 1974), p. 36. The publication of Fulbright's book is mentioned in James Critchlow, *Radio Hole-in-the-Head/ Radio Liberty: An Insider's Story of Cold War Broadcasting* (Washington: American University Press, 1995), p. 157.

32. James Critchlow, op cit., p. 165.

33. Murray Lisann, *Broadcasting to the Soviet Union: International Politics and Radio* (New York: Praeger Publishers, 1975), pp. 154–55.

34. Oleg Tumanov, *Tumanov: Confessions of a KGB Agent* (Chicago: Edition Q, 1993), pp. 66–95.

35. Reagan mentions the radios in a 1979 radio broadcast that is reprinted in *Reagan in His Own Hand*, op cit., p. 128.

36. Quoted in Don Irwin, "World Being 'Stonewalled,' Reagan Says," *Los Angeles Times*, September 11, 1983, pp. 1, 26, and Stephen Engelberg, "New Tenor, New Tone at the VOA," *New York Times*, August 3, 1984.

37. Kenneth Adelman, "Speaking of America: Public Diplomacy in Our Time," *Foreign Affairs*, Spring 1981, p. 928.

38. "US International Information Policy," NSSD 2–83, March 12, 1983, pp. 1–2, and "United States International Broadcasting," NSDD–45, July 15, 1982, pp. 1–4 (FOIA).

39. Walter Jajko, "Political Subversion of Western Europe," Richard F. Staar, ed., *Public Diplomacy: USA versus USSR* (Stanford, California: Hoover Institution, 1986), p. 64.

40. Alfred Paddock, "U.S. Informational and Cultural Program," in Staar, op cit., p. 91.

41. John W. Feuerstein, Dale J. Robertson, Kenneth J. Van Patten, *An Overview of the Jamming of International Shortwave Broadcasts* (McLean, Virginia: Mitre Corporation, January 1984). Study sponsored by USIA and VOA.

42. See *1985 Annual Report of the Board for International Broadcasting*, Washington, D.C.

43. VOA, Memo from Phil Nicolaides to VOA Director James Conkling, September 21, 1981 (FOIA).

44. *New York Daily News*, August 13, 1981.

45. VOA, "Background Notes on VOA Reportage," Internal memo from Alan Heil to James Conkling, November 2, 1981, p. 3 (FOIA).

46. Laurien Alexandre, *The Voice of America: From Detente to the Reagan Doctrine* (Norwood, NJ: Ablex Publishing Corporation, 1988).

47. *U.S. Advisory Commission on Public Diplomacy 1986 Report*, p. 26.

48. R. Eugene Parta, "Soviet Area Audience and Opinion Research (SAAOR) at Radio Free Europe/Radio Liberty," in K.R.M. Short, ed., *Western Broadcasting Over the Iron Curtain* (New York: St. Martin's Press, 1986), pp. 227–44.

49. "Dimensions of Civil Unrest in the Soviet Union," National Intelligence Council Memorandum, NIC M 83–10006 SC 02188/83, April 1983, pp. 1–29 (FOIA).

50. "Domestic Stresses on the Soviet System," Central Intelligence Agency NIE 11–18–85 (November 1985), pp. 10–13 (FOIA).

51. U.S. Congress, House, Committee on Appropriations, *Department of Commerce, Justice, State, the Judiciary and Related Agencies, Hearings before a subcommittee of the House Committee on Appropriations*, 98th Congress, 2nd session, 1982, p. 365.

52. General Kiszczak, correspondence with the author.

53. Colonel Henryk Piecuch, correspondence with the author.

54. Anatoly Marchenko, *To Live Like Everyone* (New York: Henry Holt, 1989), p. 179.

55. Ludmilla Alexeyeva and Paul Goldberg, *The Thaw Generation: Coming of Age in the Post-Stalin Era* (Boston: Little, Brown and Co., 1990), pp. 181–82.

56. "Inspiraowanie i Programowanie Dzialalnosci Antysocjalistycznej w Polsce Przez 'Kulture,' 'Aneks' i 'Kontakt' w latch osiemdziesiatych," Akademia Nauk Spolecznych Centrum Studiow Polityki i Propagandy, DRI no. 15 (69)–16 (70), p. 2; Hoover Institution Archives, Stanford University.

57. Charles Wick, interview with the author.

58. "Nagrania video i Magnetowidowe Oraz Telewizja Satelitarna w Dzialal-nosci Propagandowej Przeczwnika Politycznego," Glowny Zarzad Polityczny W P: Zarzad Propagandy i Agitacji (Warsaw: May, 1986).

59. General Kiszczak, correspondence with the author.

60. Polski Instytut Spraw Miedzynardowych Instytut Badania Wspolczesnych Problemow Kapitalizmu, *Polityka Stanow Zjednoczonych Ameryki Wobec Polski W Swietle Faktow I Dokumentow* (1980–1983), pp. 4–19.

61. Text of speech "Dywersja Ideologiczna I Agresja Propandaowa Przeci-wko Polsce," May 1986, Hoover Institution Archives, Stanford University.

CHAPTER XVII: REVERSAL OF FORTUNE

1. Ronald Reagan, *An American Life* (New York: Simon and Schuster, 1990), p. 289, and Caspar Weinberger, interview with the author.

2. William Casey, *The Secret War Against Hitler* (Washington: Regnery, 1988), p. xiv.

3. William J. Casey, Address to the John Ashbrook Center for Public Affairs, Ashland College, October 27, 1986.

4. State Department Telegram, From: American Embassy Moscow, To: Secretary of State, Date: June 8, 1981, Subject: Senior Soviet Economic Planner on Afghanistan and Poland, p. 2 (FOIA).

5. State Department Telegram, From: American Embassy Moscow, To: Secretary of State, Date: April 21, 1982, Subject: Candidate Politburo Member Demichev on Poland, Afghanistan, and START, p. 2 (FOIA).

6. Alan Riding, "Central Americans Split on U.S. Voting," *New York Times*, August 4, 1980.

7. National Security Decision Directive–17, "National Security Decision Directive on Cuba and Central America," January 4, 1982, p. 2 (FOIA).

8. "DoD Support for the DCI," Department of Defense Memorandum, September 6, 1983 (FOIA), "Remarks prepared for Delivery by the Honorable Caspar W. Weinberger, Secretary of Defense, at the Conference on Low Intensity Warfare," January 14, 1986, Office of the Assistant Secretary of Defense (Public Affairs), Washington, January 14, 1986, p. 6.

9. "Perceptions," *Washington Post*, August 8, 1983, and Thomas W. Walker, *Reagan Versus the Sandinistas: The Undeclared War on Nicaragua* (Boulder: Westview Press, 1987), p. 42.

10. Captain Kevin J. Dougherty, "The Indirect Application of Military Power: U.S. Policy Toward Nicaragua," *Military Review*, October 1994, p. 54.

11. Yevgeny Bay, "Soviet Union–Cuba: 'The Pandora Affair'—Havana's Leadership Reveals Secrets of Relations with Moscow," *Izvestiya*, April 27, 1993.

12. The author is grateful to John O. Koehler, who shared his copies of these letters.

13. Special National Intelligence Estimate, "Soviet Policies and Activities in Latin America and the Caribbean," Central Intelligence Agency, SNIE 11/80/90–82 25, June 1982, p. 19 (FOIA).

14. *Washington Post,* February 27, 1983.

15. Taken from Deborah Hart Strober and Gerald S. Strober, eds., *Reagan: The Man and His Presidency—The Oral History of an Era* (New York: Houghton Mifflin, 1999), p. 290; Edmund Morris, *Dutch*, p. 50; and Lou Cannon, *President Reagan: The Role of a Lifetime* (New York: Simon and Schuster, 1991), pp. 441–51.

16. Story told by Langhorne Motley, quoted in Strober and Strober, op cit., p. 289.

17. Stasi memorandum of September 24, 1984; John O. Koehler collection, Hoover Institution Archives, Stanford University.

18. "Statement by the Cuban Party and Government on the Imperialism Intervention in Grenada," October 25, 1983, p. 2.

19. Congressional Research Service, *The Soviet Union in the Third World, 1980–1985: An Imperial Burden or Political Asset?* Report for the House Committee on Foreign Affairs, September 23, 1985 (GPO, 1985), p. 435.

20. "Costs of Soviet Support to Cuba," State Department Briefing Paper, p. 1 (FOIA).

21. "On Measures to Strengthen Our Counteractions to the American Policy of 'Neoglobalism," Resolution of the Central Committee, July 31, 1986, p. 1, TsKhSD, Fond 3, Opis 102, Dokment 230.

CHAPTER XVIII: STUBBORN RESISTANCE

1. State Department Telegram, From: American Embassy Moscow, To: Secretary of State, Date: November 6, 1981, p. 3 (FOIA).

2. Dobrynin, *In Confidence*, p. 495.

3. *Pravda*, October 28, 1982.

4. Wohlforth, op cit., p. 31.

5. Leonid Zamyatin, "Detente and anti-Detente: Two Tendencies in World Politics," *Literaturnaya Gazeta*, September 29, 1982.

6. Detinov, op cit., p. 92.

7. Raymond Garthoff, *The Great Transition: American-Soviet Relations and the End of the Cold War* (Washington: Brookings, 1994), p. 77.

8. State Department Telegram, From: American Embassy Moscow, To: Secretary of State, Date: October 21, 1981, Subject: Soviet 'Public Opinion' on International Issues, p. 2 (FOIA).

9. Oleg Gordievksy, *The KGB: The Inside Story* (New York: HarperCollins, 1990), pp. 583–606.

10. Andrei A. Kokoshin, *Soviet Strategic Thought, 1917–1991* (London: Massachusetts Institute of Technology Press, 1998), p. 130.

11. Dobrynin, op cit., pp. 522–23.

12. Speech by Yuri Andropov to a closed session of the Warsaw Pact's Political Consultative Committee in Prague, May 4, 1983 VA–01/40473, Bundesarchiv-Militararchiv, Freiburg.

13. NIE 11–4–82, "The Soviet Challenge to U.S. Security Interests," Central Intelligence Agency, pp. 2, 5.

14. Special National Intelligence Estimate, "Soviet Potential to Respond to US Strategic Force Improvements, and Foreign Reactions," SNIE 11–4/2–81, October 6, 1981, p. 8.

15. G.K. Tsinev, "O zadachakh Upravleniya i Shestykh podrazdelenii Komiteta Gosudarstvennoi Bezopasnosti po vypolneniyu ustanovok maiskogo vsesoyuznonogo soveshchaniya rukovodyashchego sostava voisk i organov KGB i posleduyushchikh reshenii Kollegii Komiteta po zashchite ekonomiki ot podryvnoi deyatel'nosti protivnika i sodeistbiya ekonomicheskomu razvitiyu strany," *Deyatel 'nost gosudarstvennoi besopasnoti SSSR na sovremennom etape* (Moscow: F.E. Dzerzhinskiy Red Banner Higher School of the Committee for State Security, 1983), pp. 235–36.

16. Anatoly Dobrynin, op cit., p. 499.

17. Session of the Politburo, May 31, 1983, TsKhSD, F. 89, op. 42, D. 53, LI. 1–14.

18. Joseph S. Bermudez, Jr., *Terrorism: The North Korean Connection* (New York: Crane Russak, 1990), pp. 82–83.

19. Captain Kazimierz Kreja, "Subversive Influence of the West on the Youth of Poland," Academy of Internal Affairs, Warsaw, 1986, Hoover Institution Archives, Stanford University.

20. Igor Tsarev, "A 'Diamond-Studded Sky.' Should the Military Who Maintains They Have Stopped Preparing for Star Wars Be Trusted?" *JPRS Central Eurasia: CIS/Russian Military Issues*, October 20, 1993 (JPRS-UMA–93–039).

21. General Y.V. Votintsev, "Neizvestnyye Voyska Ischeznyvshey Sverkhderzhavy," *Voyenno-Istoricheskii Zhurnal*, no. 8, 1993.

22. These incidents are reported in National Intelligence Council Memorandum For: Director of Central Intelligence, From: Herbert E. Meyer, Vice Chairman, National Intelligence Council, Subject: What Should We Do About the Russians? June 26, 1984 p. 1; Donald Fortier Files collection, OA 90706, Ronald Reagan Presidential Library.

23. APRF, f. 3, op. 82, d. 177, 84–86.

24. Abraham Becker, *Economic Leverage on the Soviet Union in the 1980s* (Santa Monica: RAND Corporation, July 1984), p. 66.

25. *Izvestiya*, October 28, 1992, and Dobrynin, op cit., p. 512.

26. For Ryzhkov's statement, see *Izvestiya*, June 8, 1989. For information on Soviet military budget increases in the early 1980s, see Marshal Ogarkov's comment in *Izvestiya,* May 9, 1983, and the General Staff statement in *Pravda*, March 9, 1985. See also Army General V. N. Lobov, "Voennaya reforma: istoricheskie predposylki i osnovnye napravleniya," *Voenno-Istorischeskii Zhurnal*, no. 11, 1991, p. 3.

27. Yuri Andropov, "O zadachakh organov gosudarstevennoi bezopasnosti v svete reshenii XXVI s'ezda KPSS," *Deyatel'nost gosudarstvennoi besopasnoti SSSR na sovremennom etape* (Moscow: F.E. Dzerzhinskiy Red Banner Higher School of the Committee of State Security, 1983), p. 28, and KGB Report no. 2126/PR, November 11, 1983, in Christopher Andrew and Oleg Gordievsky, *Instructions from the Centre: Top Secret Files on KGB Foreign Operations* (London: Hodder and Stoughton, 1991), pp. 16–22.

28. Report on the Work of the Committee for State Security of the USSR for 1986, TsKhSD, Fond 89, Perechen 51, Dokment 9.

CHAPTER XIX: ALL IN THE NAME OF PEACE

1. See Sergei Tikhvinskiy, "Lessons of Genoa," *Izvestiya*, April 10, 1982, and State Department Telegram, From: American Embassy Moscow, To: Secretary

of State, Date: April 15, 1982, Subject: Soviets Recall Lessons of Rapallo Treaty: Capitalist Encirclement Can Be Broken, p. 3 (FOIA).

2. U.S. International Communication Agency, Office of Research, Briefing, Paper, B–12–23–81; Elizabeth Noelle-Neumann, *Die NATO-Experten und das Publikum: Das Problem der Akzeptanz von Verteidigungspolitik* (Allensbach: Institut für Demoskopie, 1988), Table A11.

3. State Department Cable, From: American Embassy Bonn, To: Secretary of State, Date: January 20, 1982, Subject: A Concerned Conservative Viewpoint: Lothar Spaeth on German-American Relations, p. 2 (FOIA).

4. On Brezhnev and the peace movement, see "About Soviet Campaign for Disarmament," Soviet Secretariat of the Politburo, Communist Party of the Soviet Union, no. 9/4, May 21, 1976, and "Financial Aid to World-wide Peace Committee," Secretariat of the Politburo, no. 126/8, September 26, 1978; "Plans of anti–NATO Activities," Secretariat of the Politburo, no. 206/15, April 15, 1980. Documents obtained by Vladimir Bukovsky. For Andropov's comment, see "Session of the Politburo," May 31, 1983, TsKhSD, F.89, Op. 42, D. 53, Ll. 1–14.

5. Don Oberdorfer, "International Panel Calls for Steps to Stem Spiraling Arms Race," *Washington Post*, June 2, 1982, reports that Arbatov aggressively worked on the panel and his efforts were "hard won." His reports back to the Kremlin are "Participation in Palme's Committee for Peace and Disarmament," Secretariat of the Politburo, no. 237/54, November 14, 1980, "Approval for Participation in Palme's Committee for Peace and Disarmament," Secretariat of the Politburo, no. 241/14, December 10, 1980, and "Arbatov's Reports on Participation in Palme's Committee for Peace and Disarmament," Secretariat of the Politburo, no. 36, December 23, 1980. Documents obtained by Vladimir Bukovsky.

6. For the East German intelligence view on non-communist peace movements, see for example their files on the British Campaign for Nuclear Disarmament, MfS AP31334/92 and HA XX 2MA 20585, Vols. 1–3. See also Andrew Alderson and David Bamber, "CND Chief Was Stasi Secret Agent," BBC Online, issue 1577, Sunday, 19 September, 1999.

7. "On measures connected with the 50th birthday of the chairman of the Social-Democratic party of Finland (SDPF), K. Sorsa," CPSU International Department, December 16, 1980. Document obtained by Vladimir Bukovsky.

8. These were known instances and all of these individuals were expelled from these countries. See Danish Ministry of Justice Press Release, April 17, 1982, and J.A.E. Vermaat, *Ons Leger*, October/November, 1981.

9. "Vowing to Persist, Peace Groups in Europe End Weekend of Protests," *Philadelphia Inquirer*, April 4, 1983.

10. Josef Joffe, "Soviet Diplomacy and Public Opinion: The Case of West Germany," Janos Radvauyi, ed., *Psychological Operations and Political Warfare in Long-Term Strategic Planning* (New York: Praeger, 1990), p. 83.

11. Hubertus Knabe, "Der lange Arm der SED," *Aus Politik und Zeitgeschichte*, September 1999 and from the German archives see, "Zusammengerechnet erhielt die DFU damit jahrlich 4 836 000 DM aus der DDR," SAPMO-BA DY 30 IV B 2/2.208/5 Bl. 34.

12. Detinov, op cit., p. 136.

13. Thomas J. Downey, "On Congress and U.S. Security," *World Policy Journal*, vol. 1, no. 2.

14. The best history available on this episode is Jeffrey Herf, *War by Other Means: Soviet Power, West German Resistance and the Battle of the Euromissiles* (New York: Free Press, 1991).

15. Peter-Ferdinand Koch, *Die Feindlichen Bruder* (Munich: Scherz, 1994), Markus Wolf, *Spionagechef im geheim Krieg*, pp. 185, 210–211.

16. Timothy Garton Ash, *In Europe's Name: Germany and the Divided Continent* (London: Vintage, 1994), p. 320.

17. Aleksandr G. Savelyev and Nikolay Detinov, *The Big Five: Arms Control Decision-making in the Soviet Union* (New York: Praeger, 1995), p. 68, and Aleksandr Bessmertynkh, comments in William C. Wohlforth, ed., *Witnesses to the End of the Cold War* (Baltimore: Johns Hopkins University Press, 1996), p. 74.

18. See, for example, NIE 11–4–82, "The Soviet Challenge to U.S. Security Interests," Central Intelligence Agency, p. 2.

19. "Reagan Again Says Soviet Union Influences Anti-Nuclear Group," *Washington Post*, December 11, 1982.

20. World Peace Council, *Peace Courier*, 1989, no. 4.

21. See from the Stasi archives HA XX AKG 188 039321 and HX XX AKG 11 03921.

22. Report on the Work of the Committee for State Security of the USSR for 1986, TsKhSD, Fond 89, Perechen 51, Dokment 9.

23. Grigoriev, op cit., p. 59.

24. *Gallup 1983*, p. 210.

25. W. Averell Harriman, "If the Reagan Pattern Continues, America May Face Nuclear War," *New York Times*, January 1, 1984. Kennedy's comments are from the *Congressional Record*, March 15, 1984, pp. E1027–28; McGovern's comments are from the *Washington Post*, September 4, 1983, and Hollings in *Washington Post*, February 14, 1983.

26. Dobrynin, op cit., pp. 546, 548, 550.

27. Memorandum of January 3, 1983, quoted in Wjatschelsaw Daschitschew, "Aubenund Sicherheitspolitik Rublands gegenuber Europe," *Berliner Europa-Forum* 6 (1997) no.: 15–23, pp. 19–20.

28. For dissension inside the administration, see "Reagan Is Said to Hold Firm on Defense Buildup," *Washington Post*, November 13, 1982 and "Dwindling Support for Arms Buildup," *Washington Post*, February 14, 1983. McFarlane quoted in Beth A. Fischer, *The Reagan Reversal: Foreign Policy and the End of the Cold War* (Columbia: University of Missouri Press, 1997), p. 61.

29. Leiterinformation "zu einigen oktuellen Erscheinungen in der Politik der USA," Hauptverwaltung A Abteilung VII, Berlin, 10 August 1984 VII/6/1457/84, pp. 3–4.

30. Comments of Oleg Grinevsky from Understanding the End of the Cold War, 1980–1987: An Oral History Conference, Brown University, May 7–10, 1998, translated and transcribed by Jeffrey W. Dillon, edited by Nina Tannenwald, Provisional Transcript, May 1999, pp. 15–16.

CHAPTER XX: REAGAN MAKES GORBACHEV POSSIBLE

1. Memorandum For: Director of Central Intelligence, From: Herbert E. Meyer, Vice Chairman National Intelligence Council, Subject: Why Is the World So Dangerous?, Date: 30 November 1983, CIA Memorandum NIC #8640–83, pp. 1–8.

2. Shultz, Statement at the Conference on Disarmament in Europe, *Department of State Bulletin*, March 1984, p. 36.

3. "Soviet Union—U.S. Policy Toward the Soviet Union," letter case 8490095, file OA 90706, Donald Fortier files, Ronald Reagan Presidential Library.

4. William P. Clark, interview with the author.

5. Mohammad Yousaf, interview with the author; see also Muhammad Yousaf and Mark Adkin, *The Bear Trap: Afghanistan's Untold Story* (London: Leo Cooper, 1992).

6. Yousaf, op cit., pp. 194–95.

7. Defense Intelligence Agency Memo, From: DIA Washington DC JSI-7, To: DIACURINTEL, Subject: USSR-Afghanistan Relations, Date: April 27, 1987 (FOIA).

8. State Department Telegram From: American Counsul Peshawar, To: Secretary of State, Subject: Jamiat-i-Islami Comment on Mujahideen attacks into Soviet Territory, May 2, 1987, pp. 1–2 (FOIA).

9. William J. Casey, "Collapse of the Marxist Model: America's New Calling," speech to the Union League Club, New York, January 9, 1985.

10. Alexei Izyumov and Andrei Kortunov, "The Soviet Union in the Changing World," *International Affairs* (Moscow), no. 8 (August 1988), p. 52.

11. Correspondence with the author.

12. *Biuletyn Informacyjny*, no. 77, September 1983, reprinted in Teresa Rakowska-Harmstone, "Communist Regimes' Psychological Warfare Against Their Societies: The Case of Poland," in Janos Radvanyi, ed., *Psychological Operations and Political Warfare in Long-term Strategic Planning* (New York: Praeger, 1990), p. 103.

13. Correspondence with the author.

14. *FBIS* (Federal Republic of Germany), April 16, 1985, p. J1. *FBIS* (USSR International Affairs, United States and Canada), December 26, 1985, p. A4, *Financial Times*, November 23, 1984, p. 7, and *Businessweek*, April 4, 1983, p. 95.

15. Alan Fiers, interview with the author.

16. U.S. Treasury Department, "International Oil Pricing, 1983," Executive Summary, pp. 1, 3. Document courtesy of Edwin S. Rothschild.

17. 1984 CIA study quoted in "USSR: Facing the Dilemma of Hard Currency Shortages," Central Intelligence Agency: Directorate of Intelligence, May 1986.

18. Ed Meese, interview with the author.

19. John Poindexter, interview with the author.

20. Roger Robinson, interview with the author.

21. Glenn Campbell, interview with the author.

22. Caspar Weinberger, interview with the author.

23. Caspar Weinberger, interview with the author.

24. Georgi Arbatov, *The System: An Insider's Life in Soviet Politics* (New York: Times Books, 1993), p. 203; "Enter Gorbachev," The Second Russian Revolu-

tion, BBC TV Series, Part 1, 1991; includes extensive interviews with Soviet officials on this subject.

25. Karen Brutents, "Osvobodivshyesya strany v nachale 80–kh godov," *Kommunist*, 3 (1984), pp. 103–107.

26. Interviews in "Messengers from Moscow," A Barraclough Casey Production in association with Thirteen/WNET and PACEM Productions, Inc., for the British Broadcasting Corporation. Post-Production Script, 1994, pp. 34–35.

27. Dr. Vitali Nikolaevich Tsygichko, comments to BDM study, pp. 153–54.

28. Gyula Horn, *Freiheit, die Ich meine* (Hamburg: Hoffmann and Campe, 1991), p. 10.

29. Christian Schmidt-Hauer, *Gorbachev: The Path to Power* (Topsfield, MA: Salem House, 1986), p. 107.

30. Don Oberdorfer, *The Turn* (New York: Poseidon, 1991), p. 89.

31. Andrei Gromyko, *Memoirs* (New York: Doubleday, 1989), p. 307.

32. Memorandum of Conversation, Second Shultz-Gromyko Meeting, Geneva, January 1985, p. 3, 4 (FOIA).

33. Quoted in Martin Walker, *The Cold War* (New York: Vintage, 1994), p. 283.

34. Georgy Shakhnazarov, comments in *Understanding the End of the Cold War*, op cit., p. 27.

35. For information on Gromyko's speech, see Christian Schmidt-Hauer, p. 113–14. For information on Gromyko and Dobrynin, see Arbatov, *The System* (New York: Random House, 1992), pp. 293–94. For a firsthand account, see Sergei Grigoriev, "The International Department of the CPSU Central Committee; Its functions and role in Soviet foreign policymaking and its rise and fall following the major reorganization of the central party apparatus under Gorbachev," Harvard University John F. Kennedy School of Government, Strengthening Democratic Institutions Project, December 1995, p. 54.

36. Mikhail Gorbachev, *Izbranne rechi i stat'i* (Moscow: Politizdat, 1987), Vol. 2, p. 131.

37. U.S. Department of State Telegram, From: American Embassy Moscow, To: Secretary of State, Subject: Is There Life After Geneva? Soviet Views on the November Meeting and U.S. Soviet Relations, October 29, 1985, pp. 5, 7 (FOIA).

CHAPTER XXI: THE AGING LION VS. THE YOUNG TIGER

1. " 'Fine-tuning' Reagan," *Washington Post*, October 6, 1985.

2. "President Calls for 'Fresh Start' With Soviets," *Washington Post*, October 25, 1985.

3. The illustration is from Donald T. Regan, the chief of staff at the time. "He [Reagan] was in his mid-seventies and perhaps wasn't as robust as he might have been twenty years earlier," he told *The American Experience*. "So there was this thing of the aging lion against the young tiger."

4. Sergei Tarasenko, interview on *The American Experience*, PBS television.

5. Episode is recounted by George Shultz in his foreword for *Stories in his Own Hand: The Everyday Wisdom of Ronald Reagan*, edited by Kiron K. Skinner, Annelise Anderson, and Martin Anderson (New York: Free Press, 2001), pp. xi–xii.

6. "Gorbachev's Economic Agenda: Promises, Potentials, and Pitfalls," Central Intelligence Agency Directorate of Intelligence: An Intelligence Assessment, September 1985, p. iii; classified "secret" (FOIA).

7. Senator Pete Wilson recounts this story, as told to him by Reagan in Peter Hannaford, ed., *Recollections of Reagan: A Portrait of Ronald Reagan* (New York: William Morrow, 1997).

8. Anatoly Chernyaev, *Understanding the End of the Cold War*, op cit., p. 43.

9. Shultz and Reagan quotes are from "Tense Turning Point at Summit," *Washington Post*, November 23, 1985.

10. Suzanne Massie, Strober and Strober, op cit., p. 335.

11. Ronald Reagan memorandum, ca. 1985, Ronald Reagan Library, Personal Papers, handwriting file, quoted in Edmund Morris, *Dutch*, p. 544.

12. Aleksandr Bessmertynkh quoted in Adriana Bosch, *Reagan: An American Story* (New York: TV Books, 1998), p. 263.

13. Comments at Brown University Conference, p. 84.

14. Notes from the Politburo Sessions of February 23 and 26, 1987; Anatoly Chernyaev's notebook, Archives of the Gorbachev Foundation.

15. Robert McFarlane, interview with the author.

16. Mohammad Yousaf, interview with the author. See also Yousaf and Atkin, op cit.

17. Notes from the Communist Party of the Soviet Union Central Committee Session, March 24, 1986, Anatoly Chernyaev diary, courtesy of the Gorbachev Foundation.

18. Mikhail Gorbachev, *Political Report of the CPSU Central Committee to the 27ᵗʰ* Party Congress (Moscow: Novosti, 1986), p. 19.

19. Mikhail Gorbachev mentions this in his speech to Nizhniy Tagil Workers, Moscow Domestic Services in Russian 1545 GMT, April 27, 1990. The CIA was tracking this budgetary problem as well. See "USSR: Sharply Higher Budget Deficits Threaten Perestroika: A Research Paper" (Directorate of Central Intelligence: September 1988), p. 5.

20. "USSR: Sharply Higher Budget Deficits Threaten Perestroika" (Directorate of Intelligence: Central Intelligence Agency, September 1988), p. 3.

21. Notes from the Politburo Session of October 30, 1986, Anatoly Chernyaev diary, courtesy of the Gorbachev Foundation.

22. Notes from the Communist Party of the Soviet Union Central Committee Session, May 8, 1987, Anatoly Chernyaev, diary, courtesy of the Gorbachev Foundation.

23. "Oma im Altkauter," *Der Siegel*, no. 24, 1990.

24. Ministerium für Staatssicherheit Archiven, Zur Rolle des Terrorismus und des Terrors in der Klassenauseiandersatzung zwischen Imperialismus und Sozialismus, no date, reproduced in Manfred Schell and Werner Kalinka, Stasi und kein Ende (Frankfurt, 1991), p. 230.

25. "Eine perverse Kombination," *Der Siegel,* no. 25, 1990.

26. Leiter information Uber einige aktuelle Akzente der Politik der USA gegenuber der UdSSR zu Beginn der zweiten Amtszeit Reagans, Berlin 6.3. 1985 VII/6/ 392/85. Stasi Archives. The document is marked "Top secret."

CHAPTER XXII: THE TRAP

1. Lyn Nofziger tells the story in Strober and Strober, op cit., p. 347. Account was confirmed in an interview with the author.

2. Gorbachev's Modernization program: Implications for Defense (Directorate of Intelligence: Central Intelligence Agency, March 1986), p. iv (FOIA).

3. The exchange is taken from the official transcript, which appears in Foreign Broadcasting Information Service FBIS–USR–93–133, pp. 1–11.

4. Quoted in Frances Fitzgerald, *Way Out There in the Blue: Reagan, Stars Wars and the End of the Cold War* (New York: Simon and Schuster, 2000), p. 358.

5. Quoted in Strober and Strober, p. 347.

6. Quoted in Frances Fitzgerald, op cit.

7. Anatoly Chernyaev's Notes from the Politburo Session, October 16, 1986; Archive of the Gorbachev Foundation.

8. Meeting of the Politburo of the CPSU, October 22, 1986; Cold War International History Project Archives, translated by Loren Utkin, and Anatoly Chernayev's Notes from the Politburo Session of October 30, 1986, Archive of the Gorbachev Foundation.

9. National Security Decision Directive Number 261, "Consultations on the SDI Program," NSDD–261, February 18, 1987; classified secret (FOIA).

10. L VII LXI, no. 1904/86, "Assessment by progressive circles of the scandal within the Reagan Administration," December 31, 1986. This is a Russian KGB document, translated into German, that was found in the Stasi Archives. John O. Koehler Collection, The Hoover Institution Archives, Stanford University.

CHAPTER XXIII: FREEDOM TOUR

1. *Report of the President's Special Review Board* (Washington, D.C.: President's Special Review Board, 1987), p. 54.

2. "White House Persuasion Won High Profile Speech in Berlin," *Washington Post*, June 11, 1987.

3. John O. Koehler, Stasi, pp. 348–49; the directive is part of the John O. Koehler Collection, Hoover Institution Archives.

4. "President Reagan in West Berlin: 'This Wall Will Fall,'" *Washington Post*, June 13, 1987.

5. Bessmertynkh comment is taken from William Wohlforth, ed., *Witnesses to the End of the Cold War* (Baltimore: Johns Hopkins University Press, 1996), p. 312. On military cuts see the memoirs of Marshal Akhromeev, Chief of the General Staff, *Glazami marshala I diplomata*, pp. 211–15.

6. "Reagan Lauds Gorbachev in Farewell," *Washington Post*, June 3, 1988.

7. Igor Korchilov, *Translating History: Thirty Years on the Front Lines of Diplomacy with a Top Russian Interpreter* (New York: Scribner, 1997), p. 158.

8. Igor Korchilov, op cit., p. 80.

9. Natan Sharansky, "Afraid of the Truth," *Washington Post*, October 12, 2000.

10. "Public Impressed: President 'Stands Up Well to Everyone," *Washington Post*, June 1, 1988, and "At the Summit Movement on Arms, Standoff on Rights; Reagan Meets Dissidents, Pledges U.S. Support; Gorbachev Voices Criticism," *Washington Post*, May 31, 1988.

11. "First Breath of Freedom Stirs in the Air," *Washington Post*, June 1, 1988.

12. Igor Korchilov, op cit., p. 174.

13. Gary Lee's observation is noted in Lou Cannon, op cit., p. 459.

CHAPTER XXIV: GOODBYE

1. "A Year Later, Prague Loses Its Euphoria," *Washington Post*, November 17, 1990, p. A9.

2. "Poles Give Reagan a Hero's Welcome; ex-President Honored for His Unwavering Support of Solidarity," Reuters, *Orange County Register*, September 16, 1990; "The Old Warrior at the Wall; for Reagan a Triumphant Return to Berlin," *Washington Post*, September 13, 1990; "In Solidarity's Cradle, Poles Applaud Reagan," *Philadelphia Inquirer*, September 16, 1990.

EPILOGUE

1. Quoted in publisher's note, Ronald Reagan, *The Creative Society* (New York: Devin-Adair, 1968), p. i.

INDEX